Books by Christopher Isherwood

NOVELS

A Meeting by the River
A Single Man
Down There on a Visit
The World in the Evening
Prater Violet
Goodbye to Berlin
The Last of Mr. Norris
(*English title*: Mr. Norris Changes Trains)
The Memorial
All the Conspirators

AUTOBIOGRAPHY

My Guru and His Disciple
Christopher and His Kind
Kathleen and Frank
Lions and Shadows

BIOGRAPHY

Ramakrishna and His Disciples

PLAYS (*with* W. H. *Auden*)

On the Frontier
The Ascent of F6
The Dog beneath the Skin

TRAVEL

The Condor and the Cows
Journey to a War (*with* W. H. *Auden*)

COLLECTION

Exhumations

TRANSLATIONS

The Intimate Journals of Charles Baudelaire
(*and the following with Swami Prabhavananda*)
The Yoga Aphorisms of Patanjali
Shankara's Crest-Jewel of Discrimination
The Bhagavad-Gita

My Guru and His Disciple

MY GURU AND

HIS DISCIPLE

Christopher

Isherwood

Farrar · Straus · Giroux

NEW YORK

To Don Bachardy

This is neither a complete biography of Swami Prabhavananda nor a full account of my own life between 1939 and 1976. It is my one-sided, highly subjective story of our guru-disciple relationship. Many people who were closely associated with Prabhavananda or with me, during that period, have little or no part in this particular story and therefore appear in it only briefly or not at all.

C.I. June 1979

My Guru and His Disciple

One

Toward the end of January 1939, Wystan Auden and I arrived in New York, by boat from England. I have described the events and decisions which led to this journey in my book *Christopher and His Kind*. It was our second visit to New York; we had spent a few days there in the summer of 1938, on our way home to England from China. Now, although our plans weren't definite, it seemed that we might be staying for a long time, perhaps permanently.

Our first visit had been a tourist visit, uniquely magic. As far as I was concerned, it could never be duplicated. The tension of New York life had been thrilling when it had had a time limit; now it quickly began to demoralize me. Less than two months after our arrival, I wrote in my diary:

This has been a bad sterile period for me. I've done practically nothing. Every day I think: Now I must get busy, now I must start work. But at what? My money is rapidly running out. Wystan has the prospect of a lecturing job, later on. My whole instinct is against lecturing or exploiting my reputation in any way. I would like some sort of regular humble employment. I got to know Berlin because I was doing work which related me to my social environment in an anonymous unpretentious way, as a foreigner teaching his own language. I must be anonymous until I discover a new self here, an American me.

Wystan is as energetic as I'm idle. He writes a great deal, in his best manner—poems and articles and reviews —he makes speeches, goes to parties and dinners, is brilliantly talkative. It's as if he and I had changed roles. He's the confident one, now. He is making himself at home here.

So I despaired and did nothing, blaming New York for my jitters. I now realize that they weren't caused by New York, or by my money worries, or even by the probability of war in Europe, but by an emptiness inside myself, of which I wasn't yet fully aware.

I was empty because I had lost my political faith—I couldn't repeat the left-wing slogans which I had been repeating throughout the last few years. It wasn't that I had lost *all* belief in what the slogans stood for, but I was no longer wholehearted. My leftism was confused by an increasingly aggressive awareness of myself as a homosexual and by a newly made discovery that I was a pacifist. Both these individualistic minority-attitudes kept bringing me into conflict with leftist majority-ideology.

I called myself a pacifist because Heinz, the German boy I had lived with for five years during the nineteen-thirties, was about to be conscripted into the Nazi army and I found it unthinkable that I should ever help to cause his death, however indirectly. I had therefore decided to refuse to take any part in the war effort, if war came. But this was a merely negative decision. What I now needed to learn were positive pacifist values, a pacifist way of life, a Yes to fortify my No; it was the lack of values which was making me feel so insecure. The strength Wystan showed in contrast to my weakness was based on the Christian values which he had learned from his mother, as a child, and which he had never entirely abandoned. He didn't discuss these with me at that time, knowing what a violent prejudice I had against the whole concept of religion as I then understood it.

Pacifism was the basis of a friendship I now made with John van Druten. John was easy and witty and charming, very much a man of the theater, but he was also a moralist, anxious to impose ethical standards on his life and on his plays, even when they were the lightest of comedies. After careful discussion, we made up a list of questions concerning the role of the pacifist in wartime and sent it to three prominent pacifists, George Lansbury, Rudolph Messel, and Runham Brown. All of them took the trouble to answer us.

Messel was the most radical of the three. He wanted the pacifist to sabotage the war machine, demanding total disarmament, unilateral if need be. He hoped the war would turn into a revolution. The Nazi aggressor must be allowed to invade the country without opposition. A bloodless victory, Messel added, would be no advertisement for Nazism, anyway.

Brown wrote that a pacifist should at all times try to be a useful member of society. In wartime he should work harder than ever, on some kind of social-relief project which was independent of government control and unrelated to the war effort. He should practice civil disobedience to the aggressor, no matter what the consequences.

Lansbury's letter agreed substantially with Brown's. Its tone touched John and me deeply; you could almost hear the voice of this gentle, fearlessly honest eighty-year-old warrior for peace: "You, like many others, find it extremely difficult to realise your idealism in the midst of the kind of world in which we are living. All the same, comrade, whatever was true yesterday, is true today. If you, and millions of other young men of all nationalities are once more thrown into this hell of war, nothing will come out of it but more and more confusion. Our way of passive resistance has never yet been tried out, but war has been tried through all the centuries and has absolutely failed."

The dedication and courage of these three men was inspiring, but they couldn't help me much in my present condition. They were in England, preparing to play their part in the expected war crisis. Even if I were to go back there, I shouldn't be able to discuss my personal problems with them; they would be far too busy. They might give me work to do, but I wasn't yet sufficiently sure of myself to become their follower. I needed a lot more time to think, and someone to help me clarify my thoughts.

So Gerald Heard was increasingly in my mind. He and his friend Chris Wood had emigrated to Los Angeles in 1937, together with Aldous Huxley and his wife, Maria. I had seen a good deal of Gerald and Chris while they were still living in London, and I already knew Gerald well enough to feel sure he would be understanding. The Huxleys I had never met. I was eager to talk to Aldous, whose *Ends and Means*, published two years earlier, was regarded as a basic book for pacifists.

I knew, from somewhat vague gossip, that Heard and Huxley had become involved in the cult of Yoga, or Hinduism, or Vedanta—I was still contemptuously unwilling to bother to find out exactly what these terms meant. To me, all this Oriental stuff was distasteful in the extreme. However, my distaste was quite different from the distaste I felt for the Christians. The Christians I saw as sour life-haters and sex-forbidders, hypocritically denying their rabid secret lusts. The Hindus I saw as stridently emotional mysterymongers whose mumbo jumbo was ridiculous rather than sinister. That Heard and Huxley could have been impressed by such nonsense was regrettable. I explained their lapse by saying to myself that it was typical of these hyperintellectuals to get caught unawares from time to time and led astray by their emotions. But surely such a lapse could be only temporary? I intended to avoid discussing the subject with them, as tactfully as I could. After all, it was their intellects that I needed to consult.

So I now began corresponding with Gerald. To my surprise and relief, he wrote nothing about Yoga—indeed, his tone was reassuringly practical. His thinking seemed to be chiefly in terms of group formation. Pacifists must be organized into groups which were small enough to be cohesive, every member accepting total responsibility for every other. Order and creative accuracy must be opposed to disorder and destruction. We must create a doctorate of psychologically sound, well-equipped healers . . . Gerald's phraseology wasn't always clear to me but it sounded authoritative; he seemed to know what he was up to. The idea of belonging to a like-minded group appealed to me strongly. Since my decision to be a pacifist, I had felt isolated, fearing that many of my friends must disapprove.

When I first wrote to Gerald, I didn't suggest coming

to California, but he himself urged me to, in his reply to my letter. From then on, I took it for granted that I would come, sooner or later. Quite aside from wanting to talk to Gerald and Huxley, and to get away from New York, I had always had a romantic longing to visit the Far West. Now that this journey was actually in prospect, I realized that I needed to share it with an American, so as to see the country through his native eyes as well as my foreign ones. Luckily for me, there was a young American ready to be my fellow traveler. I will call him Vernon.

Vernon and I had met and become lovers during my first stay in New York. After I went back to England we had written to each other, and when I returned in January, he was waiting on the dock to meet me. To begin with, we had taken a room together in the same hotel as Wystan. Later, when Wystan and I rented an apartment, Vernon had moved in with us.

He and I left New York on May 6, by bus. Bus travel was cheap in those days, so we could afford to make a big detour to the South, by way of Memphis, New Orleans, Houston, and El Paso; we also stopped off to see the Grand Canyon. It was almost two weeks before we reached Los Angeles.

I had felt sad to be leaving Wystan behind, but nothing would have induced him to come with us; he was busy and happy in New York. Of course we assured each other that our parting would be only temporary, and indeed Wystan did come out to California briefly, later that year—and hated it. We were together many times during the remaining thirty-odd years of Wystan's life. But our relationship was altered, not because the strength of our love had grown less, but because we no longer had to rely on each other. When we had sailed from England that January, leaving behind us nearly everyone we knew, our futures seemed interlocked for good or ill; we were a mated, isolated couple. America was to have been our joint adventure. But it was America which, literally, came between us.

Chris Wood, when I met him again in Los Angeles, appeared to be no different from the London Chris I had known, except that he was sunburned. But Gerald was certainly changed. The London Gerald had been a characteristically clean-shaven type. The Los Angeles Gerald wore a beard. True, this beard had a reason for its existence; he had grown it because he couldn't shave while lying in bed with a broken arm—the result of a fall in the snow in Iowa during a lecture tour with Huxley. But that had happened at the end of 1937, and the beard was still there; indeed, it showed signs of careful grooming and was trimmed to a point. It gave his face an upward, heaven-seeking thrust which was disconcertingly Christlike. And whereas the London Gerald had been neatly and even elegantly dressed, the Los Angeles Gerald wore jackets with ragged cuffs and jeans which had holes or patches in the knees. The London Gerald had struck me as being temperamentally agnostic, with a dry wit and a primly skeptical smile. The Los Angeles Gerald was witty, too, but he had the quick eager speech and the decisive gestures of a believer.

A believer in what? That remained for me to discover, and the discovery was a gradual process. Gerald was a master of the oblique. If I asked him a direct question, I got an answer which rambled like a river over a vast area of knowledge, carrying me past the shores of pre-history, anthropology, astronomy, physics, parapsychology, mythology, and much much more. The glimpses he allowed me of these shores were tantalizing and I would beg him to extend them, forgetting or not caring what my original question had been.

Gerald simply wasn't the sort of person one could come to and say, "Please summarize your views, so I can decide if I agree with them." Nor could I carry out my intention of accepting Gerald's pacifism while rejecting his religious beliefs. I'd begun to realize that the two were completely interdependent.

And, anyhow, Gerald subtly but absolutely refused to be rejected. If I disagreed with a statement of his—or with his use of certain words—he dismissed my disagreement by implying that it was merely semantic. He was so sure of himself that he could afford to apologize to me. He was sorry, he said; he had expressed himself clumsily. He should have stated his case in apter words —to me, especially, whose skill with them so far exceeded his own. He hadn't forgotten how to flatter.

Despite his vast learning, he treated me as an equal. He had an air of conferring with me, never of teaching me. "You remember, of course, that odd book of Smith's on the customs of the Micronesians?" would be a typical opening of one of his expositions. During our first weeks together, I would keep telling him that I'd never read Smith, or Jones, or Robinson, or Brown, as the case might be. Later I learned to let such rhetorical questions go by without comment. They were rhetorical because Gerald always told you, anyway, what Smith had said that was relevant to the subject being discussed. In the same manner, he would declare that "I should like your opinion on Smith's theory" and then proceed to inform me what *his* opinion was, and hence mine—since disagreement between us wasn't possible, according to his rules of intercourse.

I was anxious to hear more about the pacifist groups which he had written of in his letters. What kind of preparation did he think would be necessary for the members? Paramedical training? A study of Gandhi's tactics of non-violence? No, Gerald didn't show any interest when I mentioned either of these. All he would discuss was a form of self-preparation at what he called "the deep level." To become a true pacifist, you had to find peace within yourself; only then, he said, could you function pacifistically in the outside world.

Gerald had already started his own drastic program of self-preparation; every day he sat for three two-hour periods of meditation—in the early morning, around noon, and in the early evening. During these six hours he was engaged, as far as I could gather, in somehow fixing his thoughts upon what he called "this thing"— "this thing" being the source of inner peace which he was trying to contact. I think it was Gerald's natural fastidiousness which prevented him from calling it "God"—to say that he was looking for God would have sounded pretentious, ungentlemanly. Perhaps, also, he guessed that I would have a prejudice against the word. If he did, he was right. I loathed it.

My interpretation of the word "God" had been taken quite simplemindedly from left-wing anti-religious propaganda. God has no existence except as a symbol of the capitalist superboss. He has been deified by the capitalists so that he can rule from on high in the sky over the working-class masses, doping them with the opium of the people, which is religion, and thus making them content with their long working hours and starvation wages.

I soon had to admit, however, that Gerald's "this

thing"—leaving aside the question of its existence or non-existence—was the very opposite of my "God." True, it was by definition everywhere, and therefore also up in the sky, but it was to be looked for first inside yourself. It wasn't to be thought of as a Boss to be obeyed but as a Nature to be known—an extension of your own nature, with which you could become consciously united. The Sanskrit word *yoga*, ancestor of the English word "yoke," means union, and hence the process of achieving union with this eternal omnipresent Nature, of which everybody and everything is a part.

During the past few years, I had kept declaring that I knew religion was a lie, because I knew that I hadn't got an eternal soul. Now, after talking to Gerald, it became obvious to me that I had been misusing the word "soul" to mean my ego-personality. I had merely been saying (quite correctly) that my ego-personality, Christopher, was subject to change, like my body, and therefore couldn't be eternal. If I did have a soul, it could only be "this thing," seen in relation to Christopher. I might call it "mine" for convenience when thinking about it, but I must remind myself that Christopher could never possess it. If the two were ever to become united, Christopher would cease to exist as an individual. He would be merged in "this thing"; not vice versa.

The question remained: Why should I believe in "this thing" at all?

Among the various areas of knowledge that Gerald was opening up to me was the history of mysticism. For the first time, I was learning that there had been thousands of men and women, in many different countries and cultures throughout recorded history, who had claimed to have experienced union with what is eternal within oneself. That their accounts of this experience were essentially similar was certainly impressive, but it didn't prove anything, as far as I was concerned. Even when these people belonged to the modern world, they seemed utterly remote from me. Mightn't they all have been self-deluded, however sincere?

Gerald countered my objections with a compliment. My attitude showed, he said, that I was approaching the problem in exactly the right spirit. Credulity was the greatest obstacle to spiritual progress; blind faith was just blindness. He quoted Tennyson's line about "honest doubt" and told me that Ramakrishna (whoever that was) had urged his disciples to keep testing him, as a moneychanger rings coins to hear if they are false. It was no use just passively accepting the dogmas of the Church or the words of the Scriptures: I knew, of course, what Vivekananda (whoever that was) had said: "Every man in Christian countries has a huge cathedral on his head and on top of that a book." No—the only way to begin the search for "this thing" was to say to oneself: "I'll keep an open mind and I'll try to follow the instructions in meditation which my teacher gives me. If, after six months of honest effort, I've had absolutely no results, then I'll drop it and tell everybody that it's a sham."

This sounded fair enough. And I was impressed by Gerald's restraint. He didn't urge me to start meditating then and there. He didn't tempt me by describing the benefits he got from his own meditation—quite the opposite; he spoke of it in the same tone I would have used when complaining of my struggles to get a book written: it was a lot of hard work and most of the time it was frustrating. "When one comes to this late in life, one's mind's already so wretchedly out of condition."

Oh yes, Gerald impressed me enormously. Already I believed that *he*, at least, believed he was making some progress in contacting "this thing" inside himself. He couldn't be lying to me; he hadn't any motive for doing so. He couldn't be shutting himself up for six hours a day in his room and pretending to meditate merely in order to impress Chris Wood. I didn't deny that Gerald was a playactor, with an Irish delight in melodrama and arresting phrases. Indeed, I believed in him *because* he was theatrical, because he costumed himself as a ragged hobo, because his beard was Christlike but trimmed, because some of his lamentations over the human lot had a hint of glee in them and some of his scientific analogies a touch of poetic exaggeration. I should have been much more suspicious of him if he had presented himself as a grave infallible oracle. My own nature responded to his theatricality and found it reassuring, for I was a playactor, too.

What made his company so stimulating was that he seemed to be so intensely aware. Awareness was his watchword. According to him, you had to maintain continual awareness of the real situation, which is that "this thing" exists and that we are therefore all essentially united. Whenever your awareness weakened, you slipped back into acceptance of the unreal situation, which is experienced as space-time and which imposes disbelief in "this thing" and belief in individual separateness. Gerald would quote Jesus admonishing the apostle Simon Peter: "Simon, Simon, Satan hath desired to have you, that he may sift you as wheat." Gerald uttered the word "desired" with a kind of snarl, baring the teeth on one side of his mouth. Then, quite uncannily, he would mime Satan himself, separating the mortal ego-husk from the immortal wheat grain and blowing it to perdition with a gleeful puff of his breath. "Satan," in Gerald's interpretation, was the distracting, disintegrating, alienating power of space-time, operating through its agencies —the radio, the movies, the press. "It's the very *devil!*" Gerald would exclaim in a whisper, his pale blue eyes wild, like those of a man in a haunted house, beset by terrors. (He had developed the theme in a book published that year, *Pain, Sex and Time.*)

Lao-tze's *Tao Te Ching* was Gerald's favorite gospel of pacifism. He often repeated a sentence from its sixty-seventh chapter: "Heaven arms with pity those whom it would not see destroyed"—meaning that to feel concern for others is the only realistic attitude, because it is a recognition of the real situation, our oneness with each other. Feelings of love and compassion are not merely "good" and "right," they are ultimately self-protective; feelings of hatred are ultimately self-destructive.

Lao-tze says that we should be like the water, because fluidity always overcomes rigidity; rocks and prejudices get washed away in the end. To illustrate this, Gerald used to say that Man, who has survived the dinosaurs and managed to evolve without growing wings or gills or poison glands, is descended from a small, weak, but adaptable tree shrew. (A famous biologist later assured me that Gerald's sense of poetic truth had carried him too far; Man is more probably descended from a large and aggressive ape.)

Gerald agreed with Lao-tze that one should never put the other party in the wrong if that can possibly be avoided. Martyrdom may be heroic if it is unavoidable, but you must be very sure that you have done everything permissible to save your persecutors from the spiritually self-destructive act of killing you. Otherwise, your death will be an act of passive aggression for which you will be partly to blame. Gerald would say with a sigh: "I'm afraid that that exceedingly odd individual, Jesus of Nazareth, *deliberately* got himself lynched."

But Gerald disapproved of Jesus far less than of his Church. Gerald said that he could never become a Christian as long as the Church claimed for itself a monopoly of divine inspiration—which Hindus and Buddhists do not—and as long as it represented the crucifixion as the supreme and crowning triumph of Christ's career. Here, Gerald was joining Bernard Shaw in his condemnation of "crosstianity." Which I found amusing, because Gerald's meditative bearded beauty, high temples, and long red nose seemed to present the composite image of a Shavian Christ.

Gerald referred to the life he was trying to lead as "intentional living." Its purpose was, as he put it, to "reduce" the "strangulated" ego; he was fond of using words in their medical sense. The intentional life required not only long meditation periods—he insisted that his own six hours were an absolute minimum—but also an attempted moment-to-moment vigilance over one's every thought and action, since every thought and every action helps either to create or to remove the obstacles to union with "this thing." No thought or action, however seemingly unimportant, can be regarded as neutral.

What were these obstacles? Gerald, who had a tidy mind and an inclination to think in trinities, would tick them off on his long, expressive fingers—addictions, possessions, and pretensions. Addictions included their opposites, aversions. They therefore ranged from, say, a lust for blonds, heroin, or toffee to a disgust-fear of cripples, gangrene, or lizards. Gerald regarded addictions as the least harmful of the three categories. Pretensions were the worst, he said, because there is one of them which can outlast all other obstacles. You may conquer your addictions and unlearn your aversions; you may unload yourself of your possessions; you may resign from your positions of honor and retire into humble obscurity. But then, and only then, the most deadly of all the pretensions may raise its head; you may begin to believe that you are a spiritually superior person and therefore entitled to condemn your weaker fellow creatures. (Was Gerald himself in danger of yielding to this final temptation? Yes—if only because he did seem capable of overcoming all the other obstacles along the course which led to it. I could imagine that Gerald might one day begin to take himself too seriously as a religious teacher. But, surely, not for long. He was too much of a comedian not to become quickly aware of the funny side of his holiness.)

As a concept, "intentional living" fascinated me. I saw how immensely it would heighten the significance of even the most ordinary day, how it would abolish boredom by turning your life into an art form. Indeed, it was related to the attitude which a novelist should have, ideally, toward his work on a novel. With one huge difference, however. The novelist is involved only with his novel and only during work hours; the intentional liver is involved with his whole life experience, and throughout every waking moment of every day until he dies. The finality of such an involvement scared and daunted me. To Gerald's austere temperament, it strongly appealed. The negative side of his involvement was his hatred of space-time, and he gloried in his hatred. "It's only when the sheer *beastliness* of this world begins to hurt you—like crushing your finger in a door" (here he winced, miming the physical pain) "that you're ready to take this step."

Gerald accepted the Hindu and Buddhist doctrine of reincarnation—that life within space-time is a cycle of birth-death-rebirth; you are born again and again, whether you like it or not, as a consequence of your past deeds (your *karmas*). You can only free yourself from this cycle by achieving union with your real nature and thus breaking your bondage to space-time. That was why Gerald was working so hard to make sure that this life would be his last.

I simply could not share Gerald's feelings, much as I respected his beliefs. How could I hate space-time when it contained so much that was lovable and beautiful, including Vernon? Admittedly, my feelings for Vernon were hotly sexual and possessive. I found nothing essentially evil in this, but it was an entanglement with worldly life—an entanglement which was growing more extensive, for now we needed a home and at least one car; transportation in the sprawling Los Angeles area being as much of a problem then as it is today. Chris Wood had guaranteed our security for the next few months by lending me two thousand dollars. But I should have to pay them back sooner or later by going to work, and I couldn't work legally until I had got on the U.S. immigrant quota and become a permanent resident of the country instead of a mere visitor. And once I had done this, what kind of job could I hope for? It had been all very well for me, in New York, to decide that I would like "some sort of regular humble employment." After spending a few weeks in Los Angeles, I realized that the economic depression was still on, and that all "humble employment" was being competed for by thousands of better-qualified applicants. The only available work I was really qualified for was writing movie scripts in a studio. So the only options open to me were to earn a great deal of money or none at all. I consulted a movie agent about my chances. She had never heard of me as a writer and obviously thought me a hopeless case; things were very slow just now in the studios, she told me. So I worried and worried, thereby entangling myself ever more deeply in worldliness.

This made me feel that I must overcome my last remaining prejudices and try meditation. That might at least help me to take short rests from worry during the day. I already knew that Gerald himself had had lessons in meditation from a Hindu monk who was living nearby, Swami Prabhavananda. I now asked him to tell me what the Swami had taught him. Gerald became teasingly secretive, however. It was absolutely forbidden, he said, to repeat your teacher's instructions to anyone else. Such instructions varied from pupil to pupil, according to individual needs and temperaments. It would be like letting a fellow patient drink your medicine. Gerald even hinted, in his melodramatic way, that, if he were to teach me what he had been taught and I were to try it for myself, I might suffer terrible psychic consequences, maybe even go mad.

Then, relenting, he gave me some sensible and simple advice. I wasn't to attempt actual meditation of any kind. I was just to sit quiet for ten or fifteen minutes twice a day, morning and evening, and keep reminding myself of "this thing"—what it was and why one should want to make contact with it. That was all.

Now that I had made up my mind to try it, the mere idea of meditating filled me with a strangely powerful excitement. I thought of it as an attempted confrontation with something hitherto unencountered but always present in myself. When I try to recall how I felt, I think of entering an unexplored passage in a house which is otherwise familiar to me. The passage is in darkness. I stand at one end of it, on the threshold between the known and the unknown. I feel a certain awe but no fear. The darkness is reassuring and not alien. I have no need to ask, "Is anything there?" My instinct assures me that *something* is. But what? "This thing"? (Whatever that is.) Or merely my own unconscious? (Whatever that means.) At present, the question seems academic. I am content with simply being where I am, on the threshold of the dark passage.

The only distraction I was aware of, in those days, was created by my own embarrassment; I was acutely aware of myself playing this exotic game, and I seemed to be playing it in the presence of all my friends, over there in England. "Christopher's gone to Hollywood to be a yogi," I heard them saying—it would be Hollywood rather than Los Angeles, because "Hollywood" represents the movie world and all its phoniness. I knew, of course, that my real friends wouldn't sneer at me so viciously. Some might be pained or dismayed, nearly all would be puzzled, but they would take it for granted that my motives for doing what I was doing were at least honest. No, it was I myself—or, rather, a hostile minority in me—who was sneering.

Vernon certainly didn't sneer. Being young and curious about all ideas which were new to him, he was greatly interested and started questioning Gerald. He may have done some meditating on his own. The fact that I didn't ask him about this suggests that I was feeling guilty because my sits were so irregular. I think I felt the inevitable dissatisfaction of a beginner who hasn't been given any definite instructions. I can't remember why it was that I didn't immediately contact Gerald's Swami Prabhavananda. Maybe the Swami was away from home. Anyhow, it wasn't until late in July that Gerald took me to see him.

Two

In those days, and until the freeway was cut through Hollywood during the nineteen-fifties, Ivar Avenue climbed steeply from Hollywood Boulevard straight up to Franklin Avenue. There, Ivar appeared to stop. But it didn't. A short distance to the right, along Franklin, there was a left turn onto an extra bit of it. This turnoff was easy to miss. Many of Prabhavananda's visitors did miss it, the first time they came looking for him. Characteristically, Gerald liked to regard this as symbolic: where wells of eternal truth exist within space-time, they are always carefully hidden.

If, however, you made the turnoff successfully, you found yourself on a stretch of narrow road which was only a block in length. Here the ground was more or less level, for you were now, so to speak, on top of the first step of the staircase of hills looking over the city toward the ocean. Hollywood Boulevard lay below you, busy with shops and restaurants. At night it sparkled brilliantly and often swept the sky with arc-lamp beams if there was a film premiere at Grauman's Chinese Theater. But, up here on Ivar, you felt secluded within a sleepy hillside suburb of little houses nesting amidst flowering bushes and vines.

Halfway along the road, on the right-hand side, a surprise awaited you; a squat Hindu temple with white plaster walls and onion domes, their pinnacles painted gold. A flight of steps led up to it, with cypresses on either side.

At number 1946, on the street corner next to the temple, stood a wooden bungalow—then one of the city's most typical structures, originally adapted from the bungalows of the Orient, and perhaps for this reason small-windowed, with a shadowy interior, as if to provide coolness in a much hotter climate than ours. In this bungalow, Prabhavananda and two or three other people were living.

I have absolutely no memories of my first visit. Can this have been because Gerald talked so dazzlingly that the Swami's personality became dimmed, along with anybody else's who may have been present? I had known him to have this effect on me before. Nevertheless, this visit accomplished all that was necessary, from my point of view: the Swami and I arranged that I should come back alone a few days later, so that he could give me some instructions. Our second meeting is recorded in my diary; it was on August 4.

This time, he didn't receive me at the bungalow but in a small study which was part of the temple building. I found him waiting for me there when I arrived. I was immediately aware of the atmosphere of calm in this room, rather uncomfortably so. It was like a sudden change in altitude to which I should have to get accustomed.

The Swami is smaller than I remembered—charming and boyish, although he is in his middle forties and has a bald patch at the back of his head. He looks slightly Mongolian, with long straight eyebrows and wide-set dark eyes. He talks gently and persuasively. His smile is extraordinary. It is somehow so touching, so open, so brilliant with joy that it makes me want to cry.

One of the Swami's characteristics isn't mentioned here; he chain-smoked cigarettes. Since I, too, was a heavy smoker, this wouldn't have bothered me.

I felt terribly awkward—like a rich, overdressed woman, in the plumes and bracelets of my vanity. Everything I said sounded artificial and false. I started acting a little scene, trying to appear sympathetic. I told him I wasn't sure I could do these meditations and lead the life I am leading. He answered, "You must be like the lotus on the pond. The lotus leaf is never wet."

I said I was afraid of attempting to do too much, because, if I failed, I should be discouraged. He said, "There is no failure in the search for God. Every step you take is a positive advance."

I said I hated the word "God." He agreed that you can just as well say "The Self" or "Nature."

He talked about the difference between yoga meditation and autohypnosis. Autohypnosis or autosuggestion makes you see what you want to see. Meditation makes you see something you don't expect to see. Autosuggestion produces different results in each individual. Meditation produces the same result in all individuals.

I explained how I had always thought of yoga as silly superstitious nonsense. The Swami laughed. "And now you have fallen into the trap?"

In this account, there is one enormously important omission. My vague reference to "the life I am leading" seems to refer merely to a worldly life in the conventional sense; my efforts to get employment and money. I must have told the Swami about these, too, thus prompting him to advise me to be like the lotus leaf—which is a standard Hindu precept. But the question I had actually come to ask him was a far more serious one. If his answer was unsatisfactory to me, there would be no point in our ever seeing each other again.

I wish I could remember exactly how my question was worded. No doubt it was put apologetically. Perhaps I blushed and stammered. In essence it was: Can I lead a spiritual life as long as I'm having a sexual relationship with a young man?

I do remember the Swami's answer: "You must try to see him as the young Lord Krishna."

All I then knew about Krishna was that the Hindus regard him as an *avatar*—one of the incarnations of "this thing," who are believed to be born on earth from time to time; and that Krishna is described as having been extraordinarily beautiful in his youth. I understood the Swami to mean that I should try to see Vernon's beauty —the very aspect of him which attracted me to him sexually—as the beauty of Krishna, which attracts devotees to him spiritually. I should try to see and love what was Krishna-like in Vernon. Well, why not? I told myself that I didn't just desire Vernon, I also loved him. This was a way to prove it. I was aware, of course, that if I was successful, I should lose all desire for Vernon's body. But the Swami had only said "try." There was no harm in trying—especially when we weren't actually in bed together.

I wasn't at all discouraged by the Swami's reply; indeed, it was far more permissive than I had expected. What reassured me—what convinced me that I could become his pupil—was that he hadn't shown the least shadow of distaste on hearing me admit to my homo-sexuality. I had feared a blast of icy puritanism: "You must promise me never to see that boy again, or I cannot accept you. You are committing a deadly sin."

From that moment on, I began to understand that the Swami did not think in terms of sins, as most Christians do. Certainly, he regarded my lust for Vernon as an obstacle to my spiritual progress—but no more and no less of an obstacle than lust for a woman, even for a lawfully wedded wife, would have been. Christian sins are offenses against God and each one has its fixed degree of magnitude. The obstacles which the Swami recognized are offenses against yourself and their importance is relative to each individual's condition. In fact, the Swami's attitude was like that of a coach who tells his athletes that they must give up smoking, alcohol, and certain kinds of food, not because these are inherently evil, but because they may prevent the athlete from getting something he wants much more—an Olympic medal, for instance.

I doubt if I had already heard, at this time, of the *kundalini*. But I will write about it here because it is relevant to the subject of sex and chastity.

According to Hindu physiology, the kundalini is a huge reserve of energy situated at the base of the spine. Its name means "that which is coiled up," and hence it is sometimes referred to as "the serpent power." We are told that, when this power has been aroused, it rises upward along the spinal canal. In doing so, it passes through several centers of consciousness, known as *chakras*. A chakra is not an anatomical organ; its nature is described as "subtle," as distinct from "gross." Subtle matter is invisible to gross eyesight and can be seen only in spiritual visions.

In the great majority of people, the kundalini seldom rises above the three lowest chakras; therefore, its power causes only material desires, including lust. When, however, a person becomes sufficiently spiritual, the kundalini rises to the higher chakras, thus causing greater and greater degrees of enlightenment. In exceedingly rare cases, the kundalini may reach the highest chakra, the seventh, and cause *samadhi*, which is the ultimate experience of union with what is eternal within oneself.

Regarded from this standpoint, chastity isn't even a virtue; it is a practical necessity. By being chaste, you conserve the kundalini power which is absolutely necessary for your spiritual progress.

I found this image of the kundalini most helpful as a corrective to puritanism. The religious puritan regards certain parts and functions of the mind-body as "pure" and others as "impure." He refuses to admit that there can be any relation between the two groups. Meanwhile, the anti-religious puritan thinks that he is effectively damning religion when he declares that it is nothing but repressed sex. There is only one kundalini, one power behind all these functions. Why call it either pure or impure?

At the end of our interview, the Swami wrote out a sheet of instructions for me—what I was to try to do when I meditated:

1. Try to feel the presence of an all-pervading Existence.

2. Send thoughts of peace and goodwill toward all beings—north, south, east, and west.

3. Think of the body as a temple, containing the Reality.

4. Meditate on the Real Self. The Self in you is the Self in all beings. I am infinite Existence, infinite Knowledge, infinite Bliss.

August 5. I find number one the easiest—especially at night. It would be quite easy in the desert. Here, you keep hearing cars, steam hammers, distant radio, the clock, the icebox motor—and have to remind yourself that the Existence is also within these mechanisms.

Number two is easy as long as I think of typical people in each country. For some reason, it is most difficult to send goodwill toward the South Americans or anywhere south of the equator, perhaps because I've never been there. The points of the compass bother me, too. Where is everybody? This would be easiest on top of a mountain or a skyscraper.

Number three: very difficult. Much involved with thoughts of sex.

Number four: relatively easy. When I think in terms of writing, I can easily see that the writer taps a great store of universal knowledge. The more daring, the more persistent he is, the more he finds out . . . "Infinite Bliss" —infinite possibility of bliss inside each of us. Why do I make myself miserable? Fear and desire are simply a blockage in the pipe. Get them out, and the water will run. It's there all the time.

This evening, on bedroom floor, in the dark. Unsatisfactory. Stuck at number one, because I couldn't get over the feeling that everybody was asleep and therefore no longer part of "Consciousness." Posture is difficult. My back hurts. But I feel somehow refreshed.

The mention of "posture" in my diary reminds me that even my first, pre-Swami sits had been made cross-legged on the floor. This wasn't in imitation of Gerald, who preferred to sit on a chair. I think I preferred the floor because I wanted to set my meditation in some way apart from my normal experience of life. Seen from floor level, even a familiar room looks different; it was as if I had put myself into another dimension.

All that the Swami required was that one should take a position in which the spine was held straight. I could meditate on a chair, provided I sat upright. It wasn't important to cross your legs, he said. Hindus only did it because they were accustomed from childhood to sit that way.

I never achieved the classic lotus posture, in which both legs are crossed over the thighs; my legs were too stiff. But I did find that I could make myself quite comfortable cross-legged if I eased the tension by putting a pillow under my coccyx. Before long I could hold this position for at least an hour, keeping a straight back. I even began sitting on the floor like this at parties—thereby getting a reputation, no doubt, as a show-off.

I have already shown how Gerald not only introduced me to the Swami but first prepared my mind to receive the Swami's teaching. Without his help, I would surely never have found my way to 1946 Ivar Avenue. For this, I shall be grateful to him as long as I live. I shall also be grateful to him that he never tried to make me his own disciple; that would have ended in absurdity. Gerald and I belonged to the same social class, both of us were ex-Londoners with many mutual friends, we were sensitive to every nuance of each other's phraseology and humor. Although Gerald was a strict celibate, he viewed my sexual life with tolerance. Despite differences in our temperaments, we were entirely at ease together. For these very reasons, we could never have entered into a satisfactory teacher-pupil relationship. Neither of us could have taken his role seriously.

What I did take most seriously, however, was Gerald's judgment of other people. Those mild blue eyes of his had shrewdly weighed the claims of so many pretenders to spiritual knowledge; that long, sensitive nose had sniffed out so many fakes. It was Gerald's acceptance of Prabhavananda which made me willing to accept him, at any rate until I was able to form an opinion of my own.

I can't remember now by what degrees and through whom I found out the facts about Prabhavananda's past life and background. This anyhow seems the right place to tell what is essential.

He was born on December 26, 1893, at Surmanagar, a village in Bengal near the town of Bankura, northwest of Calcutta. His name, during the first twenty years of his life, was Abanindra Nath Ghosh.

Abanindra's parents were normally devout Hindus. He accepted their religious beliefs, but he wasn't a deeply meditative or reclusive boy. He liked playing football and other games, and had plenty of friends.

However, by the time he was fourteen, he had read about Ramakrishna, the holy man already regarded by some as an avatar. Ramakrishna had been born in a village not very far away, and had spent his adult life at a temple just outside Calcutta. Abanindra had also read about Ramakrishna's chief disciples, Vivekananda and Brahmananda, who had founded the Ramakrishna Order of monks after Ramakrishna's death in 1886. He felt a mysterious power of attraction in their names.

Then one day, by seeming chance, Abanindra met
Sarada Devi. She had been Ramakrishna's wife and was
now regarded by his disciples as their spiritual mother—
"Holy Mother," they called her. One of her attendants
told Abanindra who she was; otherwise, he would have
taken her for an ordinary countrywoman, sitting bare-
foot, without the slightest air of self-importance, outside
a village inn. When he approached and bowed down to
touch her feet in reverence, she said, "Son, haven't I
seen you before?"

When Abanindra was eighteen and a student in Calcutta, he visited the Belur Math, the chief monastery of
the Ramakrishna Order, which is beside the Ganges, on
the outskirts of the city. He wanted to see the room in
which Vivekananda used to stay; since his death in 1902,
it had been maintained as a public shrine. When Abanindra left the Vivekananda Room, he found himself
for the first time face to face with Brahmananda. And
Brahmananda said to him, "Haven't I seen you before?"

The effect of this encounter upon Abanindra was
far too powerful and subtle to be described in a
few words. I shall keep referring to it throughout this
book. All I need say here is that Abanindra longed to
meet Brahmananda again. So, a few months later, he
impulsively spent the money he had been given for
tuition fees on a ticket to Hardwar, because he knew that
Brahmananda was visiting a monastery there. He arrived
in the middle of the night, unannounced, but Brahmananda didn't seem at all surprised to see him. He allowed
Abanindra to stay a month, accepted him formally as his
disciple, and then sent him back to Calcutta to continue
his education.

Although Abanindra felt such devotion to Brahmananda, he wasn't yet intending to become a monk. At
college he came under another strong influence. Or-

ganized militant opposition to British rule was now growing, and many students were involved. Abanindra decided that his first duty was patriotic. He must devote himself to the cause of India's freedom; in order to be able to do this single-mindedly, he vowed not to marry until it was won. He joined a revolutionary organization and wrote pamphlets for it, which were secretly distributed. Because he looked so boyish and innocent, his comrades entrusted him with some revolvers which had been stolen from a British storehouse; he hid them in his room. These young men were mostly untrained— Abanindra wasn't even sure how to use his revolver—but they were risking their lives just as much as the veterans of the movement. One of them threw a bomb at the Viceroy and had to escape from the country. Another, who was Abanindra's close friend, was arrested and died in prison, probably as the result of being tortured. The authorities called it suicide.

Abanindra was now studying philosophy. He began coming regularly to the Belur Math because one of the swamis there could instruct him in the teachings of Shankara. His instructor kept urging him to become a monk, but Abanindra would argue with him, saying that the monastic life is escapist, a refusal to accept one's political responsibilities.

During the Christmas vacation, Abanindra stayed at the Math (monastery) for a few days. It was then that another extraordinary incident took place. Here is Abanindra's account of it, written many years later. ("Maharaj" was the name by which Brahmananda was known familiarly in the Order; its approximate meaning is "Master.")

One morning, as usual, I went to prostrate before Maharaj. An old man was also in the room. Suddenly he asked Maharaj, "When is this boy going to become a monk?" Maharaj looked me up and down, and his eyes had an unforgettable sweetness as he answered quietly, "When the Lord wills." That was the end of my political plans and ambitions. I remained at the monastery.

During the years which followed, Abanindra was at the Ramakrishna monastery in Madras. He attended Brahmananda whenever he was allowed to, which was not often, because Brahmananda had to travel from one monastery to another in the course of his duties as Head of the Order. However, Brahmananda was present when, in the autumn of 1921, Abanindra took his final vows (*sannyas*) and became Swami Prabhavananda. (*Prabhavananda* means "one who finds bliss within the Source of all creation"; *ananda*, meaning "bliss" or "peace," is the suffix usually added to a swami's given name.)

In 1922, Brahmananda died. In 1923, Prabhavananda was told by his seniors that an assistant swami was needed at the center in San Francisco and that they wished him to go there. (There were already several such centers, founded by Vivekananda during his second and last visit to the United States, 1899–1900. These centers were often called Vedanta societies, meaning that they were dedicated to the study and practice of the philosophy which is taught in the Vedas, the most ancient of the Hindu scriptures.)

Since Brahmananda's death, Prabhavananda had been hoping to be permitted to lead a contemplative life, practicing intensive meditation, at a monastery in the Himalayan foothills. He felt quite unfitted to teach anybody. In his own words, "I was barely thirty, I looked like twenty, and I felt even younger than that." But his seniors rebuked him for his lack of confidence. How could he presume to imagine that success or failure depended on his own efforts? Had he no faith that Brahmananda would help him? "How dare you say you cannot teach? You have known the Son of God!"

When Prabhavananda lectured for the second time at the San Francisco Center, he was suddenly at a loss for words and had to excuse himself and walk out of the room. But this was only beginner's stage fright. He soon became an effective speaker, as well as an efficient assistant to the swami in charge. Within two years, he was sent to Portland, Oregon, to open a center there.

While he was living in Portland, Prabhavananda was invited to Los Angeles, to give a series of lectures on Vedanta philosophy. It was then that he got to know Mrs. Carrie Mead Wyckoff. Thirty years earlier, as a young woman, Mrs. Wyckoff had met Vivekananda while he was in California. Later she had become a disciple of Swami Turiyananda, another of Ramakrishna's direct disciples, and he had given her the monastic name of Sister Lalita—Lalita was one of the handmaidens of Krishna. Henceforward, people usually called her "Sister."

Sister was now a widow and she had just lost her only son—it seemed natural for the elderly lady and the youthful swami to form a kind of adoptive relationship. Sister returned with him to Portland and kept house for him at the center. Then, in 1929, she offered him her home, 1946 Ivar Avenue, to be the center of a future Vedanta Society of Southern California. They moved into it as soon as arrangements to carry on the work in Portland had been made.

At first the Society was very small. The living room of the house was easily able to hold Prabhavananda's congregation. An Englishwoman whom they called Amiya came to live with them; later they were joined by two or three other women. They had barely enough money to live on.

Then, around 1936, the congregation began to expand. Prabhavananda had become well known locally as a speaker. It was now only rarely that anyone would telephone to ask if the Swami would draw up a horoscope or give a public demonstration of psychic powers. In fact, word had got about that he wasn't a swami in the usual California sense but a teacher of religion whose title had the same significance as "Father" in the Catholic Church.

And then donors appeared with enough money to pay for the building of a temple; there was room for one in Sister's garden. It was finished and dedicated in July 1938—one year before I first saw it.

Three

In the beginning, the most important aspect of my relationship with Prabhavananda was that I was British. For, however hotly I might profess anti-imperialistic opinions, I was still an heir to Britain's guilt in her dealings with India. I was well aware of this and of the mixed feelings which guilt caused in me. While condemning the British, I felt an involuntary hostility to Hindus—just *because* my ancestors had treated them badly and *because* spokesmen of other nations kept telling the British how badly the Hindus were being treated.

Before meeting Prabhavananda, I had known few Hindus and none of them intimately. I could therefore indulge my prejudice without having to admit individual exceptions. I could picture all Hindus as victims, the kind of victims who provoke you to aggression against them. Their weakness shames you while their silent arrogance condemns you as a bully belonging to an inferior culture. It was this imagined combination of weakness and arrogance which repelled and enraged me.

Now, feeling strongly drawn to Prabhavananda, I had

to get around my prejudice by telling myself that he was indeed an exception and not even a typical Hindu. (It is significant that I chose to think of him as looking "slightly Mongolian.") Though I had been charmed by his gentleness, I refused to think of him as weak, so I dwelt on his youthful image as the student terrorist. Despite my own pacifism, I preferred a teacher who had been willing to use a revolver; I was glad that he hadn't practiced mere non-violence, lying down in passive protest on the railroad tracks. And I was glad that he still spoke vehemently, in public and in private, against British imperialism.

I am nearly certain that Prabhavananda, by the time I met him, harbored no prejudice against the British as individuals. Indeed, I often suspected that he felt more akin to us than to the Americans among whom he had now lived for fifteen years. An enemy, present or past, is more intimately related to you than a neutral can ever be.

Besides, we shared a cultural background with him. Abanindra's British tyrants had forced him to attend schools modeled on the British educational system, to learn to speak British English, not American, and to study literature and philosophy which was almost exclusively British. (Abanindra had found the philosophy unsubtle and materialistic but had acquired a lasting fondness for Shakespeare.)

And now Abanindra, transformed into Prabhavananda, was actually playing teacher to two highly distinguished representatives of the tyrant race. Here were Huxley and Heard coming to him as pupils, humbly intent on learning the philosophy of *his* race, which their ancestors had conquered and then presumed to teach. What a victory! No, I am not being flippant. And I don't mean that Prabhavananda was enjoying the situation spitefully. That he should have such pupils gave him genuine pride, and his pride was tempered with humility. He was constantly aware of the many things which the two of them could have taught him. He had a Hindu reverence for knowledge as such, even though much of their knowledge was of a sort which his monastic training made him regard as spiritually worthless. He really valued his association with them and continued to value it in later years when he saw them only seldom.

But were Heard and Huxley fully his pupils, even at the beginning? Were they indeed accepting his philosophy as a whole, without reservations? No, I don't think they were. Both of them were eclectics—continually on the lookout for fresh formulations of ideas, new items of information which they could fit into their complex individual world pictures. Neither one of them could have put himself unreservedly under the direction of a single teacher.

And then there was the question of age. It certainly wasn't unheard-of for a swami to have disciples who were older than himself. But the Hindu concept of the relationship does have a father-child aspect; and both Huxley and Heard may well have found this embarrassing. Gerald was four years older than Prabhavananda, Aldous was less than a year younger. Yet both of them could have belonged to a senior generation, not because they looked so old but because of their air of maturity and assurance. Prabhavananda, though nearly forty-six, was still aware of his boyish appearance; it sometimes made him feel unsure of himself, as he was the first to admit.

I, on the other hand, was eleven years Prabhavananda's junior, as boyish-looking as he, and even less sure of myself. Many of the psychological props which had hitherto supported me had been knocked away. I now needed a new kind of support, and I urgently hoped to be able to accept him as my first and only religious teacher, my *guru*.

He was considerably shorter than I was. This made me able to love him in a special, protective way, as I loved little Annie Avis, my childhood nanny, and as I should love Stravinsky. His smallness sometimes seemed baby-like, because it was combined with an animal lack of self-consciousness about his physical functions. He belched loudly without excusing himself. He also expelled the mucus from his sinuses with harsh snorting noises which embarrassed the fastidious. (In later life, he stopped doing this—probably because his sinuses cleared after he gave up smoking.)

As a youth he must have had a lithe, athletic body which I would no doubt have found sexually attractive. He was still slim and carried himself erect. I was aware of a strong sexuality in him which seemed to be controlled, rather than repressed or concealed. He would remark, quite often and without embarrassment, that some girl or woman was beautiful. His honest recognition of the power of sex attraction and his lack of prudery in speaking of it was a constant corrective to my inherited puritanism.

The breadth and smoothness of his forehead gave him a calm, truthful look. His nostrils were very wide; I wondered if this was the result of the deep inhalations and exhalations which he recommended as a method of quieting the mind before meditation. His lips were big and expressive, without any suggestion of austere restraint; when they parted a little, the two extra-large front teeth peeped out, comically rabbitlike. His skin was golden but not dark. When he wore his monastic robes—of which the yellow color symbolizes renunciation—the effect was striking; he seemed all gold. But that was only when he gave lectures in the temple. Otherwise, he nearly always wore informal Western clothes: a white shirt with or without a tie, a woolen pullover, gray flannel slacks, and leather slippers.

Oriental eyes are often somewhat dismissively described as beautiful. Prabhavananda's eyes, if you considered them simply as features, were not remarkably so. They didn't dazzle or dominate you at first glance. They were soft, dark, and moist, with yellowish whites. Therefore, whenever I describe their effect upon me, the reader must remember that I am really describing how Prabhavananda—or "this thing"—was using them on that particular occasion.

His voice was naturally soft. But when he lectured, he spoke loudly and clearly, without effort. His English was fluent, with some quaint pronunciations which delighted me. He said "fussht" for "first," "etarnal" for "eternal," "okezzshionally" for "occasionally," "whirrelled" for "whirled," "Mr. Hard" for "Mr. Heard."

"This house belongs to Maharaj. Maharaj is watching over it, over all of you. I can do nothing on my own. I am only his servant." This was what Prabhavananda would tell me, and everybody else who came to the Center, again and again.

Such statements embarrassed me a little at first. I reacted to them with a nervous smile. But I was aware that Prabhavananda didn't make them lightly; that they didn't merely express a conventional piety, as in the phrase: "This is God's house."

You could say that his belief in the presence and protection of Brahmananda was all the religion he needed. It was through Brahmananda that he felt himself in communication with "this thing." Actually, during his monastic life in India, he had met most of Ramakrishna's direct disciples and had spent much more time with some of them than he had spent with Brahmananda himself. Knowing these disciples must have confirmed Prabhavananda's faith. He spoke of them with the deepest reverence. But Brahmananda was his guru, and remained unique.

Could I pretend to understand what such a devotion must mean? No. My own experience of relationships was so different and so inferior. I couldn't help thinking of any sort of love relation as a bargain struck between two parties. The parties might keep to it for a short or a long while or even until death, but they could never regard it as absolutely firm. Neither one of the parties could be trusted not to violate it at any moment without warning—thus enabling the other party to impose penalties or employ the blackmail of forgiveness.

Prabhavananda explained that Brahmananda didn't love others in this person-to-person way. Having realized God, who is love, he had *become* love. Those who came into his presence felt that love; he gave forth love while remaining incapable of possessiveness or jealousy.

I could understand this statement as an intellectual proposition; emotionally, it was unintelligible to me. And I had difficulty in relating it to Brahmananda's behavior during that brief, extraordinary scene of Abanindra's decision to join the monastery. Brahmananda's answer, "When the Lord wills," seemed disconcertingly passive, almost indifferent—even though it was accompanied by a look of "unforgettable sweetness." Was this because Brahmananda was already aware that Abanindra had subconsciously made up his mind to become a monk?

And, beyond this mystery, there was an even greater one: What had both Brahmananda and Holy Mother meant by asking, "Haven't I seen you before?" Must one suppose that they had been associated with Aba-

nindra in a previous life? And did that mean that
Abanindra was already a member of their inner circle
and that his becoming a monk in this life was therefore inevitable? I decided not to try to make sense out
of any of this for the present. I put it into what Gerald
aptly called "my suspense account."

When Prabhavananda insisted that he himself wasn't
really running the Center, the image which occurred to
me in trying to understand this situation was that of a
party of rock climbers, roped together. The highest
climber we could see was Prabhavananda. But, above
him, up there out of sight, was Brahmananda, the actual
leader of the party. Brahmananda had already reached
the summit, the goal of the climb. Therefore he must
have seen to it that the top end of the rope was firmly
belayed. The climbers could all follow him to the summit, provided that they didn't lose their determination
to go on climbing. Even if they slipped and fell, it could
only be for a short distance. The rope would break their
fall and hold them while they found a new toehold on
the cliff face.

It was very important to me that Prabhavananda described himself as a servant; that made me feel closer
to him. It meant that I needn't expect him to be perfect
and try to explain away his weaknesses. From this standpoint, his major addiction, chain-smoking, seemed sympathetic, even reassuring. The humility expressed by his
attitude to Brahmananda must surely protect him from
spiritual pride. Instead of claiming the greatness of a
spiritual teacher, he was showing us an example of a
great disciple—which was what we most needed, being
disciples ourselves.

Nevertheless, the basic question remained: Was
Brahmananda indeed up there, and was there contact
between him and Prabhavananda? Perhaps the day

would come when I should be able to get a direct answer to this, through meditation. All I could hope for at
present was some kind of half answer obtained indirectly
through Prabhavananda, by studying his words and actions and trying to get a glimpse of what was behind
them.

My only tool for Prabhavananda study was my own
intuition. It certainly wasn't infallible. It had made mistakes in the past, especially when I had demanded quick
judgments; it functioned slowly. Still, it was all I had
and better than nothing. It already assured me that
Prabhavananda wasn't in the least crazy and wasn't in
any sense a charlatan. But, for all his sanity, honesty,
and intelligence, he could still be a wishful thinker, sincerely self-deceived. Would it ever be possible for me to
feel certain about this, one way or the other?

Four

What I have just written is misleading in one respect;
it suggests that my relationship with Prabhavananda was
now established and continuous. Well, in a sense, it
was. I thought about him many times every day, taking
it for granted that he would be available whenever I
needed him. But the astonishing fact remains that, during the rest of the year and the spring and summer of
1940, I very seldom went to see him.

I will try to explain why.

Sometime in July 1939, Berthold Viertel, the poet and
film director, had returned home from England via New
York. I had first met him in 1933 in London, where we
had worked together on the script of a film he was to
direct (see *Christopher and His Kind*). We had become
close friends.

Berthold, his wife, Salka, and their three sons had a
house near the beach in Santa Monica Canyon. Though

Berthold and Salka were both Jews from Central Europe, they couldn't exactly be called refugees, since they had settled in the United States several years before Hitler came into power. Both had worked for the Hollywood studios, Salka as an actress as well as a writer.

Berthold had now been commissioned to direct a film and wanted me to help him with the script. It was to be about a young German officer who becomes a Nazi and is later disillusioned; quite ordinary stuff for those days, but when Berthold began to improvise on it, it sounded thrilling—what stuff didn't? I agreed eagerly, although he warned me that there would be very little money in it for either of us—the producer was of the kind called "independent," a more ominous word then than now. (Indeed, the film was never made and ended in a lawsuit—which I had to settle out of my own pocket.)

Since 1933, refugees from Hitler's Reich had been arriving in Los Angeles. Salka, because of her connections at the studios and elsewhere, was able to find many of them work, especially the writers, actors, and musicians. Her home had become one of their favorite meeting places.

I myself belonged to this refugee world by adoption, having lived in it during my wanderings through various European countries, between 1933 and 1938. In those days, I had known a lot of its inhabitants, some intimately, and had been accepted by them almost as one of themselves, all the more so because I was traveling with an anti-Nazi German, Heinz. As far as an outsider could, I empathized with their self-mocking, witty despair and nearly sane paranoia.

These people were already dwelling in a future, a wartime, which very few native Californians could even imagine. To myself, as a European, the war atmosphere which the refugees breathed was more native than the ignorant peacefulness of the California air. They drew me into their midst by an overwhelming psychological suction. While I was with them, I actually worried less, because I felt that they were all sharing my worry with me. I took to spending more and more time in their depressing yet comforting company and became reluctant to leave it.

In September, a week or two after the outbreak of war in Europe, Vernon and I moved from the house we had been renting in Hollywood, into furnished rooms. These rooms were in Santa Monica Canyon, only a short walk from the Viertels but a long drive from where Chris Wood and Gerald Heard lived, and an even longer drive from the Vedanta Center.

Early in 1940, I got a job at M-G-M. This was chiefly thanks to the Viertels, who knew a producer there, Gottfried Reinhardt, one of Max Reinhardt's sons. We were to make a film out of James Hilton's novel *Rage in Heaven*. My fellow screenwriter was Robert Thoeren, an Austrian. So I remained within the refugee world even at the studio. Gottfried, Robert, and I often spoke German together when we were discussing the script.

Looked at from outside, my life could have been described as busy, successful, and social. I was earning five hundred dollars a week, low-bracket pay by movie standards, Arabian Nights wealth by mine. I wasn't inspired by my film work but I was fond of my fellow workers and enjoyed our parlor game of plot construction. In the evenings, at the Viertels' and elsewhere, I mingled with famous and fascinating people: Aldous and Maria Huxley (who had a house nearby), Garbo, Charlie Chaplin, Anita Loos, Thomas Mann and his family, Bertrand Russell. And yet, deep down, I was miserable. I felt steeped in that dull brutish inertia which the Hindus call *tamas*, the lowest condition of the psyche. My misery expressed itself in various minor ailments. These were being treated by a doctor, whose large fees I could now easily afford.

The days go by and I don't see the Swami, don't start meditating. This isn't mere laziness. The opposition is enormously strong. Incredible as it seems, part of me actually wants to wallow in black lazy misery, like a pig in filth.

My diary adds that Vernon has finally caught my depression, "like a South Sea islander who nearly dies of a common cold imported by a trader."

March 6, 1940. I've seen the Swami. He says if I'm too busy to meditate I should think about the word Om, which is God. But I can only become aware of God by thinking all around him. Om says nothing. It's just a comic noise. I'm afraid the Swami is altogether too Indian for me. I must talk to Gerald again.

The Sanskrit word *Om* is used by Hindus as the basic name of God, because it is thought of as being the most comprehensive of all human sounds. Fully pronounced, it combines utterance by the throat, the mouth, and the lips—approximately *Ah-oo-mm*. This I already knew. But there were moods in which my anti-Hindu prejudice made me rhyme *Om* with *Tom*, thus turning it into "just a comic noise"—as in om-tiddly-om-pom.

In July, I went at least twice to a class Prabhavananda was giving on the Upanishads (those portions of the Vedas which contain the teachings of Vedanta philosophy; the rest contain prayers, hymns, rules of conduct, and instructions for the performance of rituals).

Seated on a cushion, he smilingly exposed the ignorance of his class. He is gentle, persuasive, and humorous. He speaks quietly, with an absolute, matter-of-fact authority. To him, spiritual truths are unanswerable facts, like the facts of geography. You don't have to get excited about them, or argue or defend. You just state them . . . I notice that he has a taste for very elegant, pointed shoes.

Someone mentioned the Holy Ghost. The Swami was asked to explain It, and said that he couldn't, he wasn't a Christian. So everybody present had a try, and the difference in our definitions was a sufficient comment on the muddle of Christian theology. To every suggestion, the Swami replied, "No—that is too far-fetch-ed." At last he sent one of the girls out for Webster's Dictionary. Some of the class were quite scandalized. "You won't find it there," they told him. But the Swami was confident: "Webster's Dictionary can tell you everything." He was wrong, however. Webster said only: "Comforter, Paraclete." The Swami promised to "ask Mr. Hard." He seems to have great confidence in Gerald.

On July 29, I got further instructions from Prabhavananda. He told me to meditate on the *Atman*, the indwelling God, "this thing" within each one of us: "Imagine that there is a cavity within you. In the middle of this cavity there is a throne, in the form of a red lotus. In the middle of this lotus, a golden light is burning. Approach this light and say 'Oh Self, reveal Yourself to me.' "

My comment on this was:

My imagination revolts from this: it sounds like a stage scene at the Radio City Music Hall. But I shall try to do it. I have put myself into the Swami's hands and I must follow his instructions, just as I follow Dr. K.'s. We always want to choose our own medicine. A rose, for example, wouldn't seem nearly so silly to me. But perhaps the lotus is better, just because I don't like it.

"The Swami is too Indian for me" was a complaint I would return to, again and again. But, even while persisting in my prejudice, I had to admit to myself that the very Indianness of Vedanta was helpful to me. Because of my other, anti-Christian set of prejudices, I was repelled by the English religious words I had been taught in childhood and was grateful to Vedanta for speaking Sanskrit. I needed a brand-new vocabulary and here it was, with a set of philosophical terms which were exact in meaning, unemotive, untainted by disgusting old associations with clergymen's sermons, schoolmasters' pep talks, politicians' patriotic speeches.

I had now met Aldous Huxley many times—usually with Maria, but occasionally by himself at M-G-M, while we were both working there. (*He* was earning fifteen hundred dollars a week, and sending most of it to help relatives and friends in wartime Europe.) I already felt at ease with Maria, who was charmingly outspoken; she asked me frank questions about my personal life, which I answered with equal frankness. When the three of us were together, we behaved like intimate friends. When Aldous and I were alone, I felt uneasy because I was aware—indeed, it was Gerald who had made me aware —that Aldous, with all his liberalism, found homosexuality and the homosexual temperament deeply distasteful. I am sure that he liked me personally and that he fought against his prejudice. He was a nobly fair-minded man. Nevertheless, my uneasiness remained.

That Aldous and I were both officially disciples of Prabhavananda didn't strengthen the bond between us, as far as I was concerned. I was beginning to realize that Aldous and Prabhavananda were temperamentally far apart. Prabhavananda was strongly devotional. Aldous was much more akin to his friend Krishnamurti, who was then living at Ojai, a couple of hours' drive from Los Angeles. Krishnamurti expounded a philosophy of discrimination between the real and the unreal; as a Hindu who had broken away from Hinduism, he was repelled by devotional religion and its rituals. He also greatly disapproved of the guru-disciple relationship.

According to my diary (July 31), I must have told Aldous at least something about Prabhavananda's latest instructions to me, thus prompting Aldous to tell me that Krishnamurti never meditated on "objects"—such as lotuses, lights, gods, and goddesses—and even believed that doing so might lead to insanity.

This conversation disturbed me very much. Suppose Gerald is barking up the wrong tree? But I'm also aware that these doubts are not quite candid; they are being prompted by the Ego as part of its sabotage effort.

My indiscretion in talking to Aldous about Prabhavananda's instructions was inexcusable. Indeed, it was worse than an indiscretion, since I must have known in advance that Aldous would be critical, and would thus disturb me and strengthen my doubts.

The refugees weren't the only ones who drew me into their midst and away from Prabhavananda. There was also an assortment of men and women whom I will call "Seekers," because many of them would have so described themselves. I met them through Gerald, who had now become a central figure in their circles, not only in Los Angeles, but throughout the country. Chris Wood protected him from the Seekers' phone calls by refusing to take messages for him, but his mail was enormous and urgent. "It's funny," I once said to him, "how these people invariably write to you airmail special delivery, when all their questions are about eternity."

Some of the Seekers had unquestionable integrity and courage—even perhaps saintliness: a man who had become a clergyman because he had had a vision of Christ when he was fighting in World War I, a Japanese who had been persecuted by his countrymen for his pacifism, an ex-burglar who had practiced mental non-violence while being beaten up by prison guards. As for the rest, many might have been called cranks but almost none of them fakes. I couldn't imagine any of them as disciples of Prabhavananda—some because they were too exclusively Christian, others because they put the need for social action before spiritual training, others because they were entangled in the occult, others because they were trying to use what they called religion to heal sickness, promote longevity, ensure success in business and joy in marriage—all this with perfect confidence in the purity of their motives.

What was I looking for, amidst these people? What made me sit through their lectures and join them in hours of earnest discussion? I might have answered truthfully that I was interested in some of them as practitioners of pacifism. I could have claimed that the rest were at least teaching me tolerance: during my pre-California life I wouldn't have been seen dead with them. Their earnest air of dedication, their gently persuasive voices, and their pious vocabulary would have turned my atheistic stomach.

But I had to admit to a deeper motive. I was associating with the Seekers in order to find weaknesses in their faith and contradictions in their creeds; to prove to myself, if possible, that they were seeking a non-existent treasure. If their treasure was non-existent, then Prabhavananda's might be, too.

Thus I kept rediscovering in myself an active underground force of opposition to Prabhavananda's way of life—insofar as it threatened to influence mine. In my diary, I called this force my ego—what I actually meant was my self-will. "Nothing burns in Hell except self-will" was a favorite quotation of Gerald's, from the *Theologia Germanica*, XXXIV.

Speaking of hell, I am thankful that I at least had the good sense not to personify my self-will as the Devil and imagine myself to be the prey of an awesomely malign superpower, whose strength I couldn't be expected to resist. What I was struggling with was something quite intimate and unalarming, something that had an animal, not a superhuman nature; something that was partly a monkey, partly a dog, partly a peacock, partly a pig. One must be firm with it, one must keep an eye on it always, but there was no reason to hate it or be afraid of it. Its plans for my future weren't devilish, they weren't even clever. It merely wanted to maintain the usual messy aimless impulse-driven way of life to which it was accustomed. It would actually rather wallow in "lazy black misery" than be interfered with by Prabhavananda.

Five

By August 1940, the war had long since ceased to be
called "phony," even in California. It was a solid presence which cast its shadow all over the United States.
The Nazis had occupied France and threatened to invade England. Americans had begun to tell each other
fatalistically, "We'll be in it soon."

The future promised us bureaucratic discipline, denial
of comfort, frustration of self-will. So my anti-Prabhava-
nanda underground panicked and was ready to lie low
and give up its sabotage efforts, for the time being. In
contrast to the grim activity of the outside world, the
Vedanta Society way of life suddenly appealed to it, as
being quiet and snug. While the rest of me tried to
meditate, it could at least sit still and do nothing.

*August 9. To see the Swami. Sat in the temple while he
and several of the holy women who live at the Center
finished their evening rites. The bottoms of the women*

were enormous, as they bowed down to adore. Could concentrate on nothing else.

("The holy women" was one of Gerald's phrases. Used by him, it chiefly expressed affectionate humor, but also some misogyny. He and I agreed, at that time, in finding women hard to coexist with as fellow worshipers. They so often seemed to us to be calling attention to their presence, especially when decked out in their best saris with tinkling bracelets, and the saris naturally enlarged the bottoms. Our prejudice would never have included Sister Lalita, however. In the temple she was the most self-effacing of us all.)

The Swami called me into his study afterwards. He gave me new and much more elaborate instructions.

First, I am to think of people all over the world—all kinds of people at all kinds of occupations. In each one of them, and in all matter, is this Reality, this Atman, which is also inside myself. And what is "myself"? Am I my body? Am I my mind? Am I my thoughts? What can I find within myself which is eternal? Let me examine my thoughts and see how they reflect this Atman.

August 12. Meditation night and morning. It is much easier now, since the Swami's new instructions, because I can begin with the external world and work inward. I start by thinking of Heinz. Then of the airmen fighting over the Channel. Then Hitler, Churchill. Then Teddy, our dog in Portugal, the ocean with all its fish, etc. etc.

August 13. Huge German air attacks on England. Invasion is expected hourly. I feel terribly depressed, but not frantic. It's amazing how much my "sits" help, however

badly and unwillingly I do them. They clear the mind of
that surplus of misery which is entirely subjective and
unnecessary, and helps no one—which, in fact, merely
poisons the lives of everybody around you and makes
their own troubles harder to bear. Too much unhappiness over external tragedies is as bad as too little. Both
softening and hardening of the heart can become vicious.
I begin to understand what Eliot means in Ash Wednesday: "Teach us to care and not to care."

August 18. Today I finished an almost unbroken week of
"sits." My chief effort is to stand outside the Ego, to
try to catch a glimpse of the world with a non-attached
eye. But the Ego, with its gross body and great swollen,
sullen pumpkin head, is like a man who <u>will</u> stand right
in front of you at a horse race; you can only catch
glimpses of the race by peeping under his arms or between his legs. It is terribly difficult, but the mere discipline of trying brings its own rewards—cheerfulness,
long periods of calm, freedom from self-pity. Vernon is
the invariable barometer of my failure or success. Yesterday afternoon, when we were laughing together, he suddenly said, "If only it could always be like this!"

(I should mention here that Vernon and I were just
about to move into a rented house back in the Hollywood area. This wouldn't necessarily isolate me from
the world of the refugees but it would enable me to visit
the Vedanta Center much more easily.)

September 7. Looking in through the glass door of the
living room at Ivar Avenue, I saw the Swami sitting
alone. He must have been meditating—his face was
utterly transformed. It was very still and almost frighteningly attentive, like a lion watching its prey before it

jumps. Then he became aware of my presence and rose to greet me, his usual gay polite Bengali self.

According to my diary, I found it easier to meditate in the shrine room of the temple than in my room at home:

The atmosphere is extraordinarily calming, and yet alive, not sleepy. Someone said to me that it's like being in a wood. This is a very good description. Just as, in a wood, you feel the trees alive all around you, so in the shrine the air seems curiously alert. Sometimes it is as if the whole shrine room becomes your brain and is filled with thought. Of course, the smell of the incense also helps. It induces a special mood by association—just as the smell of antiseptics induces the passive mood of the hospital patient.

If you entered the temple when it wasn't being used and when the curtains were drawn together, concealing the shrine, it looked like a small lecture hall which was remarkable only for the good taste and simplicity with which it was furnished. Light gray walls, a light gray carpet, rows of light gray seats facing a pulpit on a platform. On the walls were photographs of Ramakrishna, the Holy Mother, Vivekananda, Brahmananda, an image of the Buddha, the alleged face of Christ on the Turin shroud. There were no decorations, Indian or other, except for the word *Om*, which was carved on the pulpit.

When the curtains were drawn apart, you saw that there was a little windowless shrine room beyond the platform on which the pulpit stood. Within this shrine room, on a pedestal of two steps, stood the shrine itself. It was about four feet in height and had been made in India out of a dark wood which was intricately carved and gleamingly polished; four double Corinthian pillars supporting a dome. Under this dome, a photograph of Ramakrishna stood in the middle. To the right of it was a photograph of Holy Mother; to the left were images of Buddha and Krishna and a Russian icon of Christ. Photographs of Brahmananda and Vivekananda were on a lower level, together with images of some minor Hindu deities.

During the Sunday lecture, the curtains were parted and the shrine exposed, decked with garlands of flowers and lit by candles in glass candlesticks which had sparkling pendants. It looked exotically pretty, and no doubt a casual visitor to the temple, seeing it for the first time, would regard it merely as a charming focal point in the scheme of decoration. But this shrine really was a shrine, in the primary meaning of the word. It contained relics of Ramakrishna, Holy Mother, and some of their disciples, including fragments of bone which had been preserved after their bodies had been cremated. The Hindus, like the Catholics, believe that such relics generate spiritual power which can be communicated to worshipers who expose themselves to it. But this is only half of the process. What the worshipers receive, they must return to the shrine through acts of worship; thereby they "recharge" the shrine, and thus themselves, continually. It was therefore a rule that ritual worship must be performed before the shrine every single day.

When driving along Sunset Boulevard, I would sometimes feel the impulse to park outside a certain church and go into it. Before kneeling in one of the pews, I would genuflect to the altar and cross myself. I always felt slightly guilty of theatricalism as I did this, and excused the action to myself as being a gesture of mere conformity, since I was in a Catholic church.

What was I actually doing there? I might have answered that, by meditating in our temple, I had discovered in myself a strong devotional inclination which I had been suppressing throughout most of my adult life. Because of this inclination, I now felt drawn to *any* sacred place. A Catholic church was more like our temple than a Protestant church would have been, because it contained a shrine. The consecrated Host was present in the tabernacle on the altar, and people kept coming in throughout the day to kneel before it and adore it.

This was true, but not the whole truth. Because of my Protestant upbringing, going into a Catholic church still gave me a slight sense of daring, of doing what was forbidden. This was what made my visit exciting. To genuflect and cross yourself was scandalous behavior, by the Protestant standards of my youth. To bow down before a Hindu shrine wouldn't have been scandalous in the same way; it would have been just heathen and therefore meaningless.

Having entered the pew, I became a Vedantist again and meditated according to my instructions. I felt nothing incongruous in doing this. After all, we had Christ's icon on *our* shrine, so why shouldn't I regard myself as a welcome guest—welcomed by Christ, at any rate, if not by his priesthood? However, I never stayed on in the church if a service was about to be held; that would have seemed to me like trespassing. And I never dipped my finger in the stoup of holy water. That, I felt, would have involved me in an alien and therefore dangerous kind of magic.

About the middle of August, a young American named Denny Fouts had arrived in Los Angeles. Denny would represent himself to new acquaintances as having been a spectacularly successful homosexual whore. It was true that he had had a number of affairs with rich men and that they had given him a lot of money. He made much of this, speaking of having been "kept" by them, and watching your face as he used the word to see if you would wince. (I have described him as "Paul" in my novel *Down There on a Visit*, which also contains a sketch of Gerald as "Augustus Parr.")

At first I had found Denny's tactics tiresome. Then he had surprised and intrigued me by showing great interest in Vedanta and in the Swami. Long conversations with him had gradually convinced me that his interest was absolutely serious. It seemed to be related to some terrifying insights he had had while taking drugs.

October 26. Lunch with Denny, who is anxious to start a new life—get a shack in the hills, a menial job, and immediately renounce everything: sex, drink, and the Gang. He's very nervous and much worried about his motives—is he wishing to do this for the right reasons? But surely, at the start, the reasons don't matter? If you are doing this for the wrong reasons, I told him, you'll very soon find out.

Meanwhile, Denny still goes to parties and gets drunk and talks nothing but religion, to the great amusement of his friends, who call him "the drunken yogi."

Today I took him to the temple, where we sat for some time in the shrine (or "the box," as Gerald calls it). I couldn't concentrate—I was thinking all the time of Denny—trying to "introduce" him to Ramakrishna, and hoping he wouldn't be put off by the photographs on the shrine, and the flowers, and the ivory and brass figures. It does look rather like the mantelpiece in an old-fashioned boudoir. Actually, Denny liked it all very much, but was dismayed because he had thought what a wonderful place it would be to have sex in.

By this time, I had become possessive of Denny, regarding him as my personal convert, the soul I had saved. And I was eager to bring him to Prabhavananda. I expected to get credit from both parties; Prabhavananda was to praise me for my valuable catch, Denny for my understanding, all-pardoning guru.

Their meeting was a disaster. I wasn't present, but, from what Denny told me about it later, I guessed that he had struck the wrong note from the beginning. He must have been aggressive and theatrical and strident, painting himself as the lowest of sinners and daring Prabhavananda to reject him. This approach might have made an impression on some Christian ministers. But Prabhavananda wasn't interested in show-off sinners, any more than he was interested in self-satisfied holy men. All he watched and listened for was the look and sound of truth.

When Denny had finished his performance, Prabhavananda discouraged him from trying to make a drastic change in his life, telling him that what he needed was hard work; he had better go out and get himself a job.

Denny was terribly disappointed and hurt. As soon as we got back to his room, he threw himself down on the bed and burst into tears, sobbing that he was rotten, everybody despised him, and he'd better kill himself with heroin as soon as possible.

I protested, of course—as anybody would. In fact, I said far more than I meant. I told him that I didn't despise him, that I admired him and liked him and wanted to be his friend.

At first I was slightly shocked by what seemed to me to have been an inflexibility and lack of understanding in Prabhavananda's behavior. Also, my feelings were hurt by his rejection of the first disciple I had brought to him. He immediately sensed this, the next time we were alone together. With his usual gentle reasonableness, he explained that, in the religious life, if you try to do too much in too great a hurry, you are sure to have a reaction and perhaps lose your faith altogether. Maharaj had always been suspicious of sudden hysterical "conversions." Soon I began to realize that Prabhavananda had shown sound judgment.

Nevertheless, I was now committed to doing something about Denny. So I took him up to see Gerald, after telling Gerald what had happened at the Vedanta Center. Perhaps I slanted the story a little, to prejudice Gerald in Denny's favor; in any case, this was a sly tempting of Gerald to demonstrate his superior charity. Denny assisted me by turning on all his powerful charm. Gerald was quickly won over.

As for myself, I continued to see Denny quite often, and was soon able to feel sincerely what I had told him— that I did like him and did want to be his friend. I was able to admire him, too, for Denny declared that he wasn't going to be discouraged by what Prabhavananda had said. He was determined to start meditating and living "intentionally," under Gerald's guidance. He and I remained friends throughout all the ups and downs of his life during the next few years, but he never forgave Prabhavananda. This was a constant cause of friction between us.

November 7. Some while ago, driving home through the evening traffic along Sunset Boulevard, I was attacked by one of those spasms of cramp which often follow Dr. K.'s injections. It was so violent and so unexpected that I exclaimed "Oh God!" aloud. And now something extraordinary happened. The word, which I have mis-used ten million times, produced a kind of echo in my consciousness, like the vibration after a bell has been struck. It seemed to vibrate down, down into the depths of me. It was so strange, so awe-inspiring, that I longed for the cramp to return. I thought: "I have called upon God." After a moment, I had another spasm, but this time there was no echo. The word was just another word.

How much unhappiness there is in the world! No need to search for it across the ocean, in bombed London or China or Greece. The other evening, outside my win-dow, a little boy cried to his mother: "You don't want anyone to play with me!" Even the most trivial unkind-ness is heartbreaking, if one weren't so deaf and blind. Very occasionally, I'm aware of this. The other night (it sounds absurd when I write it) I ran the car over a tin can on our parking lot, and felt almost as bad as if I'd killed an animal. "Oh God," I said to myself, "must we always keep smashing things?"

Tomorrow morning, I'm going up to the temple to be initiated by the Swami. I know he is only doing this to encourage me—because, as he told Gerald, I am "arnest" —but I feel terribly inadequate. Lately, I've been getting up too late and missing my morning hour.

November 8. Picked up Gerald in the car and was at the temple by seven-thirty. When I went into the shrine, the Swami was already seated. I took my place on his left, holding a little tray with the flowers which one of the women had given me to offer; two red roses, a white rose, and a big white daisy. First the Swami told me to meditate as usual. Then I had to offer the flowers—the red roses to the photographs of Ramakrishna and Holy Mother, the daisy to the icon of Christ, the white rose to the Swami himself, as my guru. Next, he told me to meditate on Ramakrishna in the central cavity of the heart. Then he taught me my Sanskrit mantram, which I must never repeat to anybody, and gave me a rosary, showing me how to use it.

A *mantram* consists of one or more Sanskrit words, a holy name or names, which the guru gives to his disciple and which the disciple is required to repeat and meditate on throughout the rest of his life. The giving of the mantram is the essential act of the initiation ceremony. The guru may also give the disciple a rosary; this can be thought of as a physical gift which embodies the spiritual gift of the mantram.

The rosary beads used by the Ramakrishna Order are made of small dried kernels of the berry of the rudraksha tree. There are 108 beads, plus a bead which hangs down, out of line with the others, and has a tassel attached to it. This bead is said to represent the guru.

Repeating your mantram is called making *japam*. When making japam with your rosary, you repeat your mantram once for each bead. On reaching the tassel bead, you reverse the rosary and start it the other way around. Out of the 108 repetitions of the mantram which make up one turn of the rosary, a hundred are said to be for your own devotions, and the remaining eight to be on behalf of the rest of mankind. Since these eight represent a labor of love and not part of your personal efforts toward spiritual progress, you must not count them in reckoning how much japam you are going to make each day—one turn of the rosary counts as one hundred only. The average amount of japam made by an energetic devotee would be between five thousand and ten thou-

sand daily. The value of the rosary is that it measures
your japam for you; you aren't distracted from it by
having to count. But you are also encouraged to make
japam at times when you can't use a rosary—when you
are engaged in some manual work or driving a car.

In my diary, there is no mention of any others having
been initiated that day. Later on, as the Center grew,
Prabhavananda would usually initiate several people at
a time, each one in a separate ceremony. However, a
number of devotees must have arrived later that morning, for this was the birthday of Holy Mother. By nine
o'clock, I was back in the temple, having my first experience of a full-scale *puja* (ritual worship).

*The Swami offered flowers, incense, water for washing.
He made spots of red on the foreheads of Ramakrishna
and Mother with sandalwood paste. Food was brought
in, a complete meal: soup, curry, and chocolate cake
with whipped cream. The Swami's nephew acted as
prompter, reading the directions for the acts of ritual in
Sanskrit. At the end of the ceremony we each offered
a flower.*

*After this, we went into the Swami's study, where
there is a grate, for the fire ceremony (homa fire). All
our actions, good and bad, were symbolically offered up
and purified in the fire. The Swami made a sign on our
foreheads with the ash, to symbolize the opening of the
third eye, the eye of the spirit.*

*Then lunch, very gay, with lots of people. The food
offered in the temple had been mixed in with what we
ate, so this was actually a kind of communion service.
They do this every day. The consecrated food from the
temple is called prasad.*

*The Swami admitted that he oversmokes. "You must
listen to me," he giggled, "not follow me." He told us*

that during his first years here he made no converts at all. Now he has about twenty-four.

Drove Gerald home. We agreed that this sort of thing could never be transplanted to the West. Ritual is valuable, certainly—but perhaps only for the person who actually celebrates it. The holy women seemed more concerned today with the mere domestic bustle of preparing and serving food. At least that was the impression I got as an outsider.

Nevertheless, all this Hindu domesticity doesn't repel me. Precisely because it is so domestic. Ramakrishna really does seem to be established in that household. They fuss over him like a guest of honor. There is no dividing line between the activities of the temple and their daily lives. And, after all, if you admire the man at all, why not make him feel at home? Why not reproduce, as far as possible, the ceremonies he used to practice and the style of life he was accustomed to? It's really a matter of common politeness—like eating Chinese food when the Chinese Ambassador comes to dinner.

I was still, as is obvious from the above, seeing the Vedanta Center very much through Gerald's eyes— from an anthropological rather than a spiritual standpoint. Nevertheless, I had just entered into a relationship with this little Bengali and his establishment which was far more binding and serious than a marriage—I who had always had an instinctive horror of the marriage bond! Would I have involved myself in this way if I had clearly understood what it was that I was doing? Not at that time, I think. I didn't understand because I didn't yet believe in the spiritual reality of the involvement.

Prabhavananda must have known very well what he and I were letting ourselves in for. According to Hindu belief, the tie between the guru and his initiated disciple cannot be broken, either in this world or on any future plane of existence, until the disciple realizes the Atman within himself and is thus set free. Meanwhile, the disciple may neglect, reject, or even betray the guru, but the guru cannot disown him. In such cases, the guru must continue to guide the disciple mentally, from a distance, and protect him through prayer.

I had to take it for granted that Prabhavananda had long since faced up to and accepted this tremendous responsibility; it was, after all, his justification for being a swami. The mantram which Brahmananda had given him implied the obligation to pass on its power to others by giving them mantrams of their own. The Christians claim that their line of apostolic succession still carries the authority of spiritual power, even though it is now nearly two thousand years long. How short, by comparison, was the line that led us back to Ramakrishna! It was as though we at the Vedanta Center were disciples of a disciple of one of the apostles of Jesus.

Prabhavananda often told us he believed that no one who came to seek instruction at the Center did so by mere accident. "Ramakrishna chose you, *all* of you," he would declare, with conviction. "He led you to this place." In other words, we had to thank Ramakrishna's grace rather than any good karma of our own, accumulated through our previous lives. Did I believe this? I would have liked to—good luck gives one far more satisfaction than a reward of merit. But, for the present, I put Prabhavananda's statement into my "suspense account." By this time, it contained many items whose disposition couldn't be determined—and might never be.

How did Gerald regard my initiation? He certainly hadn't discouraged me from accepting it. He himself had already been initiated. So had Huxley. But both of them, as I have said, were temperamentally eclectic. I don't believe either would have felt that the initiation ceremony imposed limits on him or committed him to a special loyalty.

I suppose Gerald assumed that I would feel the same way. He can't have regarded me as having now become Prabhavananda's exclusive property, for he kept discussing with me his plans for a monastic community in which I was to be included. He had provisionally named it Focus.

Gerald was now no longer thinking in broad terms, of interrelated groups dotted about the country. Focus was to be independent, and very small—just Gerald and an English friend of his and Denny and I. Gerald had already arranged for Denny to go and work on a farm in Pennsylvania, because the farm was being run on biodynamic principles—involving the use of compost heaps. He wanted Denny to become a biodynamic expert and then put his knowledge into practice at Focus, since we were to grow our own food.

It seemed that life in our community was to be turned strictly inward, with all of us focused on "this thing," and the time left over between our meditation periods allotted to vegetable growing, household chores, frugal meals, and rationed sleep. Maybe we would never go outside the place at all.

Surely neither Denny nor I—for Gerald's friend I can't answer, since I didn't know him—would have lasted at Focus a single month. Did I ever seriously intend to join it? I don't think I knew, myself.

I was still living with Vernon, still working at M-G-M. I knew that I should be obliged to make a move of some kind, before long. Now that the United States had started conscription, conscientious objectors were to be drafted for firefighting and other forestry duties and sent to camps in the nearby mountains. At present I was over draft age, but I felt sure that men in my age group would be called up in the nearly certain event of war. So why shouldn't I volunteer now, just as many people were volunteering for the Armed Forces, instead of waiting passively to be pushed? (I did do this, some while later, but was told that volunteers for service in the camps were not being accepted.)

Six

November 12, 1940. Headache this evening, and rheumatism in my hip. So I did my meditation sitting upright on a chair in my room. Perhaps because of the headache, concentration was much easier than usual. My mind soon became calm. Sitting with closed eyes in the darkness, I suddenly "saw" a strip of carpet, illuminated by an orange light. The carpet was covered with a black pattern, quite unlike anything we have in the house. But I could also "see" my bed, standing exactly as it really stands. My field of vision wasn't in any way distorted.

As I watched, I "saw," in the middle of the carpet, a small dirty-white bird, something like a parrot. After a moment, it began to move, with its quick stiff walk, and went under the bed. This wasn't a dream. I was normally conscious, aware of what I saw and anxious to miss no detail of it. As I sat there, I felt all around me a curiously intense silence, like the silence of deep snow. The only sinister thing about the bird was its air of utter aloofness and <u>intention</u>. I had caught it going about its business—very definite business—as one glimpses a mouse disappearing into its hole.

November 13. I told the Swami about the parrot, this evening. He said it was a "symbolic vision," not a hallucination. On the whole, he seemed pleased. He thought it a sign that something is happening to my consciousness. Probably, he said, there will be other visions. I must take no particular notice of them, and not regard them as a matter for self-congratulation. They have no special significance. The psychic world is all around us, full of sub-creatures, earthbound spirits, etc. To be able to see them is just a knack, a minor talent. Dogs see spooks all the time. It is dangerous to let them interest you too much. At best, they are a distraction from the real objectives of the spiritual life. At worst, they may gain power over you and do you harm.

I also asked the Swami about sex. He said that all sex —no matter what the relationship—is a form of attachment and must ultimately be given up. This will happen naturally as you make progress in the spiritual life. "The more you travel toward the north, the farther you are from the south." But he added that force is no good. A man came to Brahmananda and asked to become a monk; he had castrated himself to be free from sex. Brahmananda wouldn't receive him into the Order. When the Swami was a young monk, he once asked Brahmananda to release him from sexual desire. (Brahmananda had the power to do this.) But Brahmananda smiled and answered, "My son, if I did that, you would miss all the fun of the struggle."

To encourage me, the Swami quoted a saying of Ramakrishna: "He who has been bitten by the cobra is sure to die . . . The cobra has bitten you, Mr. Isherwood," he said with a giggle. "You won't live long!"

November 30. About two weeks ago, I had another vision. The same orange light but redder, this time, like firelight. I thought, it's happening again. A face began to form. It was my own face. I looked at it, quite consciously, for several seconds before it disappeared.

When I started to tell the Swami about this, he looked dismayed and exclaimed in alarm: "Not that parrot?" (Because, says Gerald, the parrot might eventually have "come through" and been visible to other people. Most embarrassing. And then the Swami would have had to exorcise it. We'd have a three-day sit at the temple, and, goodness, how much Ramakrishna would eat!)

However, when I explained, the Swami was pleased and told me I'd seen my own "subtle body." He asked me if the face wasn't much handsomer than my own physical face. As a matter of fact, it was: very distinguished, rather like a Red Indian, with light blue eyes.

(The Atman in man is said to be covered by a number of *koshas*, sheaths. The outermost of these is the gross body, which is visible and tangible to other human beings at all times. Beneath this is the subtle body, not ordinarily visible to others, which vitalizes and holds together body and mind. Unless the individual becomes united with the Atman, this subtle body will not disintegrate with the gross body at death but will survive to form the basis of a new gross body when the individual is reborn.)

January 5, 1941. To the temple. The Swami lectured on the universality of religion, and against sects and fanaticism. Today he looked very young and sounded vigorous and political. I could picture him in the days before he joined the monastery, as a young student agitator and terrorist, fighting for a free India. He kept thumping his fist on the pulpit. As usual, he worked in a little nationalism—the Hindus were tolerant, the Christians and Mohammedans were not.

January 6. Sometimes I feel that my whole day depends on the first ten minutes after I wake up. Which kind of waves will first break the surface of undifferentiated consciousness? The war, personal resentments, my health, the studio, the weather—anxiety, depression—they wait just outside the illuminated field of thought, ready to move in and impose their ugly vulgar little pattern, the pattern of the day. But suppose one puts some other arrangement of one's own, consciously, in the middle of the field? Then they cannot combine.

January 11. The Swami is in bed, with a slight heart attack. So I had to do something as a substitute for his lecture. Read poems aloud—by Herbert, Vaughan, Emily Brontë, Tennyson, Swinburne; and the duel scene from The Brothers Karamazov.

January 14. Gerald lectured to the class at the temple, on the difference between meditation and contemplation. Meditation is the stage of effort in which we struggle to fix our mind on the Object by means of images, similes, and metaphors. Contemplation is effortless. When we achieve it, we are unaware of the passage of time; our mind has become one-pointed. The need for images stops. We pass beyond the stage of logical analysis. We cease to infer. We know.

It must have been soon after this that Gerald decided he couldn't any longer be publicly associated with the Vedanta Center, couldn't go on lecturing at the temple or helping Prabhavananda edit our magazine. This decision wasn't sudden. Gerald had first discussed it at length with several of his friends, including me. Having made up his mind, he wrote Prabhavananda a letter of resignation.

I suppose I must have been shown this letter, but I can't remember what was in it; perhaps because there is a confusion in my memory between what Gerald privately said to me before writing it and what he actually—and no doubt more tactfully—wrote.

Gerald's basic accusation was that Prabhavananda's way of life violated the monastic standards of austerity; it was too social, too comfortable, too relaxed. The Swami had Hindu notions of hospitality and would often invite guests to lunch—some of them not even devotees, but just their relatives or friends. Appetizing meals were served—that is, if you liked curry—and they were not necessarily vegetarian. The Swami had a car at his disposal. He chain-smoked, which set a bad example to those who were struggling with their own addictions. The women waited on him hand and foot and he accepted their service as a matter of course. His relations with them—though doubtless absolutely innocent—could easily cause misunderstandings and suspicions among outsiders. For, after all, he *was* the only male in a household of females.

Even if Gerald's letter was tactfully worded, it hurt Prabhavananda's feelings deeply. "Mr. Hard had the cheek to write to me like that!" he exclaimed indignantly, in my presence. Later he answered Gerald indirectly in an article, "Renunciation and Austerity," which he wrote for the magazine. Here are two quotations from it:

> You would identify the life of renunciation with a life of poverty and discomfort and you would say that if a spiritual teacher lives in comfort and in a plentiful household he is evidently not living the consecrated life. Your view is too simple. A man of true renunciation concerns himself neither with poverty nor with riches. If the poor man hugs his few trivial possessions, he is as much attached and as much a worldly man as the rich man. Only the poor man is worse off—because of his envy.
>
> Mere outward austerity is a degenerate form of ritualism. A spiritual soul never makes any demonstration of his renunciation or of his communion with God. He even sometimes raises external barriers to shield himself from the eyes of the curious.

(Was the Swami's chain-smoking an "external barrier," I wondered?)

Gerald kept repeating that his personal affection for Prabhavananda remained unchanged. Prabhavananda couldn't, in any case, disown Gerald, his disciple; Gerald was much present, I am sure, in Prabhavananda's mind and prayers throughout the rest of his life. But, after this, they didn't see each other often. And when they did, they behaved with noticeable politeness.

Huxley was distressed. It is a disaster, he said, when two sincere practitioners of the spiritual life fall out with each other—especially since there are so few of them, anyway. "Judge not that ye be not judged," he murmured to himself, several times—which suggested that he thought Gerald had been in the wrong.

Others may have thought so, too—or at least that Gerald's criticism of Prabhavananda could be as justly turned against himself. If the outside world might object to the Swami's life among women, mightn't it object, even more strongly, to Gerald's sharing a house with Chris Wood, who was unashamedly homosexual? If the Swami was to be accused of living comfortably, might not Gerald be accused of living in seeming poverty while enjoying invisible wealth in the form of food, lodging, transportation, and other services and goods provided by his friends? Gerald had said that the question of the Swami's moral reputation was important because he had publicly set himself up as a religious teacher. But it could be retorted that Gerald was teaching *his* kind of religion just as publicly and on a much larger scale through his books.

Undoubtedly, a great deal of Gerald's dislike of the atmosphere at the Vedanta Center was an expression of his own very different temperament. He recoiled from the women, with their chatter and laughter and bustle, because they were lively and vital and he was a life-hater. Although he could justify his attitude philosophically, saying that he longed to die in order to be free of space-time, there was an extra sourness to some of his remarks which seemed merely dyspeptic. As when, for example, he showed disgust for the human body as such, saying that the penis looks like a bit of loose gut hanging down from the abdomen; the hatred behind the simile was curiously shocking. Or when, on seeing me return sunburned and sweaty, in shorts, from cycling with Chris Wood, he exclaimed reproachfully, "What a *grip* on life you've got!"

Looking back after all these years, I don't think Gerald

was being in the least hypocritical when he wrote that letter to Prabhavananda. At the same time, it is obvious to me that Gerald's dissociation of himself from the Vedanta Center was tactically necessary, in view of the new involvement which awaited him in the near future. In other words, his first move toward that future—the establishment of Trabuco College—was to break his ties to any particular religious group, and thus regain complete freedom of action.

I am not suggesting that Gerald consciously foresaw this already. But there is a part of the mind which does foresee and plan, far ahead of our conscious intentions; and it has its own ways of hinting to us what it intends, though without making itself embarrassingly clear. If Gerald had ignored the hinting of that planner and gone on collaborating with the Swami, I believe that the moment might well have come when the Swami would have had to dissociate himself from Gerald.

Gerald's break with Prabhavananda had a side effect; it made me more valuable to the Vedanta Center. Not that I could ever make good the loss of Gerald's spellbinding lectures and the increase they had caused in attendance and in cash donations. But I could at least give readings whenever the Swami was unable to appear, and I could take over the assistant editorship of the magazine.

I don't think Prabhavananda had seriously expected that I would resign in sympathy with Gerald. Nevertheless, I felt that I had acquired the status of a non-deserter in his eyes and that he was fonder of me in consequence. Soon I found myself drawing closer to him for another, quite different reason.

In the middle of February, Vernon and I parted—

not so much in anger as in mutual exasperation. We still loved each other, but not enough. We kept being jarred to the bone by each other's self-will, and neither of us would give way.

We moved out of our house; I went to a hotel, Vernon found rooms not far off. I wished he would go back to New York and thus put a barrier between us. While he remained in Los Angeles, there was a danger that we might settle for a truce which wasn't a reconciliation and couldn't last. I missed him horribly. Without him, everything, from the war to my job at M-G-M, became less bearable. I saw Gerald nearly every day, largely because I could talk about Vernon to him. He did his best to be a sympathetic listener, which only made the situation more painful. My real support came from visits to Prabhavananda, because I couldn't talk to *him* about Vernon—or at least not in the same self-pitying, self-tormenting way; I would have been ashamed to. Most of the time, I sat silent in his presence. Silence came naturally to him, and he accepted the silences of others without question. Meanwhile, I tried to draw strength from the atmosphere which I could nearly always feel surrounding him.

At his suggestion, I spent my first whole day of silence at the Center fasting and meditating. This sounds like an impressive austerity, but in practice it wasn't. You weren't allowed to talk to other people, but you could ask the Swami questions, about spiritual and philosophical problems. You were to take no solid food between dawn and dusk, but you might drink as much water or fruit juice as you wanted. You weren't required to spend the whole day in the shrine room; you could read in the Swami's study, or walk in the garden or up and down the street. I read several of the essays in Sri Aurobindo's book on the *Bhagavad-Gita*, the first of the Hindu religious classics I was to study. The Swami told me to make japam while I walked and to give everybody I met on the street a mental blessing. You weren't to think of yourself with a feeling of superiority, as a holy man blessing worldlings; you were simply saluting the Atman within each fellow human being.

When I sat in the shrine room, the smell of stale incense made me drowsy, and occasionally I dropped off into a doze. Yet the time didn't seem wasted. It was like being on a long railroad journey in a foreign country at night. At least, I said to myself, the train must be taking me *somewhere*.

No doubt. But I knew it wasn't taking me toward Vernon. In facing the shrine, I was turning my back on him. How cruelly unnatural this seemed. For I was disowning not only our sexual relationship but something more precious to me—our daily and nightly togetherness and the comfort of its contacts, its exchanged smiles and words of intimacy. Remembering all these, I felt snivelingly sorry for myself—until I was stopped by a great wave of sympathy for Prabhavananda.

How much more alone he was than I, exiled among us aliens! What a stifling little prison 1946 Ivar Avenue must be for a still vigorous, subtly intelligent man of powerful emotions, cut off from everything he had known and loved in his youth. Imagine what it must mean to have to accept our distasteful Western ways, our grossness of perception, and be resigned to trying to teach us, every day until he died. Yes, this was a life sentence, stretching out before him in its appalling tameness and sameness. How could he bear it? How had he borne it so long?

Prabhavananda's answer was staring me right in the

face. It was embodied in that quaint piece of Oriental furniture which so improbably contained a fragment of incarnate God. But could I ever find it there for myself—that other, almost unimaginable kind of togetherness? I wasn't even sure yet that I wanted to find it. Maybe the price was too high.

Seven

In March 1941 I moved into an apartment which had unexpectedly become vacant, just around the corner from the house in which Gerald and Chris lived. Early in May, the first term of my contract with M-G-M expired. I told the studio that I didn't want to renew it, giving as my reason that I expected to be drafted soon as a conscientious objector. My employers were polite about this, seeming almost to approve. Perhaps, in the psychological confusion of that ante-bellum period, any kind of war involvement, even as an objector to war, appeared somewhat enviable and admirable to those who were still civilians.

Then Denny arrived back from Pennsylvania. The biodynamic farm hadn't been a success, chiefly because he and the farmer hadn't liked each other. Meanwhile, Denny had been classified by his draft board as a conscientious objector (4-E). He would be called up to work in a forestry camp in the fairly near future.

I had invited him to stay with me at the apartment. For as long as we might be together, we decided to try an experiment in intentional living, following a relaxed version of Gerald's schedule—three hours of meditation a day, instead of six.

Every morning, when our alarm clock rang, we got out of our beds in silence and began our first hour of meditation, he in the living room, I in the bedroom. He washed and dressed first, then fixed breakfast while I washed and dressed. As we sat down to eat, we broke our silence by saying "Good morning." After breakfast, I did the dishes and whatever minor housecleaning was necessary. After this, we took turns reading aloud to each other from some "religious" book. One of these was William James's *Varieties of Religious Experience,* which we both condemned for its sloppy, imprecise style and academic approach to its subject. Actually, we were showing off to each other. We liked to think of ourselves as being now in a kind of front-line trench, actively engaged in spiritual combat and therefore entitled to sneer, as combat troops sneer at a war story by a non-combatant. Denny's favorite comments were "*Mary,* how pretentious can you get?" and "How she *dare!*"

At twelve, we began our second hour of meditation. Then we had lunch. If we went out in the car during the afternoon, we took our book with us and the non-driver read it to the driver. This was supposed to keep us from watching for sexy pedestrians. It didn't, but it did divide the driver's attention by three—book, pedestrian, road—instead of by two, and was therefore the cause of several near-accidents. Our third hour was from six to seven. Then we had supper, the meal we both looked forward to—it was leisurely, with no duties ahead of us. We seldom went out after it, because we had banned movies as distractions. We were usually in bed by nine-thirty.

We had agreed that we would give up sex, including

masturbation. This was made easier by the fact that we didn't find each other in the least sexually attractive. However, while keeping to the agreement, we talked about sex constantly, boasting of our past conquests and adventures. No doubt the underground opposition forces in Denny and myself were working together to sabotage our experiment. But their strategy was crude and unlikely to succeed. If our sex talk excited us, up to a point, it also acted as a safety valve. We might have built up a far greater lust pressure if we had strictly refrained from mentioning the subject.

On the whole, those weeks of May and June were unexpectedly happy. After the loneliness which followed my parting from Vernon, I found Denny's companionship exactly what I needed. The day lived itself, our timetable removed all anxieties about what we should be doing next. We were continually occupied, and everything we did seemed enjoyable and significant. The apartment was curiously delightful to be in, because of the atmosphere we were creating. I don't remember our having one real quarrel.

It was our experiment which held us together. Neither of us could make it work alone, even for a day; we had to cooperate. There was no time for moods, sulks, caprices; if any psychological trouble showed signs of developing, we had to acknowledge its presence at once and then proceed to discuss it out of existence. There was no question of one of us succeeding and the other failing; this wasn't a competition. There was only one alternative to continuing the experiment—dropping it altogether. That we should drop it became less and less likely as the weeks passed and Denny's call-up to the camp grew more and more imminent. Why give up so late in the game?

Denny contributed more to the success of our experiment than I did, both materially and morally. He was an inventive cook and he had the knack of homemaking. He wasn't ashamed to demand comfort from his surroundings. My puritanism felt guilty about demanding comfort, although I enjoyed it if it was provided for me. More importantly, it was Denny who made the greater effort to keep us following our daily schedule. As I now see, this was because he had much more to lose than I had if we failed. This was the last bridge he hadn't burned.

Denny was then at a critical stage in his life. He had returned to the States after a series of quarrels with his wealthy lovers, well aware that he had behaved every bit as badly as they had, if not worse. Then he had broken with the friends in Los Angeles who had laughed at him for becoming interested in Vedanta. Then (according to his version) Prabhavananda had rejected him as despicable, rotten, and unworthy to receive spiritual instruction. Then he had gone to work on the biodynamic farm and had failed to make good and thus be a credit to Gerald. And now, finally, his relations with Gerald himself were deteriorating.

No doubt there had always been some friction between them. Denny could be sharp-edged, sour, and rude, and he was chronically suspicious of the motives of others. (In *Down There on a Visit*, I have presented the Denny–Paul character as a kind of touchstone which reveals whatever elements of falseness are present within the people who are exposed to it.) Denny couldn't resist challenging Gerald's authority as a teacher and mocking his old-maidish fastidiousness, his affectations of speech, his evasiveness, his Irish blarney. Gerald, who was extremely sensitive to any hint of criticism, began to withdraw, injured. Soon Denny—and therefore I—had stopped seeing him unless it was absolutely necessary. I can't pretend that I had tried very hard to prevent this from happening. I realized that it would be far easier to live with Denny if I kept him to myself as much as possible.

Through the Huxleys, we heard of a lady who taught hatha-yoga exercises. We wanted to learn these for purely athletic reasons, so we were glad to find that she didn't set herself up as a spiritual guru, like some other hatha-yoga practitioners. The exercises did make us feel wonderfully healthy. They also filled up most of the time we had free from other occupations.

Our teacher, though perhaps a lot older than she looked, was the embodiment of suppleness and serpentine charm. A serpent who was also a perfect lady, she never lost her social poise. Having explained that the air which is passed through the body in the air-swallowing exercise should come out "quite odorless," she merely smiled in playful reproach when we discharged vile-smelling farts.

I felt that I ought to tell the Swami about our lessons—guessing that he might not altogether approve of them. The violence of his disapproval surprised me. He didn't object to the postures and the stretching but he warned me sternly not to practice those breathing exercises which require you to hold your breath; they can cause hallucinations, he said, and end by damaging the brain. In 1935, when he made a return visit to India with Sister Lalita, he had met one of his former fellow monks who had since left the monastery and taken up hatha-yoga. This ex-monk was the same age as Prabhavananda and therefore already in his forties, but he looked like a boy of eighteen and behaved like a half-witted child, giggling meaninglessly. The usual justification for the practice of hatha-yoga is that it strengthens the body in preparation for spiritual austerities. But Prabhavananda seemed to regard it merely as an indulgence of physical vanity. "What is the matter with you, Mr. Isherwood?" he asked me reproachfully. "Surely you do not want Etarnal Youth?" I was silent and hung my head—because, of course, I did.

When I questioned our teacher—as tactfully as I could and without mentioning Prabhavananda—about the possible dangers of the breathing exercises, she laughed at the idea but then conceded that if you practiced them rigorously, for many hours each day throughout a number of years, you could perhaps do yourself harm. So I was left in a state of indecision, not wanting to disobey Prabhavananda yet not feeling that I need give up our lessons altogether.

Then, however, our teacher began to urge us to learn the yoga technique of washing out the intestines by muscular action alone; you squat in a bowl full of water, suck the water in through the anus, swirl it around inside you, expel it again, thus cleansing yourself of poisons. Until this technique has been mastered, you should use an enema every day. And meanwhile, the sphincter muscle of the anus must be made more flexible, through dilation . . . A set of rectal dilators now appeared. I use that verb advisedly because I can neither remember nor imagine our serpent lady actually giving us such unladylike objects. Did Denny perhaps procure them? The largest was a wicked-looking dildo, quite beyond my capacity but dangerously tempting to my curiosity. I told Denny that, at least as far as I was concerned, our lessons would have to stop—lest sex should sneak in through the back door. We parted from our teacher but continued to do some of the exercises at home. (Years later I took to using the breathing exercises occasionally, because I found them helpful in clearing up obstinate hangovers.)

On July 7, my monastic experiment with Denny was cut short by the opening of the La Verne Seminar. This seminar had been planned by some leading Pennsylvania Quakers in correspondence with Gerald. La Verne is about twenty miles east of Los Angeles. In those days, it was a very small town in the midst of orange and lemon groves, with a coeducational college founded by one of the Baptist sects. Since this would be vacation time, the Quakers had been able to rent the girls' dormitory building to house the twenty-five men and women who were going to take part in the seminar.

It had been agreed that there were to be three periods of group meditation and two periods of group discussion, daily. These were some of the problems scheduled to be discussed:

To what extent must the beginner in the spiritual life be prepared to discipline himself? Can we make a distinction between the duties and privileges of two ways of life—that of the householder and that of the monk? Is the life of prayer a form of escapism, or is it, perhaps, the most direct form of action? Can the other major world religions, taken together with the findings of modern science, help us revise our cosmology? Granted that the present order of things is in a state of chaos due to the war, what could be the structure and sanctions of a new order of society? Can we produce an order in which man's spiritual growth is fostered, not hindered? What have history and science to teach us about the nature and power of non-violence?

Gerald, I knew, was coming to La Verne with one personal objective; he wanted to find out how far he could go in agreement with the Quakers. In his writings, he had referred to the Society of Friends as the most promising force for spiritual regeneration within the Christian Church. But he had described the Quaker way of meditation as happy-go-lucky. Quakers sit passively waiting for the Inner Light, he said, without bothering to study what the great mystics have taught about the technique of prayer. Gerald had also deplored the Quaker preoccupation with social-service projects. The Quaker social worker, he said, is unwilling to face the truth that his activity is chiefly symbolic; its material consequences for the people he is trying to help can't possibly be foreseen and may sometimes be disastrous. The only person who stands to benefit spiritually from the project is the social worker himself—as long as he can remember that he isn't really helping his fellow men but offering an act of worship to the God within them. The worker nearly always forgets this, Gerald added, because he becomes distracted by anxieties about the material success of his project.

As for the Quakers themselves, many of them were broad-minded and genuinely humble. I think they were fascinated by Gerald's personality and eager to understand his ideas, but they couldn't help being suspicious of what they called his "Oriental" tendencies. And even the most liberal of them must have regarded his celibacy with some distaste. Quakerdom is based on the values of family life.

Until shortly before the seminar opened, I had been supposing that I should attend it on my own, since Denny would already have been called to his camp. But the call-up never came and now there was no reason why he shouldn't join me. This he did unwillingly and with a bad grace, bringing his hostility to Gerald along with him. As soon as we arrived at La Verne, Denny began watching me for signs of disloyalty to himself— that is, of friendliness toward Gerald. So now I found myself in a peculiarly false position. I felt obliged to cooperate with Gerald publicly and also to join Denny in bitching him behind his back.

Indeed, we bitched nearly everybody at the seminar. Our negative behavior expressed the discomfort we felt at being separated from our previous life together. We decided that life at La Verne was a kind of parody of it and that these professionally religious people were hypocrites, posers, windbags. From our decision, a convenient conclusion could be drawn: if they weren't acting up to their professed principles, then we needn't act up to ours.

Actually, Gerald was at his brilliant best throughout the month we spent at La Verne. As unofficial chairman, he was tact itself in checking the overtalkative and encouraging the shy to speak. And he was masterly in his summings-up of rambling speeches which nobody else had been able to follow.

In my diary there is a day-to-day account of the seminar, with descriptions of all those who took part in it. I have already borrowed some of this material for the seminar scenes in *Down There on a Visit*, setting them in a different location and inventing a sex scandal to involve the Denny–Paul character. What remains I may publish elsewhere. It doesn't belong to the main theme of this book.

If the La Verne Seminar had been a sporting event— Contemplatives versus Actives—it could be said to have resulted in a draw, one all. By the time it was over, my cousin Felix Greene had decided to give up his executive job with the Friends Service Committee in Philadelphia and remain in California with Gerald. And I had decided to go to Philadelphia and work with the Quakers.

This didn't mean that I had changed sides, philosophically speaking. My motives were practical. Feeling convinced that the States would soon be at war and that I should then have to declare myself a conscientious objector before a draft board, I wanted to get involved with an organized pacifist group which could give me the moral support I would need. I couldn't with honest conviction join any of them except the Quakers. Other such groups tended to be dominated by Christian fundamentalists who upheld the infallibility of the Bible and similar dogmas which I didn't accept.

I might, of course, have found employment with the Quakers of Los Angeles, some of whom I already knew. But it seemed to me less embarrassing to make my plunge into Quakerdom as a stranger among strangers, 2,394 miles distant from Gerald's possibly reproachful gaze.

On August 21, having at last got his call, Denny left for the forestry camp at San Dimas, not far from La Verne, but up in the mountains. The next day, I flew East to visit Wystan and to be interviewed by Caroline Norment, who was about to open a hostel for refugees from Nazi Europe under the auspices of the Friends Service Committee. Caroline and I took to each other and it was agreed that I should report for work as one of her assistants, in the middle of October.

The hostel was at Haverford, just outside Philadelphia. A large, shabby mansion, built at the beginning of the

century and once luxurious, was its headquarters. Between twenty-five and thirty refugees—men, women, and
children, Jews and non-Jews—were living there or at the
homes of neighboring Quakers. Many of them had pro-
fessional backgrounds—as teachers, lawyers, economists,
musicians—and could hope to get jobs sooner or later.
When they did so, they would be replaced at the hostel
by other refugees who were on a waiting list.

Meanwhile, the function of the hostel was to prepare
them for an independent existence in the United States.
Some needed to rest and get their health back, some
needed to learn more English. But their psychological
preparation was a greater and subtler problem. Uprooted,
disillusioned, and suspicious, they were being asked to
have faith in and adapt themselves to an abstraction
called the American Way of Life, which even their
mentors couldn't quite agree with each other in defining.
No doubt, the indoctrination was sometimes less than
tactful. No doubt, the indoctrinees were sometimes
bossed into activities they didn't see the point of. Nevertheless, while admitting the validity of Gerald's objections to the Quaker practice of social service, I felt that
we—Caroline and her assistants—were doing considerably more good than harm.

My days were spent giving the refugees English lessons, going for walks with them, accompanying them to
classes at Haverford College—to learn the American
Way of Teaching—and to social gatherings in the neighborhood—to observe the American Way of Entertaining.
I also, like everybody else at the hostel, lent a hand with
the housecleaning and washed dozens and dozens of
dishes.

The thought that I was serving God within the refugees came to me often, not awe-inspiringly, but comically. It sustained me as a private joke does, so long as

you don't tell it to anyone else. The essence of this joke was that most of these human temples of the God I was serving would have unhesitatingly described themselves as atheists.

I am sure that the refugees had many jokes about me and the rest of the hostel staff. Almost without exception, they saw the Quakers as lovable but unworldly eccentrics and Quaker pacifism as mere craziness. From their point of view, my best asset was probably that I had known pre-Hitler Berlin. They kept coaxing me to talk about it. Doing so made me slip naturally into German, in which they would join me—thus breaking our often-broken hostel rule that English must be spoken whenever possible. Even those who spoke it fluently seemed unwilling to, unless compelled. Perhaps because the language reminded them of their predicament as aliens.

What they didn't realize was the extent to which I, too, was an alien, in Quakerdom. But, unlike them, I wanted to belong to it. Already I was using Quakerese in conversation with my fellow workers: "Caroline, I have a concern." "Caroline, does thee want me to take thy letters to the mail?" I attended the Haverford Meeting House on Sundays and within a few weeks found myself standing up and speaking. Playacting? Yes, partly. But playacting about something that was entirely serious to me. There is no reason why you can't equate the Quaker Inner Light with the Hindu Atman. I was really talking about Vedanta to them, but in their idiom, not mine. It was merely my self-consciousness which made this into a theatrical performance.

At the end of those long long workdays, I was usually eager to drop into bed and sleep. But, later on, when I had discovered a sexual playmate, I would take an occasional evening off with him in Philadelphia. This seemed to me just fun, well earned. I had no conscience pangs. I had never felt that Quakerdom demanded celibacy of me; they all approved of sex, even if it was only of the lawful kind. I made one little concession to respectability, however; I always removed my Friends Service Committee button from my jacket before we went into bars where we would get drunk and the steam bath where we sobered up again.

Shortly after the attack on Pearl Harbor, regulations were issued which restricted the movements of "enemy aliens" to very small areas around their domicile—the area around our hostel contained no post office, no movie theater, no drugstore. Nearly all the refugees were still technically German or Austrian citizens and therefore subject to this restriction.

They took it very quietly. This was what their chronic pessimism had been awaiting. In their voices there was a note, almost, of relief that the inevitable worst was no longer to be delayed. "It's France, all over again," they muttered. "Next will come the detention camps."

Caroline made a vigorous speech, assuring the refugees that the regulations couldn't possibly be enforced because they were so absurd and unjust. "If we make such a mess of bureaucracy in this country, it's because we're not used to it." (This I interpreted as a gentle reproof: "You Europeans got so used to *your* bureaucracy that you didn't realize it would turn into a tyranny and destroy you.") Then she was off on the warpath to the District Attorney's office in Philadelphia. To my astonishment, the D.A. lifted all local restrictions on our hostel members immediately. Caroline took her victory as a matter of course, never having doubted that the American Way of Life would prevail. To me, this was an extraordinary demonstration of the Quakers' power over the consciences of non-Quaker Philadelphians, even in wartime.

In the middle of May 1942, a young English Quaker lectured at the Meeting House. He was on his way back to England after working with the Friends' ambulance unit in China. He had blond hair which was curly like a lamb's fleece, and a charmingly silly, innocent laugh. He seemed to me to be an ideal non-violent hero. I got an instant crush on him—and was thus moved to volunteer for a second ambulance unit, which the Quakers were then organizing. I was turned down, however, because all volunteers had to be either doctors or trained automobile mechanics.

Meanwhile, as expected, the U.S. draft age had been raised. It now included those in my age bracket.

June 17. Today I sent off form 47 to the draft board, applying for 4-E classification as a conscientious objector. When you write these things down for official consumption, they sound horribly priggish and false—because you are presenting yourself as a strictly logical, rational human being with principles, a philosophy of life, etc. Whereas I, personally, am much more like a horse which suddenly stops and says, "No. That's going too far. From that pond I won't drink."

I have reasons, of course, and a philosophy. I can explain them—quite lucidly, if necessary. But how dry and cold they would be without the personal factor behind them: Heinz is in the Nazi army. I would refuse to kill Heinz. Therefore, I have no right to kill anybody.

Of course there are a dozen ways in which you can come to the pacifist decision. And I don't doubt that there are many people who honestly arrive at it on general principles: they simply know that it is wrong for them to kill. But I have never been able to grasp any idea except through a person.

June 30. Medical examination at the draft board. All these kids seem so utterly helpless, so unprotected. You feel, "Let me go, instead of them." Their nervous little jokes. The old-timer who scares them with his army tales. The boy who's afraid he'll faint when they take his blood. (He didn't.) The young Negro's beautiful body, so dignified in its nakedness; nearly everybody else wore undershorts.

I had to wait till last because, for me as a C.O., this wasn't just a preliminary but the only examination I should get. They didn't do much beyond establishing the fact that I was alive.

The Friends Service Committee had now decided that the hostel must be closed down—partly for financial reasons, partly because no more refugees were expected to be able to get over from Europe and because those who remained with us would nearly all be able to find jobs in the rapidly expanding wartime labor market.

I myself left Haverford early in July, to return to California. Soon after my arrival there, I got a notice from my draft board that I had been classified 4-E. This meant that I could expect a call to the forestry camp within the next six weeks. Or so I imagined.

While I was away in Pennsylvania, Gerald Heard and Felix Greene had bought—with money from an anonymous donor—a ranch called Trabuco. It was sixty miles south of Los Angeles, in an almost empty stretch of country behind the coastal hills. Here Felix had caused to be built what they already called Trabuco College. Gerald said that it looked like a small Franciscan monastery in the Apennines. It was indeed dramatically picturesque, a complex of tile-roofed buildings with cloisters which commanded a vast airy view westward to the ocean. And its interior design was a model of monastic simplicity—built-in cabinets and tiled floors—requiring a minimum of dusting and sweeping.

Felix had worked all through the winter, studying and revising the architect's plans, pressuring contractors to get on with the job, dashing from place to place to snap up the last available supplies of lumber and metal fixtures before they were "frozen" by military authorities. He had also done a great deal of the construction with his own hands. "With an energy," said Gerald, "that was almost *epileptic*." Gerald's adjective suggested not only unwilling admiration but an ironic admission of responsibility. He himself had unleashed Felix and his energy upon the original modest Focus project. And now Focus, the mini-retreat for four people, was swallowed up within Trabuco College, this—to Gerald—slightly embarrassing showplace, which could house fifty.

Gerald reminded us frequently that Trabuco was to be a college in the sense of the Latin word *collegium,* "a community." He also spoke of it as "a club for mystics," non-sectarian, non-dogmatic, and as "a clearinghouse" for individual religious experiences and ideas.

Those who visited it were to meet as colleagues, not as masters and disciples, not as spiritual superiors and inferiors.

More than two months passed and I had still heard nothing from the draft board. On September 25, I got a letter from one of the boys at the forestry camp, saying that they had been expecting me to arrive some days previously. Was I technically AWOL without knowing it? Alarmed, I telegraphed the director of the camp, asking what I should do. He wrote back that if I hadn't got my induction notice I needn't worry. He wasn't allowed to admit me to the camp without it.

Meanwhile, the Swami was urging me to apply to the draft board for reclassification as a theological student, 4-D. (One of the men at the Vedanta Center in San Francisco had already been classified 4-D, so a precedent had been established.) The Swami had a frankly admitted motive for keeping me out of the forestry camp. He wanted me to come and live as a monk at the Vedanta Center, as soon as he could make arrangements to accommodate men there. This might take several months. But he also had an occupation for me which I could begin work on immediately. He had just finished a rough translation of the *Bhagavad-Gita* and needed me to help him polish it.

I told him I doubted very much that the board would agree to reclassify me when I was already as good as drafted. Why should they take the trouble to do the extra paperwork? The Swami giggled and said, "Try." To my ears, there was a slightly uncanny quality in this giggle; it sounded as if he knew something about the situation which I didn't. I sent off my application for 4-D.

September 28. Talked to the Swami on the phone. He is ready to write a letter to the draft board, backing up my appeal for reclassification. But first he wanted me to re-assure him that I really intend to become a monk. I said yes of course—but later I was bothered by all kinds of doubts. Just what does the Swami mean by "monk"? One who takes the vows of chastity and poverty? Or one who belongs, specifically, to the Ramakrishna Order, conducts lecture courses, officiates at the rituals, and goes to lunch with householder devotees in their expensive houses. I'll see him tomorrow and ask him.

September 29. As I expected, the Swami waved my doubts aside. Of course, he said, I wouldn't be asked to do things I wasn't fitted for or wasn't inclined to do.

October 12. Most days, I see the Swami and we work together on his translation of the Gita, turning it into more flexible English. This is a very valuable way of studying, because I have to make absolutely sure I understand what each verse means. Some of the Sanskrit words have meanings which sound bizarre in English, and the Swami, who has long since learnt to paraphrase them, has to be practically psychoanalyzed before he'll admit to the literal translation.
No call from the draft board yet.

There never was a call. Nor any answer to my appli-cation for 4-D. This silence was explained when the authorities later announced that they were lowering the upper draft-age limit to thirty-seven. By that time, I was well into my thirty-ninth year.

January 29, 1943. The opening of Brahmananda Cottage (as the Swami has christened the house where we're to live, at the Vedanta Center) is still fixed for the sixth of February. At the moment, this, and all that it implies, seems utterly remote and unreal. I told the Swami some weeks ago, "I've been ten thousand miles away from you."

Daydreams of a "last fling." Some part of me is irrationally convinced that somehow someone will show up to give me a glamorous final twenty-four hours of sex in the best Elinor Glyn style.

February 3. Lunch with Berthold Viertel. Talked about my move to the Center. He disapproves of it with all the jealousy of his fatherly affection. A return to the Quakers he could understand, a retirement into an ivory-tower life of novel writing he could understand. But why am I joining these obsolete Hindus? What possible relevance can their beliefs have to the world of 1943?

Berthold feels a deep suspicion of Gerald, whom he naturally associates with Vedanta and the Swami. He asked, "Would you be doing this if you'd never met Heard?"—as though he expected the question to disconcert and perhaps enrage me. "Would I have written for the movies," I countered, "if I'd never met you?"

In the afternoon, I called Denny on the phone, up at the forestry camp. He seems to be completely happy there. He has been skiing. He showed no special desire to come down and visit us.

Supper with Chris Wood. Afterwards, we went to the Club Gala. I haven't been to a place of this sort in ages, and it was so nostalgically reminiscent of all the other times—the baroque decorations and the cozy red velvet corners, the sharp-faced peroxide pianist with tender memories and a tongue like an adder, the grizzled tomcat tenor, the lame celebrity, the bar mimosa, the public lovers, the amazed millionaire tourist and the daydream sailor. I have loved them all very much. I owe them many of my vividest moments of awareness. But enough is enough. And here we say goodbye.

Or do we? Isn't this entirely the wrong spirit in which to become a monk? I am not going to the Center to forget such places. No—if this training succeeds, I shall be able to return to the Gala, or any other scene of the past, with the kind of understanding which sees what they are really all about.

Eight

Against my will, terrified, helplessly attracted, I cross the
vast empty courtyard in blazing sunlight, pull the bell
chain—*clang*, the grim ironbound wicket opens. They
are all inside, in the shadows, cowled and black-robed,
waiting for me. Within a moment, they have stripped
me of my clothes and forcibly robed me. I stammer the
irrevocable vow. I vanish into silence and an eternal
indoors, trapped by the Trappists, *a monk*!

This youthful fantasy-farce—inspired by *The Garden
of Allah* and the anti-Catholic horror tales of my Protestant upbringing—kept recalling itself to my mind and
making me grin as I took part in the events of February
6; the service in the temple, the dedication of Brahmananda Cottage with a homa fire in its living room, the
reception afterwards, at which the inmates of the Center
mingled with the householders of the congregation,
amidst much eating, photography, gush, and chatter.
The atmosphere of this last scene reminded me strongly
of life in Quakerdom.

We four male monastics were on display, embarrassed,

robeless, and quite unmonklike, in our Sunday suits. Prabhavananda wore his robes for the occasion, and only he seemed at ease, beaming and delighted because Maharaj's work was going forward, the Center was growing bigger. In recognition of my own altered status, he had now stopped calling me Mr. Isherwood and started calling me Chris—he pronounced it "Krees." (In my diary I began to reciprocate by referring to him as Swami instead of the Swami.)

Brahmananda Cottage was number 1942 Ivar Avenue. The temple stood between it and number 1946. These three buildings could hardly have been less alike—1942 was a small, Spanish-style, stucco-walled house with a tiled roof—yet they formed a kind of unit simply by being so close together; there were only a few yards between them. It seemed absurd to think of 1946 as a convent and of 1942 as a monastery in the ordinary sense of the words, for how could nuns and monks be isolated from each other when they were living at such close quarters? In fact, the inmates of the Center were now like members of a family. The men shared many occupations with the women, and they were in and out of each other's houses all day long. We only separated to sleep.

February 8, 1943. Well, now that we've slept two nights in Brahmananda Cottage, now that the mimosa is withering in the vases and the homa fire leaves no trace beyond a stain of clarified butter on the hearth—is there anything I can say about the monastic life?

No. Nothing. As a matter of fact, my unconscious hasn't even cocked an eyebrow or twitched an ear, yet.

And, for the next two or three weeks, it probably won't.
Like a drunk who has been pitched into the lockup, it
just lies there snoring, quite unaware that it can't get out.
When it begins to wake up, I suppose the trouble will
start.

The trouble started in much less than three weeks,
with Asit, Swami's nephew. (Given its proper Bengali
pronunciation, his name would have been approximately
Osshit. Since that would have sounded improper or
funny to American ears, it had been decided to call
him Ossid.) Asit was a slim lively attractive Bengali boy
of about twenty-five. He had come to the States on a
visit, some years previously, and now he couldn't go
back, because of the war. He was a student at the University of Southern California, where he had already
graduated in cinematography. He wanted to return to
India as soon as possible and be a film director.

Asit was a conventionally pious Hindu but he had no
intention of becoming a monk. It had been simply a
matter of convenience to put him up in Brahmananda
Cottage for the time being. He had seen to it that he
got the best room, in the way he got everything that he
wanted—by alternately coaxing and bullying the women.
He took it for granted that women are born to wait on
men—on Hindu men, at any rate—and the women
seemed to accept this, although they often scolded him
for his laziness and untidiness.

I myself had to sleep in a dark little anteroom, with
only a closed door between me and Asit's radio, which
he was apt to play at almost any hour of the day or
night. Since working at the Haverford hostel, I had
fondly imagined that I was well adjusted to group living.
But at Haverford I had had an isolated bedroom in a

neighbor's house and had never been exposed to this kind of invasion of privacy.

Like Swami, Asit took a special attitude toward me because I was British, but it was a different kind of attitude. His manner alternated between the aggressive, the suspicious, the deferential, and the flattering. Whenever the newspapers reported some British political action in India, he would teasingly insinuate that I shared responsibility for it. Sometimes I found this amusing, sometimes I lost my temper childishly.

When I asked Asit, as politely as I could, to please not play his radio at certain times, he was up in arms against me as an embodiment of British tyranny. So a battle of wills was joined. This battle cost Asit nothing, emotionally, because to him it was just a game—twisting the British Lion's tail. But it caused me to suffer sudden spasms of rage which could make meditation impossible.

My three brother probationers were George, Webster, and Richard. Everybody, including Swami, spoke of us as monks, but, strictly speaking, we had no right to that title, since we had taken no vows. According to the rules of the Ramakrishna Order, the first vows, called *brahmacharya*, can be taken only after a minimum probation period of five years. Our so-called nuns weren't really nuns yet, either.

George was a man of about my own age, lean and rugged and nearly bald, taciturn but capable of growly-voiced satirical remarks. His bedroom and bathroom formed a separate apartment, with an outside entrance of its own and no connecting door to the rest of the house. He had paid for this reconstruction. He was jealous of his privacy and it was seldom that he invited any of us to come inside. As time passed, he covered every inch of his wall space with photographs—enlargements (some of them huge) of the available pictures of Ramakrishna, Holy Mother, Brahmananda, and Vivekananda, and snapshots of Swami taken by George himself. On the tables and chairs were more pictures, together with statuettes of deities and jars full of flowers which had been offered before the shrine. Many of these he kept until they were withered and foul-smelling.

We made fun of George as an eccentric, even to his face, but he soon became an affectionately respected figure in our family. We respected him because he seemed to be living with such single-mindedness, spending almost all of his time in Swami's presence or else alone. He would sit on the floor in a corner, so that the rest of us scarcely noticed him, and write down Swami's remarks, even the most commonplace of them, in a notebook. Swami would often laughingly protest against this, but George had the obstinacy of devotion; nothing could stop his note taking or his photography. He also wire-recorded Swami's Sunday lectures and weekday classes. Sometimes, after most of us were in bed, he would type these up in his apartment. The recorder would relay Swami's voice at full volume, and George, as he typed, would chant even louder, in Sanskrit. You could hear him all over the house and outside on the street. I never minded George's chanting the way I minded the chattering of Asit's radio—not because the one was sacred and the other profane, but because George was George, everything he did seemed natural, it couldn't be otherwise. So you accepted it.

The remaining bedroom in Brahmananda Cottage was shared by Webster and Richard. They were both seventeen. Webster's favorite sport was judo. His short, immensely strong body was covered with curly black fuzz, as if to compensate for the hair he was already beginning to lose from his head. His face was clean-cut and shiny with health—it was the face of a slow, careful, serious thinker, obstinate but very good-natured. He had a great aptitude for carpentry and other branches of house-building. At the age of fourteen he had decided that he was going to become a monk when he was older. His mother was a Vedanta devotee, so she hadn't opposed him. It probably wouldn't have made any difference if she had.

Richard was curly-haired and brown-eyed, with a comically crafty expression which prevented his face from being conventionally handsome; he reminded me of a bear. He was much taller than Webster and his smooth-skinned body was beautifully proportioned and muscled; he had developed it by barbell exercises. Both of Richard's parents were Vedanta devotees and, at the same time, earnest middle-class moralists—which may explain why Richard felt a genuine religious vocation but resisted it violently. We never knew, from one day to the next, if he would stay at the Center. Richard didn't appear to know, himself. At least, that was the impression he liked to give. He was a subtle, teasing playactor who enjoyed keeping us guessing.

Webster loved Richard dearly and used all his influence to prevent him from leaving. When Richard disappeared for hours into Hollywood and Swami asked where he was, Webster would try to cover up for him or, in extreme cases, go out to look for him and fetch him back. Actually, Richard would be found doing something quite harmless, such as eating ice cream with friends, but he was so secretive about his absences that he might as well have been to a whorehouse. Both he

and Webster were students at Hollywood High School—
not an ideal training place for would-be monks.

*February 26. Richard was suspended from school the
day before yesterday—for doing handstands on the scaffolding around a sixty-foot smokestack in the playground.
It was during the lunch hour, with a big crowd watching.
Now, of course, he's the students' number-one hero. He
says he wants to leave here, get a job at Warner's Theater
as an usher and enjoy the pleasures of "the world." I
should be the last to laugh. If anybody can understand
Rich, it ought to be myself.*

*And yet it's a disaster. Imagine discovering this place
and this way of life at seventeen, and not being able to
hold on to it! And then having to crawl back, inch by
inch, at my age or maybe older. I'm still hanging on by
the eyelids myself after nearly three weeks. I've got to
convince myself, practically, that the shrine can give me
strength to do what I could never do alone.*

*The shrine is like a bank, in which we have put our
money and can never draw it out again. But it pays interest, so the only thing to do is to deposit more and more
and more. It's the shrine that really matters; the fact of
its being there, always, right in the midst of our household. It's particularly wonderful at night. You feel so
safe there and there is such a sense of contact. Like
sitting face to face with someone you know very well,
and not having to speak.*

*In the next room, Asit and Richard are discussing
Rich's future. I can hear every word through the door.
"Well, go ahead," giggles Asit. "Marry—get some
keeds!" And Rich, who is thoroughly enjoying the conversation, answers, "But I don't want that. I want to be
a vagabond."*

He is always telling us this. His daydream figure is the

wandering, drunken philosopher. Somehow or other, he found out about Rimbaud and pestered me until I lent him my copy of A Season in Hell. (I've brought a few books with me here, thinking of them as necessary personal possessions, like clothing. I never foresaw that they might become liabilities!) Now Rich is going around repeating delightedly, "The best thing is a good drunken sleep on a sandy beach." If Swami hears him, I shall have some explaining to do.

March 1. Richard finally decided to stay, after a last-minute interview with Swami during which he apparently went through every mood known to psychology. Part of Rich is so sincere that it makes you want to cry; part of him is quite cynically cunning—as when he plays up to Swami and pretends to be under the influence of Swami's hypnotic power.

The other day, while Swami was out, Rich sat in Swami's place on the living-room sofa and imitated him puffing at his cigarettes and curling up his toes. The girls and I pretended to be his disciples and asked him questions. "Swami," said one of them, very wide-eyed, "what shall I do? I don't have the time to meditate. I'm so involved in the cares of the world." "Aw wairl," replied Rich, absolutely dead-pan, catching Swami's accent perfectly, "jarst try to think of Gard okezzshionally." When Swami heard about this, he was delighted.

We found a prose poem which Rich had typed out and hidden at the back of the shrine. It was called "A Farewell to Vedanta." I can remember only one bit of it: "As I lifted my weights, may I lift the weight of my ignorance . . . As I climbed to heights unknown, so may I climb toward Thee."

"Heights unknown" referred, of course, to the smoke-stack. Swami and I went round to interview the principal of Hollywood High this morning and plead (unsuccessfully) to have Rich taken back. The principal was a desolate shattered figure in the midst of utter confusion. One had the impression that he and his staff had long since lost control of the huge hygienic rowdy school and its gang of sexy students. Wearily, he pointed out to us that Rich has scarcely attended a single class in any subject; some of his teachers don't even know what he looks like. As for the principal himself, he seems resigned to rudeness, ignorance, inattention, venereal disease, illegitimate babies, and sex in every form—but he still has one proud boast: no student has ever actually met a violent death on the premises, and no student shall, if he can help it. On this point, he is really obstinate. "Why," he exclaimed, "it would be in every newspaper in the country!" He took it for granted that Richard's parents would have sued the school if Richard had fallen.

As we were driving away, we passed the celebrated smokestack. It looked horribly dangerous. The scaffolding seemed insecure, and a fall could only have been onto asphalt or a spiked iron fence. Swami folded his hands, glanced upward for a second, and murmured, "May I have that courage!"

So Rich is to stay home, and study Vedanta and try to be a real monk. For a month's trial.

I was fond of Webster and Richard but I couldn't quite think of them as my brothers; after all, they were young enough to be my sons. I would have been glad indeed to have George for a brother; but, in those days, he seemed impossible to get close to. Whenever I spoke to him, he was friendly, but he kept retiring into non-communication, either by starting his note taking or going to the shrine or shutting himself up in his apartment. Even when we were washing dishes together after meals, he would chant to himself, and I didn't like to interrupt him by talking.

I also felt a distance between myself and Sister Lalita. This wasn't so much because of her age. She was an intelligent and active old lady who read radical magazines and loved gardening. (Swami complained that she would never let anything grow, because she kept changing her mind and transplanting flowers from one corner of the garden to another.) Our relations were inhibited by her extreme politeness. It seemed to me that she thought of herself as our hostess, with obligations toward us as guests. And, in addition to this, she often inspired me with awe. She had actually known Vivekananda! This fact came home to me with special force and strangeness when I watched her in the shrine room. She had an air of unobtrusiveness which was somehow majestic. She made me think of Holy Mother as Swami had described her to us, sitting quietly by the roadside, in front of the inn.

I felt entirely at ease, however, with the other women at the Center. It was easy to think of them all as being my sisters, though with varying degrees of intimacy.

Amiya, the big blond Englishwoman, was plump but still pretty; she had a soft creamy skin and sparkling eyes. She was an efficient cook and housekeeper, bossy, lively, warmhearted, talkative, devoted to Swami and to Sister. Having shared their years of poverty with them, she was inclined to patronize female newcomers. But she didn't object to us men, and she and I were soon drawn together by our Britishness. Even when I saw how her ladylike limey accent and peculiarly British tactlessness must infuriate Americans, I couldn't take their side against her.

Swami himself turned on Amiya sometimes and scolded her unmercifully, in public, so that she shed tears. She took this meekly, but I was shocked. I asked myself: Why does he have to do it in front of the rest of us? Is he taking revenge on her because she's British *and* a woman? Does he have a deep-down Hindu contempt for all women?

Once again, Swami seemed to read my thoughts, for he now often spoke of the scoldings which Brahmananda had given him. "He *pounded* and *pounded* on me," Swami said, repeating the word with an almost sensual relish; and he added that the scoldings were sometimes quite unjust. For example, Brahmananda had found fault with him because a letter in the printed heading on some stationery was seemingly broken. When Swami had brought the style book and shown him that the gap in the lettering was actually intentional and part of the design, Brahmananda ignored the explanation and continued to scold. And then, said Swami, he had begun to realize that Maharaj wasn't concerned about specific mistakes or faults, he would rebuke and humiliate you in order to correct bad tendencies which he detected in your subconscious mind.

Very well, I could take it on trust that a Brahmananda could behave with seeming unreasonableness and cruelty, and do so out of sheer benevolence. How can one hope to understand the actions of such a superhuman being? But could I believe that Swami also had this kind of discrimination? There were times when I couldn't. When Swami lost his temper, I found his performance altogether convincing. He seemed immature and petty. This raised a question: What exactly *was* Prabhavananda? Could he be simultaneously Abanindra Ghosh and Brahmananda's instrument? Could he be combining the mannerisms of his immature persona with the insight of a great saint? Well, time would show. It was my hopeful belief that, by degrees, Swami would become less of Abanindra and more of Maharaj. Meanwhile, I loved him as he was, and that included all of Abanindra.

Sarada was a girl in her early twenties, of Norwegian descent. She had studied music and dancing. Often, when she thought nobody was watching, she would execute ballet movements, humming to herself. A certain balletic gracefulness could also be noticed in her gestures as she sat before the shrine, performing the ritual. She probably spent more time in the shrine than any of us, except George, with the result that she neglected her household duties.

Amiya was fond of Sarada, but she was forced to play the humiliating role of Martha in the Gospel story, chiding her sister Mary for sitting at the Lord's feet instead of helping to get the dinner ready. She was also a bit jealous of the praise Sarada got from Swami for her devotion. Sarada didn't resent Amiya's grumbling. She must have known that she herself was often guilty of an irritating holy vagueness, an air of thick-skinned serenity which could try anyone's patience. But Sarada also had a wild, lively, unaffected side to her character. She was capable of saying straight out, without coyness, that she thought Richard "a beautiful boy." She was full of jokes about our daily life, which included the ritual and Ramakrishna himself. At first, she even shocked me slightly. This was a response conditioned by my Ten Commandments upbringing. It helped me to realize how meaningless the concept of blasphemy was in my present surroundings. There was no way of blaspheming against the kind of God we were being taught to believe in here.

Yogini was a married woman of about thirty. Her husband, whom Swami had named Yogi, was in the Army but about to be discharged for some medical reason. He, too, was a devotee and had created a sensation in camp by having a picture of Ramakrishna by his bed and burning incense in front of it every evening. He had also formed a group of fellow soldiers to study Vedanta, despite the disapproval of the chaplain. Soon Yogi and Yogini would have to decide what their future was to be. Would Yogini leave the Center and settle down elsewhere with Yogi as a married couple? Or would they both live here in partial separation, as monk and nun? Or would they separate altogether and Yogini remain here? (They finally chose the third alternative.)

Yogini was attractive, with a good figure, fresh coloring, and lots of frizzy fair hair. She laughed a great deal and seemed to take everything lightly. It was some time before I was able to appreciate the seriousness of her commitment to the religious life and the strength of her loyalty to us as her brothers and sisters. She was someone you could rely on absolutely.

One morning, a lady appeared at the Center who was from a government office which issued propaganda to foreign countries about the virtues of cultural life in the United States. She wanted me to write an article on the Vedanta Society, to show (these were her own words) "how wonderfully the United States tolerates all religions." I refused, as tactfully as I could. When I described this encounter, that day at lunch, Yogini said, "I think it's wonderful how *we* tolerate the United States."

Sudhira was a hospital nurse by profession. I believe she had first come to the Center to nurse either Sister or Amiya through an illness. She was Irish-Californian, with a strong accent on the Irish.

Sudhira had a charming, handsome face, but her essential beauty was of a rarer kind—the beauty which shows itself in the carriage of the head and shoulders, the movements of the hands, the walk. Physically, she was a great aristocrat. Sometimes, when she came into a room, quite unselfconsciously intent on carrying a tea tray, her entrance was so stately that it filled me with delight.

When Sudhira was a girl, she had fallen in love with a young airplane pilot. Three days after their marriage, he was killed in a crash. She became obsessed by the fact of his death; she longed to find out what death really is. She was already working as a nurse and now she made a point of getting herself assigned to seemingly terminal cases, so that she could observe them while they were dying. Being good at her job, she sometimes saved them —and immediately lost interest in them.

While nursing at the County Hospital, she had managed to contract most of the available infectious diseases. She had also got herself involved in numerous automobile accidents. That she had survived all these seemed to suggest that her particular kind of death addiction was only a flirtation; much as she loved to wander along the mortal frontier, she had no immediate intention of crossing it.

I soon began to build a myth around her. She was the universal Nanny, I told her. She was the figure that we meet twice in our lives, at the entrance and at the exit, to help us into this world and out of it. I begged her to be with me at my deathbed, we would have such a wonderful time together. And I told her about the poem I was writing. I was trying to describe her in mythical terms but could get no further than the first line: *Is that the needle, Nanny, you are bringing?*

Sudhira laughed, but she didn't tell me I was being silly—her Irish heart loved this kind of talk. Soon I started getting sick for short spells; thus we could spend hours chatting, instead of doing our proper jobs. Her presence tempted me to transform my life at the Center into an illness, a toxic laziness, from which I should become increasingly unwilling to recover.

Nine

March 26, 1943. Woke murmuring a line from Yeats's translation of Oedipus at Colonus: "Even from that delight memory treasures so . . ." I read Yeats often, just now. He represents a most elegant kind of sexual sublimation.

Felt a bit heavy from Sudhira's vitamin B1 shot last night. She has decided that we all need pepping up, and goes around at bedtime with the hypodermic, visiting her "customers."

Tried to think that my Real Self was already sitting in meditation before the shrine, as I herded my sleepy body out to the washroom, emptied its bladder, and sponged its face. Webster, who had called me, was in the boys' bedroom, finishing his homework by electric light. Thought: "Shall I point out that it's already daylight outside, if he'll raise the shades? Don't be such an old fusspot. But surely it's time he went into the temple? That's his affair, not yours. Shut up."

Raised the shades in the living room, thinking how much I love the daylight. In this mood, I picture myself as a wistful prisoner—the type that watches the swallows and waters a flower with his tears.

Arrived to find the shrine room empty. Tried to pray for my friends, but could feel absolutely no affection for anybody. The only thought which almost always seems valid is of the boys fighting each other all over the world. That gives me a sense of obligation. Because of their suffering, even if for no other reason, I must contribute my tiny effort toward this other way of life.

Then the usual bad feelings—vanity, because Swami came in late and saw that I was already in the shrine. Self-accusation, because I'm not in England. This still sometimes recurs—although I know perfectly well that, whatever my duty may have been in the past, it is now to stay here, and that I only wish to return because I care what the world thinks of me. Then satisfaction, because, technically, I'm still keeping all the rules. Then sex thoughts. Then resentment against various people whom I regard as threats to my convenience.

After worship, as I was going across to the other house for breakfast, a special-delivery letter was handed to me by the mailman; it was from Richard's father to Swami. I touched it to my head in mock salutation before giving it to Swami, and immediately felt that the joke was silly. Swami read the letter, which had an enclosure for Rich, while I watched him inquisitively and Sudhira brought in spoon bread and eggs and we ate our prunes. Swami passed me the letter to read. Rich's father wasn't sure if he should take Rich's decision to leave the Center seriously, since Rich hadn't mentioned that he and Swami had discussed the matter.

Rich didn't read his part of the letter but took it away with him from the table. Sister remarked that she'd have to hire a gardener, now that Rich is leaving. When we got up from breakfast, I urged Swami to get Rich away as soon as possible. I made this sound as if I were thinking of Rich's own good. The truth is that this interim period, with Rich smoking up the living-room and listening to jitterbug music, is getting on my nerves. Also, I know that he's planning some kind of sex excursion for tomorrow night—as why the hell shouldn't he? But it makes me feel so insecure.

Asit put me into a good temper by flattering remarks about my new haircut. Burned trash in the incinerator. I often feel mad at Asit when I'm burning the trash, because he's apt to leave razor blades amidst the wastepaper, twice I've nearly cut my hand. However, this morning he hadn't left any. Felt a warmth toward him and Rich—the first decent feeling of the day.

Met Sudhira, who told me that she'd been having an argument with George about Richard. According to her, George thinks that Rich should be forced to stay here, no matter how, because the Lord is sure to work on him gradually if only he sticks around. Sudhira disagrees.

She told about a marmoset she'd had as a pet. It bit and the vet filed its teeth, and it got toothache and sat with its paw to its mouth and the tears running down its face. And Sudhira, who had hated it, began to feel sorry for it and got codeine for it from the hospital and it turned into a dope fiend, and died. She was so beautiful as she described this, with tears in her eyes.

(Presumably, the marmoset represented Richard and the moral was that you must never interfere forcibly with another person's way of life. A peculiar charm of Sudhira's anecdotes was that they seldom quite applied to the subject they were meant to illustrate.)

Returned to the kitchen to help with the dishes. Dishwashing is always enjoyable here, everybody is so cheer-

ful. I make up nonsense verses to amuse the girls. For
example:

> With many a mudra and mantram, with mutterings
> and mouthings and moans,
> The rishi flew into a tantrum, and rattled the
> avatar's bones.

> After reams of ridiculous ritual, after offerings of
> ointment and eggs,
> The cripples were kissed by Rasputin, and recovered
> the use of their legs.

Then went into the temple, to watch Sarada doing
the first part of the ritual. Swami wants me to learn it.
I had the book of instructions open in front of me and
followed. Then I went in to see Swami, who showed
me the rest. He had been talking to Richard, who had
said he wanted to be a military policeman and shoot
someone in the belly. "He's an egomaniac," Swami said,
but he couldn't help smiling. He loves Rich.

Richard did finally leave, on April 10. In my diary,
I tried to define my feelings about this:

Let those who want to leave, leave. I can't agonize over
straying sheep. Whatever else the religious life is, it isn't
tragic, because every effort and discomfort is purely
voluntary; you can stop whenever you wish. And this
talk about the world's pleasures being wretched and
tasteless is just silly, as far as I'm concerned. Sure, you
have to pay for them, but they're marvelous while they
last. You can't wish them away and groan and say you
never did like them, really. They have extraordinary

beauty and significance, and woe to the wetleg who denies it.

The world at its best isn't miserable, isn't hateful—it is mad. The pursuit of worldly pleasures as ends in themselves is madness, because it disregards the real situation, which is that we are living a life that has only one thing to teach us, how to know God in ourselves and in other people. To be sane is to be aware of the real situation. The desire, the <u>homesickness</u>, for sanity is the one valid reason for subjecting oneself to any kind of religious discipline.

May 1. Shaky after two days in bed with flu. But I want to write down a few things.

While in bed, I read Waley's translation of the Chinese novel *Monkey*. Also *The Light of Asia*, and several Buddhist writings from Lin Yutang's anthology. Having done so, I feel, very strongly, that we must not despise the body. The body is not a lump of corrupt filth, it is not evil. It is our faithful loyal servant, in sickness and in health; it really does its best. Of course, if you let it be the master, then it will display all its greed and stupidity and brutishness. If you put your dog on the dining-room table, you mustn't be surprised if it gobbles everything up. We must be very firm with the body and also very kind.

Also, I do feel that we must be ready to accept sickness—not as a burden, but as a profoundly educational experience, neither less nor more educational than health.

Sudhira has been looking after me, and telling me stories. While she was nursing in the children's ward at the County Hospital, she caught meningitis and became delirious. Two beautiful white horses appeared in her room and told her that they'd come to take her away with them to Mount Shasta, but that first they must all three of them go into the chapel and say a prayer. Sudhira actually followed them into the hospital chapel, dressed only in a short nightgown. She was kneeling at the altar rail and laughing at the awkwardness of the horses—they couldn't kneel properly—when a doctor found her and led her back to bed.

May 4. Was up all day, but am back in bed this evening, resting. Webster hurries in and out, bringing me things, like a hospital orderly, under Sudhira's command. He shows a kindness and gentleness which are almost feminine. I feel he takes our monastic relationship absolutely literally. As far as he's concerned, we're brothers, and that's that.

I have no idea "where I am." Have I made progress during these three months, or haven't I? To a certain degree, I do feel yes, I have. Just being with Swami has given me a much clearer idea of what the spiritual life ought to mean. How infinitely difficult and yet how utterly simple it is! Want to find the Atman? All right, go ahead and dig it out, like a terrier.

The worship is very helpful. I did it again today—for about the 18th time. Nearly always, I at least manage to get a great awareness of responsibility. Here am I, with all my karma upon me, presenting myself before the unthinkable majesty of what is enthroned in the shrine. "I'm sorry, sir. I'm the only one they could send today." Offering the prayers and mudras, the flowers and lights and incense, I am representing everybody I have ever known and all my unknown human brothers and sisters. This is when I think about Heinz and try to send him a message—even if he's already dead.

(A *mudra* is any one of the various symbolic hand gestures used in the ritual. My diary doesn't mention what was, for me, the most important quality of the worship; it was the best of all aids to concentration. While performing the various acts of the ritual, you were obliged to keep your mind on what you were saying and doing—all the more so, if you were a beginner. Thus you could scarcely avoid thinking about God almost continuously, for about an hour and a half. Under any other circumstances, my span of concentration would have been about one and a half minutes.)

May 19. The man came round today who exterminates vermin and termites. Sarada, who is a born missionary, had a talk with him and excitedly reported that he is much interested in Vedanta. "I'm sure he's got the makings of a devotee," she said. George commented dryly: "From ratman to Atman."

(Speaking of George reminds me of something which happened several weeks ago. Web and I—we're temporarily sharing the big bedroom because of visitors— were wakened in the dead of night by a mysterious thudding. I was sure that I knew what it was. It instantly brought back the memory of a Japanese air raid —my first—heard over Canton from far away across the river, in 1938. A raid on Los Angeles is considered just possible; we've had two or three false alarms already. I assured Web, who was excited but a trifle nervous, that this could only be a nuisance raid. A Japanese aircraft carrier must have sneaked up near to the coast in the shelter of a fog, and launched a few planes. Our chances of being hit were one in a billion . . . And then —we both realized that we were listening to George's typewriter! He produced the peculiar thudding sounds by typing with it placed on the floor. What had fooled us was that he hadn't chanted while he typed, as he nearly always does.)

Today and all night until 7:00 a.m. tomorrow morning, we have a 24-hour vigil, taking it in turns to chant
Ramakrishna's name in the shrine, an hour at a stretch
—because it is the full moon of Buddha's birthday and
because Swami thinks we are getting lazy.

Have just done my stint in the shrine room, chanting
"Jaya Sri Ramakrishna!"

(*Jaya* or *Jai* means "hail," "victory to," or "glory to."
Sri, when used as a prefix to honor a deity or saint, means
"revered" or "holy." In a secular sense, it is the equivalent of "Mr.")

The first ten or fifteen minutes are the worst, because
they are a conscious effort. Then, as Sudhira puts it,
"the thing begins to say itself." You find yourself changing gear from one inflection to another. "Jaya Sri Ramakrishna" becomes "Jaya Sri Ramakrishna," which becomes "Jaya Sri Ramakrishna." Sometimes you begin to
rock back and forth, keeping time to the chant. Sometimes you go up and down the scale, almost singing it.
Sometimes you get terrifically loud and start shouting
it. Sudhira, who loves anything emotional, says it's best
in the middle of the night. Once she and Asit and another devotee got together and made such a noise they
could be heard all over the neighborhood. The shrine
room "feels" quite different when the chanting is going
on—it's like being at a jam session.

I asked Swami: "If Vivekananda had already experienced the highest samadhi, why did he have any more
doubts?" Swami explained that Ramakrishna wished him
to have doubts. He deliberately "locked the door and
kept the key," in order that Vivekananda should return
to ignorance. Vivekananda had to doubt, for our sake.
Otherwise, we should say to ourselves: "It was very easy

for him to believe, he was simply hypnotized by Ramakrishna's personality. His belief proves nothing." What's
so reassuring is that Vivekananda went on doubting so
long before he became convinced.

Amiya and I were letting off steam together over the
horrors of American food—for example, mint jelly and
mayonnaise on fruit salad. (I must admit, I rather over-
play the role of fellow Britisher, to please Amiya.)
Yogini is the worst offender, I said; her mixtures would
shock the witches in Macbeth. Sarada came by, over-
heard us, and laughed.

At this point, my diary refers to a project which had
been in my mind for a long while already—a novel describing the making of the film with Berthold Viertel in
England, during 1933–34. All that existed of it so far
was its title, *Prater Violet*, and three "quite promising"
pages. My desire to get back to work on *Prater Violet*
was related to a general anxiety about my future as a
fiction writer. I had good reason to be anxious. In the
four years since I arrived in the States, I had produced
nothing but two *New Yorker*-type short stories.

Swami was well aware that I had written novels and
that they had scenes in them which some people considered shocking. He had no intention of reading the
novels, but he was rather amused by the idea of their
shockingness and proud of my celebrity. Somebody complained to Swami about the indecency of a scene in one
of Aldous's novels. Swami silenced him by asking gaily,
"Is it *warse* than Shekspeare?" And there was an American writer who had visited Swami and later described
him in print as "a great soul." Swami had forgotten the
writer's name but I identified him as that supershocker,
Henry Miller. (See *The Air-Conditioned Nightmare*.) I

told Swami: "You certainly choose the dirtiest writers for your disciples!"

Swami didn't tell me *not* to write any more novels. He simply took it for granted that I would devote all my available time and my literary abilities to our *Gita* translation, articles for our magazine, and similar tasks. The fiction writer was thus being forced to go underground. But he was determined to survive, and maybe these restrictions were just what he needed to provoke him into becoming active again. He was now a subversive element, whose influence would grow steadily stronger and make itself felt before long.

May 22. Right now, I'm going through an ebb-tide phase —one of those periods which have recurred throughout my life, during which I would, ordinarily, oversmoke, lounge around doing nothing, go too often to the movies, run after sex, read crime stories, drink too much, wallow in the newspapers, and feel depressed. I must watch myself or I shall be apt to grab some excuse for leaving the Center altogether. (If, for example, they were to raise the draft-age limit again, which seems possible.) The forestry camp now presents itself in a furtively attractive aspect, because it would permit a return to sexuality. I now think of sex in entirely promiscuous terms; I've no desire for any kind of relationship. I don't know if this is a good sign, or not.

Reading the life of Vivekananda, the part about his austerities, I ask myself: What were all those agonies and struggles for? *There are times when I feel that I have absolutely no idea. But then I always think: Well, can you tell me what Churchill's blood-toil-tears-and-sweat are* for? *I don't know that, either; so the balance is restored. The spiritual life is, at worst, no more unreal than the political.*

I'm starting to make a selection of Vivekananda's sayings, taken from his letters and lectures:

If living by rule alone ensures excellence, if it be virtue strictly to follow the rules, say then who is a greater devotee, a holier saint, than a railway train?

If you are really ready to take up the earth's burden, take it up by all means—but do not let us hear your groans and curses, do not frighten us with your sufferings. The man who really takes up the burden blesses the world. It is the Saviour who should go on his way rejoicing—not the saved.

The dualist thinks you cannot be moral unless you have a God with a rod in His hand, ready to punish you. Suppose a horse had to give us a lecture on morality, one of those very wretched cab horses who moves only with the whip. He begins to speak about human beings and says they must be very immoral. Why? "Because I know they are not whipped regularly."

I am glad I was born, glad I suffered so, glad I did make big blunders, glad to enter peace. Behind my work was ambition, behind my love was personality, behind my purity was fear, behind my guidance the thirst for power. Now they are vanishing and I drift.

I hate this world, this dream, this horrible nightmare, with its churches and chicaneries, its fair faces and false hearts, its howling righteousness on the surface and utter hollowness beneath, and, above all, its sanctified shopkeeping.

Let the barks of puppies not frighten you—no, not even the thunderbolts of heaven—but stand up and work.

May 24. Sister was very contrite this morning because she'd disagreed with Swami yesterday when he denounced wartime patriotism. "Well," she sighed, "that's just one more hump I'll have to get over."

Swami should be the last person to blame anyone for being patriotic. At heart he's still a flaming Hindu nationalist, and gets very heated when British policy is discussed. But I'm never really bothered by his inconsistencies. And, essentially, he's so humble. I'm sure he refers every problem back to the shrine and Maharaj. I'm glad that he's sometimes vain about his youthful appearance; that's so much better than being "above" vanity and trying to impress everyone with your holiness. Swami's great quality is that he never gets in the way of what he stands for; his figure never blocks out the light.

May 28. A blue jay, with a particularly harsh note, has got terribly on Swami's nerves. He throws stones at it, jumping into the air with a little hop and nearly overbalancing. Amiya and Sudhira like the bird, however, because it enrages Dhruva, whom they both dislike. Dhruva barks frantically at the jay, as it perches just out of his reach and screeches insults.

(Dhruva was Sister's beloved, ill-tempered old collie. He was named for one of the saints of ancient India. According to legend, Vishnu—God in the aspect of Preserver—rewarded Dhruva by taking him up to the sky and setting him there as the polestar.)

At the beginning of June, Swami left suddenly for the East, because Akhilananda, one of his brother swamis, had become seriously ill at the Vedanta Center in Providence, Rhode Island. Before leaving, Swami told me that I was to sleep in his bedroom while he was away. Since his room was in the other house, amidst those of the nuns, this was a seemingly strange decision. Perhaps

Swami, who was somewhat literal-minded about sex, thought that I, as a homosexual, would be further from temptation's reach there than while sharing Webster's bedroom. No doubt, also, he foreknew the effect that being in his room would have on me. I was extraordinarily conscious of Swami's presence there, almost as though I was sharing it with him. I wrote in my diary that I felt like apologizing to Swami every time I used the toilet, and that I hoped I should go on feeling that way as long as my stay lasted. I did.

July 1. Who should saunter in this afternoon but Richard, with his hair cropped short. He wore a blue Navy denim shirt, blue-jean pants, and a seaman's sweater. He was three weeks in the Merchant Marine, on Catalina Island, and then got himself discharged because they taught him nothing except cleaning toilets. Now he has a job as an usher at Warner's Theater. He plans to stay there two or three months, till he can join the Marine Corps.

As soon as we look at each other, we always begin to laugh, like two people who are bluffing at poker. Only, at the same time, I get the uneasy feeling that maybe Rich isn't bluffing. Rich sometimes gives you a look which is disconcertingly mature, indulgent almost, as though he were a grownup playing with a child.

July 7. Out for a turn around the block before vespers, I met Rich. He looked a real bum, dirty, unshaven, and slier than ever. He has quit his job at the theater and is going around mowing lawns. He refused supper because, as he said, he can't eat here without going into the shrine room first, and he won't go into the shrine room because he has "broken" with Ramakrishna. His scruples are part of his fascination.

Swami returned on July 14, bringing with him Swami Vishwananda, the head of the Vedanta Center in Chicago.

Vishwananda is fat, jolly, very Indian. He nearly chokes with laughter at his own jokes, and talks Bengali with Swami and Asit. Everything delights him here, especially the food; in Chicago he can't get proper curry. His Indianness makes Swami seem more Indian, too.

Vishwananda is staying in our house, thus producing a new crisis of overcrowding, especially as he has to have the big bedroom all to himself; this fills me with jealous possessive jitters. However, these I must overcome once and for all, just as I would have had to overcome them in a forestry camp. Isn't it perhaps because I'm not in camp that this problem arises at this particular time? Do we ever avoid anything?

July 16. I've just been talking to Swami. I feel such a deep relationship with him. "Love" is too possessive a word to describe it. It's really absence of demand, lack of strain, entire reassurance. I can't imagine being jealous when he seems to favor one person, because it's so obvious that his attitude toward each one of us is special, and "to divide is not to take away."

He touched my cheek with his finger and giggled, because The New Republic had referred to me as a "prominent young writer." I told him how free I've been from sexual thoughts and fantasies during the past weeks, and he said, "Yes, I saw that in your face yesterday, but don't get too confident, they will come back."

Vishwananda came into "my" washroom this morning, spilled water on the floor, and left a brownish gob of spittle in the basin. This is just the sort of thing I've got to take, and like.

Later. Vishwananda got hold of me and put me through a regular examination, making me show him the mudras we use in the ritual. Then I had to talk on the telephone to Joan, one of the M-G-M secretaries, who had called up out of the blue to gossip. When we were through, I rushed into the shrine room, prostrated, rushed out again, had lunch, slept till four, hurried down to the boulevard with Swami's watch to be repaired and a letter to Willie Maugham about the exact translation of a verse in the Katha Upanishad from which he wants to take a title for his new novel—The Razor's Edge or The Edge of the Razor—nearly lost Dhruva in the crowd, got home, sawed some wood, joined in a discussion as to whether or not Richard should forget about the Marine Corps and try to get classified as a conscientious objector, had tea, translated a verse of the Gita, ate too many peppermint drops, and am now late for vespers. This is what they call an escape from the world!

July 19. This weekend has been stormy, unexpectedly so. We had a puja and there's nothing like a good puja for stirring up lust. As we sat there in the shrine room, it came to me with the fullest force how much I should like to give up Vedanta, pacifism, everything. Yes, get into a uniform and be the same as everybody else. I really wouldn't care what happened to me, I thought, provided I could spend a few more rousing Saturday nights.

Suppose Swami's just kidding himself? Suppose there's no God, no afterlife? Well—suppose. Then death is best, at once. But if you don't want to die? Could you be satisfied with a life of cautious, rationed sensuality? I don't think you could. You've got to renounce or destroy yourself. So the minimum Buddhist position still stands—wrote he, taking another peppermint.

There is no point even in writing this down, however. In a stormy sea there's no point in doing anything but continuing to swim. Keep going through the motions —nothing more. This will pass.

July 22. What I didn't mention in my last entry was that much of my tension was concerned with a copy of the rules and regulations of the Belur Math, which has just arrived. Back at headquarters in Calcutta, they seem to be getting worried about the easygoing way the American centers are run. They want us to shape up and become strictly Hindu monastics.

My God, I thought, when I heard this, what is this gang I've joined? Is it to be turbans unwinding uphill all the way, to the very end? Swami answered my fears and doubts by asking me to write a letter to the Math for him, explaining that their Indian rules couldn't possibly apply to the American centers. "If they refuse to give way," he said, "I shall leave the Order!" What a little rock of safety he is!

(Belur Math did give way temporarily, but it continued to exert pressure to achieve its objectives, gently and with truly Oriental patience, throughout the years that followed.)

July 23. We are in the midst of a heat wave. I spend all the meditation hours rattling through my japam, so as not to be bothered with it at any other time. At present, I have no feeling for the sacredness of the shrine. If you ask me what I want, I reply: Sex, followed by a long long sleep. If offered a painless drug which would kill me in my sleep, I would seriously consider taking it; and I've never played much with thoughts of suicide before.

I inhabit a world in which people are scarcely real. Real are my sex fantasies and sex memories. Real are the devices I think up for not being woken prematurely by somebody's alarm clock. Utterly utterly unreal are Ramakrishna, religion, the war with all its casualties and suffering, and the problems of other people. I long to get away from this place. And yet, if I do manage to wriggle out somehow, I know that, in two or three months, I'll pine to get back in again.

July 26. Today has been a relatively good day. I got up early, went into the shrine at six, and then cycled down to the printers' before breakfast to take them the copy for the leaflet announcing Vishwananda's lectures. This morning I roughed out another page of Prater Violet, did three verses of the Gita and my 2,500 beads.

July 28. Salka Viertel brought Garbo up to lunch at the Center. The girls were all a-flutter and Garbo didn't disappoint them. She played up to them outrageously, sighing how wonderful it must be to be a nun and implying that all her fame was dust and ashes in comparison. Then she flirted with Swami, telling him how dark and mysterious his Indian eyes were. Sarada, of course, is convinced that Garbo's soul is halfway saved already. Swami says that now I am to bring him the Duke of Windsor, his other object of worldly admiration.

(Swami was a regular moviegoer in those days, so his admiration for Garbo wasn't to be wondered at. The Duke of Windsor was another matter. I could only suppose that Swami still pictured him as the young Prince of Wales, visiting India in the early nineteen-twenties. Since most Indians must have been expecting that the Prince would be just another embodiment of British imperial tyranny, his unassuming boyish charm must have come as a great surprise to them and been therefore all the more powerful and winning.)

August 6. I must just write a few lines in recognition of this important date: six months at the Center, six months of technical celibacy. Last year, that achievement would have seemed positively supernatural. Now I see it as the very first step, merely: less than the first. It has no value except as a reassurance that nothing is impossible.

Today, Swami Vishwananda started to teach us a chant: Ram, Ram, Ram, Jaya, Ram. It sounds so idiotic —just like the fake-Tibetan chant in The Ascent of F6. And it is a perfect example of the kind of thing I must learn to accept. If I'm too dainty-stomached to swallow a little Sanskrit, how can I possibly prove to my friends that there is something more to this place than mere quaintness?

I think how they would laugh at Vishwananda, and at moments I really hate them all—everybody outside the Center—savagely: there they sit, sneering and yet doing nothing to find out what it's all about. But I'm really hating myself—for not being strong enough to convince them.

To live this synthesis of East and West is the most valuable kind of pioneer work I can imagine—never mind who approves or disapproves.

Last night, Swami told me: "One thing I can promise you. You will never regret having come here. Never."

On August 17, I began what I described to myself as "a few days' rest from the Center." I had rented a room in a house which was opposite the Viertels' home in Santa Monica Canyon.

This wasn't by any means my first "rest." On several occasions I had spent a few nights at Chris Wood's house in Laguna Beach, or at the houses of other friends. I had also often been invited out to lunches and evening meals. Swami made no objection to any of this, as long as I wasn't needed at the Center for a particular reason.

He can't have realized, of course, that Santa Monica was an area of special danger to me, because of the erotic magic of the nearby beach. On May 14, there is a reference in my diary to this magic and to the kind of pseudo-aesthetic lust it aroused in me:

Down to Santa Monica to have lunch with the Viertels, then went on the beach with Garbo and Tommy Viertel. We walked along the shore, right to the pier. The sun was brilliant, with a strong wind—the palms waving all along the cliff, and the ocean dazzling with light and foam. The air was full of spray and falling light; it was beautiful beyond all words. The afternoon had an edge of extra-keen, almost intolerable sensation on all its sights and sounds and smells. Seeing a human body in the far distance, you wanted to seize it in your arms and devour it—not for itself, but as a palpable fragment of the whole scene, of the wildness of the wind and foam, of the entire unseizable mystery and delight of the moment. I glimpsed something, for an instant, of the reality behind sex. Something which we reach out toward, as we take the human body in our arms. It is what we really want, and it eludes us in the very act of possession.

Garbo chattered away. She was nice. I liked her better

than ever before. Later she drove me back, shooting all the stoplights. But the afternoon was more memorable than she was.

August 18. Strange—I've been looking forward to this outing for several weeks, and now that I'm here I find I'm bored. This is chiefly because of the Viertels. I'd blandly assumed that they'd be delighted to see me, and that they'd devote all their time to keeping me amused. They are quite pleased to see me, but they're all working hard and busy with their own problems.

Thus frustrated, I decided to get in touch with a young writer I had recently met, Tennessee Williams. He had come out to California to work on a picture for M-G-M. A friend had given him my address and he appeared at the Center—by ill luck, in the middle of a meditation period. But, despite the embarrassment of our surroundings, we had managed to exchange the necessary psychological signals, which meant that we would meet again.

I located Tennessee, after some search, at a very squalid rooming house called The Palisades, at the other end of town—sitting typing a film story in a yachting cap, amidst a litter of dirty coffee cups, crumpled bed linen, and old newspapers. He seemed not in the least surprised to see me. In fact, his manner was that of the meditative sage to whose humble cabin the world-weary wanderer finally returns. He took it, with discreetly concealed amusement, as the most natural thing in the world that I should be having myself a holiday from the monastery. We had supper together on the pier and I drank quite a lot of beer and talked sex the entire evening.

Tennessee is the most relaxed creature imaginable: he works till he's tired, eats when he feels like it, sleeps when he can't stay awake.

Since the coastal area had been put under a wartime blackout, the park at the top of the cliffs had become a sex jungle at night, full of servicemen and their hunters. Tennessee was in his element there. I walked with him a little way into the thrilling darkness but didn't join him in the hunt.

During the next week, we were together often. We were quite charmed by each other and already intimate, like the old friends we were destined to become. Swimming with him, or taking long early rides alone up the coast on a bicycle, I was more than usually body-conscious and pleased with my vigor. My thirty-ninth birthday was only a few days ahead, but I didn't care. I felt like a young man.

One marvelous evening, Berthold read German poetry aloud to me, including mad Hölderlin, my favorite. We were both moved to tears. I realized that he was trying to re-create the role of mentor which he had played ten years earlier, while we were working on the film. In this role, he kept making indirect attacks on the monastic life. To these I didn't react. I could never be angry with him again—for, now that he had become a character in *Prater Violet*, he was a privileged creature and, in a sense, my child. He didn't know this yet.

By this time, Denny had been discharged from the forestry camp because of some cardiac weakness. On the twenty-first, he came to visit me in Santa Monica with two friends. One of these friends was a young man of striking beauty. Describing the scene later, I used to say that my first glimpse of him had hit me "like a shot from an elephant gun" and made me "grunt" with desire.

When Denny and I were alone, I accused him of having maliciously introduced me to this beautiful temptation in order to seduce me away from the Vedanta Center. This was meant as a joke. Nevertheless, I knew that the young man's image had been stamped upon my mind and would reappear at inconvenient moments, in the shrine room and elsewhere. It would be all the more disturbing because I realized already that he himself wasn't unattainable.

That same evening, I went with Berthold to visit Bertolt Brecht and his wife, the actress Helene Weigel. I had met them for the first time two days before, with Hanns Eisler, the composer, and had immediately become aware that I was in the presence of a tribunal. My position, as a member of a religious sect, was about to be judged according to Marxist law. My judges were polite, but beneath their politeness was contempt. To them, "religion" meant ecclesiastical politics—politics of the capitalist front. But even if I had convinced them that Prabhavananda had nothing to do with vested interests of this sort, they would have remained hostile to him. Brecht said—I am not quoting his exact words—that a saint needs thousands of sinners to make his career possible; meaning that any attempt to lead a spiritual life is mere self-indulgent individualism. I sat silent, almost sorry that I couldn't defend Prabhavananda and myself with an equally silly dogmatism.

What I have been describing is a succession of encounters, all in various ways subversive, which perhaps helped to produce the absurd little anticlimactic climax of August 24.

That morning, as usual, I went down to swim. The beach was almost deserted. As soon as I was in the water above my waist, I took off my swimming trunks, as I often did, and slipped them around my neck. I loved to swim naked, although/because, while doing so, I always felt the excitement of a flirtation with Sex.

And now a man appeared, walking along the tide line. As soon as he saw the trunks around my neck, he began to grin, with pleased amusement. He stripped off his own trunks and came up to me through the water. He handled my body. I made no resistance. We were both sexually aroused and both laughing. I laughed because this wordless encounter seemed odd and dreamlike; I had already realized that he was deaf and dumb. Finding myself on the verge of an orgasm, I stopped him. He didn't seem disappointed or offended. He let go of me at once. Still laughing, he turned and waded away. It struck me that he was like an apparition which I myself had summoned; perhaps a minor and unalarming demon. Well might he laugh!

I went back to my room in a state of incredulity. Was this tiny push all that had been needed to throw me off balance? I was partly horrified, partly amused, entirely bewildered. As I stood naked in the bathroom, a voice said to me: Did you think it wouldn't count, as long as you didn't go all the way? That was the same thing as doing it, and you know it was. Well, go ahead—finish it off.

I did so, with difficulty. The act gave me no pleasure. It seemed idiotic.

My reaction was to return to the Vedanta Center as soon as possible, two days earlier than I'd planned.

Ten

August 31, 1943. My chief reason for opening this book today is my intense disinclination to write a single word. I feel just awful. Can I possibly stay on here?

When I told Swami, vaguely, that I'd had trouble with sex, he smiled and patted my head. "It's a hard life," he said. "Just pray for strength, pray to become pure." So there we are. I've got to become pure.

The diary goes on to describe emotional upsets which were currently being suffered by other members of the family—aversion, insomnia, crying fits—and continues:

One's first reaction to all this is the world's reaction: mustn't there be something radically wrong with this place, if everybody is so hysterical? But that objection arises from the fallacy that the aim of religion is to make you happy in a worldly sense. It isn't. The death of the ego was never supposed to be pleasant, and this misery may really mean that we are getting ahead with it. So let the squeezing process go on, as long as we can take it.

September 1. I have a gnawing desire to go and see Denny and cry on his shoulder. He's the only person I can discuss the situation with, quite frankly. But discussing it will only make it worse. What's done is done. Oh, wretched little ego, are you mad? What do you hope for yourself from this self-torture?

How many times must I repeat what Gerald used to tell me: "At the moment of action, no man is free"? What happened the other day could never have happened if I hadn't been lounging and slacking for days before. The whole time I was in Santa Monica, I scarcely meditated once, or told my beads, or kept up any discipline at all.

The act itself was nothing. I only mind about it because it spoilt a record and hurt my vanity. It was even a very good thing that it happened—or rather, it will have been a good thing if it jolts my complacency. It's amazing how one blinds oneself. How, with closed eyes like a sleepwalker—or like someone who is pretending to sleepwalk—one edges nearer and nearer the table on which the candy lies.

And, as always, within this defeat lies the possibility of an enormous victory. If I can resume my life here and carry on as if nothing had happened, then that'll be much more reassuring than if I'd never slipped. Morale is the only thing that matters.

At about this time, I wrote to my draft board notifying them that I would be willing to serve in the Army Medical Corps, supposing that the draft-age limit were to be raised again. A recent official ruling had guaranteed the conscientious objector's right to choose the Medical Corps. Before this, he had had no right of choice and was liable to be given any duties which were technically non-combatant. Most C.O.'s, including myself, had regarded this alternative as unacceptable—it amounted to helping somebody else fire the gun which you refused to fire yourself. Therefore, we had had to refuse service with the Armed Forces altogether.

Since I knew that the raising of the draft-age limit was now unlikely, my letter didn't represent a serious attempt to get myself forcibly removed from the Vedanta Center. Writing it was merely a move in a game which I was playing with myself, irresponsibly fiddling with the various triggers of change.

September 15. Being with Denny unsettles me, and yet I need him more than ever before, because he's the only person who can view my life as a whole, and therefore the only one who can give me intelligent advice. He isn't shocked by the squalid bits of it and he isn't repelled or mystified by Vedanta. He's always getting in digs at Swami, whom he's never forgiven, but he doesn't suggest that I should leave the Center.

His attitude was summed up the other day when he said, "Either make up your mind to be a monk or a dirty old man." Sometimes I find this kind of brutality bracing, sometimes it just annoys me, because I know, and Denny knows, that he has no right to talk to me like this, when he isn't faced with the same problem himself. If I were to leave the Center, he would be pleased in a way, because it would shock a lot of people he dislikes and because he knows I could only turn to him and depend on him more than ever—most likely, we'd start living together again. But he'd also be a bit dismayed, I'm sure, because, in a strange way, he relies on me to do his praying for him. Whatever happens, he can't lose. And I, it seems, can't win.

Sometimes I feel that everything would be solved if I could get the right kind of person to join me here. Somebody who had the same problems as myself and spoke my language. But I know that this is only a fantasy created to take the place of the relationship I really ought to be cultivating—the relationship to the shrine and what it stands for. Everything else is a substitute and would end as all substitutes end.

It's as if I'd walked into a trap at last. After all my other impersonations, I have picked up yet another funny mask and stuck my nose into it—and now it won't come off. Have I really got to spend the rest of my life with these people, or any particular group of people?

How I long for the mere sensation of freedom again! I keep remembering that phrase from the Carmen song about smuggling and the mountains and freedom: "la chose enivrante," the intoxicating thing. I don't even mean sex—it's far more trivial than that. Just to sit at the wheel of a car at a drive-in, eating pie with coffee, and know I can take off in any direction I want to . . .

No! What utter nonsense I am writing! To say that I really want "freedom" is as untrue as to say I want the vision of God. I don't know what I want. The very use of the word "I" immediately turns any such statement into a silly noise. Do I want to die? My goodness, no—for what? Do I want to live? My goodness, no—for what? I would like to lose consciousness for ever and ever, I think. But to believe in total extinction seems like sentimental optimism.

How delightful religion used to be—in the days when I wasn't doing anything particular about it! What delicious emotions, what pleasantly sentimental yearnings! Now it's just a stupid boring misery. I seem to get worse and worse. I know that I am ten times more disagreeable than I have ever been before in my life. Oh, of course, I know the answer to that one. Swami says it's like cleaning out an inkwell which is screwed to the table: you keep pouring in water and nothing comes out but dirty old ink—at least, not for a long long time.

Later: Sudhira just came in, to give me a nightcap glass of lemon and rum for my cold. Her face, with its slap-happy masochistic smile, looked moist, perhaps from crying. "Aren't you terribly lonely here?" I asked. "Yes, terribly." "So am I."

While complaining like this, I was carrying out my monastic duties with a fair show of diligence—running errands, correcting the proofs of our magazine, and performing the ritual worship quite often. Then, on September 20, I went to lunch with the Viertels in Santa Monica and had another sex encounter on the beach. This time, it was neither absurd nor unreal; I simply met an attractive young man who wanted exactly what I did.

The very next day, I got a telegram from a dear friend and sex partner who was coming to California on leave before being sent overseas with the Army. He was paying a goodbye visit to his family, who lived in a neighboring city. He wanted to say goodbye to me, too, and I realized that he expected our goodbyes to be said in bed. Was I going to refuse him—knowing that we might never see each other again? Of course not.

I had to ask Swami if I could skip the evening class. This made me feel guilty. I sat with him for a few minutes, because I didn't want to seem eager to rush off. Suddenly he turned to me and said, "You know, Chris—even if one gives up the spiritual life altogether for a while, he will come back to Ramakrishna before he dies. We know that for a fact. We have witnessed it."

Maybe because he thought I needed a change of scene, Swami arranged for me to visit the three other Vedanta centers on the West Coast. The official reason for my trip was that I should represent him at the dedication of a house in Portland, Oregon, to which the local Vedanta Center had just been transferred.

I left Los Angeles on September 30. My first stop was at the San Francisco Center, a Victorian/Hindu-style building, picturesquely domed and fretworked, which had survived the 1906 earthquake. This was an all-male household, ruled over by a handsome, masterful swami, Ashokananda. There was no pampering of the monks with the domestic comforts we took for granted in Hollywood. I found the atmosphere frugal and depressing, and wrote to Sudhira: "I never realized before how *absolutely* necessary women are. This place smells of renunciation, fog, and salad." The city itself, which I had last seen in peacetime, depressed me even more than the Center, for it was full of servicemen, waiting in crammed noisy joyless bars to be shipped out to their ominous future in the Pacific war.

The Portland Center didn't lack women, but most of them were elderly and seemed exhausted by the energy of their very young swami, Devatmananda. His motto, taken from Vivekananda, was "Face the brute!"—which meant that he tried to do everything himself. Standing on a stepladder, he handled the wire ends which awaited connection to a chandelier, as he talked enthusiastically about the future work of the Center and winced without complaint at frequent electric shocks.

The puja which accompanied the dedication of the

Center lasted for three days. My only relief from it was the time I spent with my former brother monastic, Richard. He was present because Portland was his hometown, but he was now about to leave it and join the Marines. Meanwhile, he dodged all Devatmananda's attempts to make him work and threw a heavy bread knife around in the garden, saying that he was preparing himself for "Jap hunting." One afternoon, during a party for devotees, he and I sneaked off to see a thriller called *The Leopard Man*, instead of handing round plates of sandwiches.

Three swamis had come to Portland for the ceremonies—Vishwananda, Ashokananda, and Vividishananda of Seattle. Vishwananda had already made himself completely at home, just as in Hollywood. He spent his days eating, chanting, and playing the harmonium. I loved him at breakfast, when he clapped his hands as though he were at some Asian inn, and shouted, "Bring eggs!"

On October 9, there was one more ceremony, the laying of the foundation stone for a future temple. This was to be built on a large piece of land belonging to the Vedanta Society and already being used as a retreat by the devotees, several miles outside the city.

Most of the land was covered by a birch forest, with some wooden houses in it, looking very Scandinavian. The swamis gathered, in their yellow robes, at the spot where the stone was to be laid. It started to drizzle. Ashokananda teasingly told Vishwananda to go and pray for the rain to stop. Vishwananda waddled off by himself among the trees. The rain stopped. He returned, amidst humorous but surprised applause. The ceremony began. The drizzle started again. "Go and pray some more," said Ashokananda. Vishwananda sighed: "The

second time is more difficult." But he went off obedi-
ently, nevertheless—only to return, an instant later, gasp-
ing and trotting; he had disturbed a nest of wild bees.
The rain continued and we finished the ceremony under
umbrellas.

One of the devotees, an old lady, offered to pay for
my training as a monk, because "you boys are doing such
splendid work."

After Portland, I went on up to Seattle, to stay a night
at the Center there before returning to Los Angeles.
Ashokananda and Vividishananda were with me on the
train.

As soon as we crossed the Oregon–Washington state
line, Ashokananda began what became a tiresomely pro-
longed would-be humorous bullying of Vividishananda.
When we discovered that the train had no dining car,
he declared that Vividishananda was responsible, since
Washington was his state. Vividishananda merely smiled
and said nothing.

The Seattle Center was much smaller than either of
the others I had just visited. Vividishananda had only
one monk who actually lived with him in his house. This
was a young man who had lately been demobilized from
the Army. He seemed quite as devoted to Vividishananda as George was to Prabhavananda; but, unlike
George, he took his renunciation a shade too grimly—
or so I thought. After telling me that he and Vividishananda went for a daily walk through the park, he added:
"But we shan't be able to do that when summer comes,
because the girls lie around there in swimming suits."

Vividishananda's smiling quietness was impressive. He
appeared to take religion as a matter of course—how else

could one spend one's life? I imagined myself as his disciple. He would claim my every waking moment—no time-wasting chatter, no self-indulgent scribblings, no sex fantasies. I might develop genuine austerity. But I should also develop a terminal illness and escape from him by dying within the year. Devatmananda would keep me orbiting around him in a whirl of chores; all I should ever learn from him would be how to fix the plumbing. I hadn't the temperament for utter submission to Ashokananda, even though I realized that it might do wonders for me spiritually; he would goad me to defiance and revolt. As for Vishwananda, whom I was now growing deeply fond of, my joining him at the Chicago Center could well have disastrous results for both of us. I could see myself sinking with him into gluttony, and even seducing him into becoming my drinking companion.

No—for me, it was Prabhavananda or nobody.

November 19. A lot of time has gone by, but little news. My position is exactly the same. The shrine is always with us. As long as some contact is maintained with it, all is simple and possible. As soon as contact is broken, all is horrible, tense, confused.

The other day, Swami said to me, "Do you know what purity is, Chris? Purity is telling the truth."

Two soldiers are walking past the temple. One of them looks at it and I hear him exclaim: "Boy! The guy who built that thing sure had a screwy wife!"

By the end of October, Swami and I had finished a rough draft of our translation of the *Gita*. Since then, we had been revising it, with the help of a friend of mine, Margaret Kiskadden. This revision was carried out with increasing but still unshared misgivings, as far as Mrs.

Kiskadden and I were concerned. At last, on November 22, she reached the brink of frankness and confessed that she didn't think our version was really any better than most of the others—which we had been criticizing for their obscurity and archaic un-English locutions; it was dull and it was clumsy and it reeked of Sanskrit. She further confessed that she had shown part of our version to Aldous, that they had discussed it, and that he had agreed with her opinion.

It was an awful moment, because, once she'd said this, its truth was only too obvious. I felt a wave of depression sweep over me—and Swami, seeing how I felt, suddenly turned very small and gray and shriveled, a bird on a winter bough.

And then—it was really amazing—I saw in a flash what to do. I ran back to my room with the manuscript.

Our version began: "Oh, changeless Krishna, drive my chariot between the two armies which are eager for battle, that I may see those whom I shall have to fight in this coming war. I wish to see the men who have assembled here, taking the side of the enemy in order to please the evil-minded son of Dhritarashtra."

In about half an hour, I had turned this into:

> Krishna the changeless,
> Halt my chariot
> There where the warriors,
> Bold for the battle,
> Face their foemen.
>
> Between the armies
> There let me see them,
> The men I must fight with,

> Gathered together
> Now at the bidding
> Of him their leader,
> Blind Dhritarashtra's
> Evil offspring:
> Such are my foes
> In the war that is coming.

I brought this back and showed it to them, and they were both excited. I'm excited myself, because it opens up all sorts of possibilities, and I now realize how horribly bored I was with the old translation. I don't see my way clearly yet, but obviously this method can be applied throughout the book. There should be several different kinds of verse, and I think I can vary the prose style, too. We are going to Aldous this evening, to discuss the whole thing with him.

What had I actually done, during that half hour? I had turned a passage of creaky antiqued prose into some lines of verse which were alliterated and heavily stressed in imitation of an Old English epic. Why? Because I had felt a sudden urge to get the show on the road. The prose had dragged its feet. The verse was brisk and catchy, it seemed to be going somewhere. At least, I had said to myself, I won't let the reader fall asleep on page one.

Thus described, my action sounds irresponsible, frivolous, merely desperate. But, even then, I knew that it wasn't—that I was taking this first step in accordance with an overall plan for rewriting our translation, unclear to me as yet but definitely workable. I was also beginning to see how such a plan could be justified.

Considered simply as a work of literature, the *Gita* is

not a unity, except in the sense that it is all composed
in the same kind of Sanskrit verse. It has several quite
distinct aspects. If you have to choose between translat-
ing it into English verse or prose, prose seems preferable,
because much of the material doesn't lend itself easily
to the capacities of English verse. (The Sanskrit original
is, from an English point of view, unnaturally terse and
compressed; translated literally, it would become a poem
written in telegrams.) It is at least arguable that a mix-
ture of verse and prose is better than either medium
used exclusively; that both are needed to present the
Gita in its full variety.

To begin with, the *Gita* is epic. It was composed to
fit into another, far larger epic poem, the *Mahabharata*
—the story of the descendants of King Bharata (*Maha*
means "great"), who lived in ancient India. At a certain
point in that story, Arjuna, one of its warrior heroes, is
about to lead his men in a civil war against the army of
his foster brother, who has tricked him and his natural
brothers out of the kingdom they should have inherited.
Arjuna is a friend and disciple of Krishna, who is living
on earth in human form. Krishna agrees to be with
Arjuna throughout the battle as his charioteer, but he
will not join in the fighting.

It is here that the *Gita* takes up the story, naming
the leading warriors on both sides and telling how
Arjuna asks Krishna to drive him into the no-man's-land
between the armies, so that he may see the men he is
about to fight against. When Arjuna does see them, he
realizes that many are his kinsmen or old friends, and he
exclaims that he would rather die than kill them. He
begs Krishna to advise him what to do.

Thus far, the *Gita* has preserved the epic character
of the *Mahabharata*. But now, as Krishna begins to rea-

son with and instruct Arjuna, it becomes a quite different kind of literary work, having sometimes the character of a gospel, sometimes that of a philosophical discourse. The gospel passages are often poetic in feeling; the discourse passages, translated into English, seem to demand prose; verse would only make them prosy.

Krishna himself has different tones of voice. Sometimes he speaks as God, sometimes as man. Like Jesus, he speaks as God in the aspect of Protector, telling Arjuna to take refuge in him. But he also appears to Arjuna in the aspect of God transcendent, within whose being all creation is contained. Arjuna, who has begged Krishna to grant him this vision, is terrified by its majesty, its blinding brilliance, and the thunder of its speech. Krishna calms his fears by reappearing in human form, as Arjuna's familiar friend. In this aspect, he speaks simply and affectionately. Then, as Krishna returns to his discourse, his tone changes again. He explains the nature of action, the practice of renunciation and meditation, the forces which activate the universe, and the respective temperaments and spiritual duties of different kinds of individual. While doing this, he often uses Sanskrit philosophical terms which require footnotes to explain them; they have no exact equivalents in English. His tone rises, now and then, to thrilling passages of lyrical declaration; more often, it has the quietness of absolute authority—a university lecture delivered by God.

In conclusion, Krishna tells Arjuna that he must fight, because this is his *dharma*—the duty which is imposed upon him by his own nature. Arjuna is a member of the warrior caste and he has accepted the responsibilities of a military leader. He cannot now impulsively disown his dharma and try to obey some other concept of duty; a dharma which is not naturally his will lead him into spiritual confusion. And Krishna adds: "If you say 'I will not fight,' your resolve is vain. Your own nature will drive you to the act."

(It was of special importance to me, as a pacifist, to learn that the *Gita* doesn't sanction war—as some have claimed—any more than it sanctions pacifism. It cannot, from its absolute standpoint, do either. It leaves each individual to discover what his or her dharma is.)

Arjuna has been convinced by Krishna's teachings. He agrees to fight. Thus, the *Gita* ends. The *Mahabharata,* continuing its story, tells that the battle lasted eighteen days and resulted in total victory for Arjuna and his brothers.

I don't remember that Swami ever made any objection to the method I was about to use in rewriting our translation. Yet this was a delicate subject. By questioning the literary unity of the *Gita,* I had come near to raising another question: Is the *Gita* a philosophical unity? Many scholars have declared that it isn't—that it contains additions and alterations made at later periods by philosophers of differing schools and that it shows the influence of Buddhist and even of Christian thought. Swami was too well educated not to be able to see a certain justification for such criticisms; but his whole soul rebelled against them. To him, since childhood, the *Gita* had been sacred—every line of it equally so. If I couldn't share his feeling, I could at least take his side by stirring up the prejudice of my college days to damn these dull academic dogs whose noses were trained only to sniff out a "corrupt" text.

Looking through our *Gita* today, I find many transitions from prose to verse or from verse to prose which I can't justify logically. I must have made them purely by ear and often just to keep changing the pace. But Swami, whose faith in my literary taste was stronger even than mine in his spiritual discrimination, passed nearly everything—only objecting, occasionally and very mildly, when I used a word or phrase which strayed too far from its Sanskrit original.

The rough draft of the revision was quickly finished— so quickly, indeed, that my accomplishment became a household legend; Swami even hinted that I had been divinely inspired. I was pleased with myself but also well aware that this praise came from friends who knew nothing of the world of the theater and the film studios. I, who had seen a script reconstructed before breakfast, a song composed while the actors waited on stage, knew that such so-called miracles are not uncommon. I suspect that they are often the result of simultaneous but divided activities in the creative mind. You have no faith in the version of the book or play you are working on but are unwilling to change it, telling yourself that this would mean a lot of trouble and that time is short. Meanwhile, however, a rebellious element inside you has secretly created its own anti-version, complete down to the last detail, and is waiting for a chance to produce and impose it. If the rebellion succeeds, outside observers are amazed at the speed and smoothness with which the takeover is accomplished.

Rebellions may be made smoothly, but never without causing psychological disturbance. In my own case, I suddenly felt that I couldn't work under such pressure unless I started smoking again. (I had given up the habit with difficulty in 1941, because I was upset about my parting from Vernon and wanted to raise my morale by asserting my willpower.) When I lit my first cigarette, I felt so sick to my stomach that I had to run out into the garden for air. But I persisted, and soon I was chain-smoking as compulsively as Swami himself.

Eleven

January 3, 1944. Swami and several of us went to see *The Song of Bernadette*. On the whole, Swami approved of it. He liked the deathbed scene and the vision of the Lady because, he told us, visions usually appear in the <u>corner</u> of a room, and that's what happens in this film. Needless to say, he was convinced that the roses on the Lady's feet were really lotuses. He is extraordinarily obstinate on this point. As for me, I had a real good cry, from about reel two onwards, and greatly enjoyed myself.

January 13. Yesterday, Swami gave a lecture on Vedanta to a Young Methodists' club at U.C.L.A. He was disgusted by the students' behavior. The girls sat on the boys' laps throughout.

Sarada has become a Song of Bernadette addict. Whenever anybody wants to see it, she goes along with them.

January 14. With Swami out land shopping for the new center. A realtor showed us a marvelous property high

up in the hills above Brentwood, with a view over Santa
Monica Bay and across the city to Mount Wilson and
Baldy. But it would cost hundreds of thousands to
develop. No road, even.

The idea of moving the Center away from Hollywood
to the outskirts of the city had been in Swami's mind
for some time. I don't think he regarded the matter as
urgent, but he enjoyed land shopping just for its own
sake. He had an eye for real estate, and he could become
surprisingly businesslike when asking questions about
prices and the terms of a mortgage.

*February 18. Richard's parents are here—just back from
visiting Rich at the San Diego Marine Base. He'll go overseas soon. He is the camp eccentric. Everybody knows
and likes him.*

*Perhaps the only thing that would ever reconcile me
entirely to this place would be having someone here I
could talk to as I talk to Denny; someone who, at the
same time, was convinced of the necessity for this way
of life and absolutely determined to stick it out here.*

*February 28. Swami has been sick. Now he's recovered.
He sits on the sofa and we forget him. We play, un-
mindful, like children, in the completely uninteresting
certainty of their father's love. If we cut our fingers
we'll remember and run to him at once. Our demand
on him is total and quite merciless. We demand that he
will be here, now, tomorrow, whenever we decide we
want him.*

During that spring, I again met the beautiful young
man Denny had introduced me to in Santa Monica the

previous August. I will call him Alfred, because I happen
to find that name unromantic and asexual; beauty such
as his demands a foil.

Alfred and I started seeing each other often, and soon
I felt very much involved with him emotionally. This I
called being in love with him, but it would have been
truer to say that I identified him with my desire to
escape from the Center; he embodied the joys of being
on the Outside.

Alfred himself couldn't have been sweeter about this.
Although not in love, he liked me and was ready for sex
whenever I wanted it. Throughout the next year, he
treated me with the consideration and understanding of
a true friend. I sometimes treated him as one of the
seven deadly sins, which might be overcome by overindulgence. In such moods, my attitude was: Let me go
to bed with you so I can get tired of you.

*April 13. Was horrid to Sudhira, because she'd allowed
a friend of hers to read one of my stories. The rational-
ization for my behavior was that, a day or two ago,
Swami said to someone in my presence: "Why do you
read novels? All books that do not give the word of God
are just a trash." So I worked this up into a sulk, the
usual kind—that I'm not "understood" here, that Swami
hates Art, and that this is what keeps all my friends
away from the Center, etc.*

*Actually—don't I know it all too well?—I'm merely
sulking because I want to run off and play around Alfred.
I worked off some spite at the committee meeting of the
Vedanta Society by announcing that I'd resign from
being president this year.*

*April 14. Swami, sitting on the steps outside the temple
this morning, asked me so sweetly why I'd resigned from*

the committee. I put it that I dislike taking any official position here because I want to feel free to walk out at a moment's notice. Swami accepted this as though it were the whole truth—and, as usual, his love and utter lack of egotism melted me completely. I suppose that's what Brahmananda did to you; you felt he was more on your side than you were yourself.

April 17. My day of silence. Eight hours in the shrine. Boredom. Blankness. Storms of resentment—against Asit, against India, against the possibility of being given a Sanskrit name. Extraordinary how violently I react against this; yet I know that Swami won't ever insist on it, if he sees that I really mind.

(To me, "Christopher Isherwood" was much more than just my name; it was the code word for my identity as a writer, the formula for the essence of my artistic power. So, to force me to take another name would be an act of hostile magic. You would be tampering with my identity and reducing my power . . . Like all matter-of-fact explanations of a magical process, this sounds ridiculous, of course. Which is, no doubt, why I refused to accept it at that time and remained puzzled by the violence of my reaction, calling it "extraordinary.")

"Decided" not to become a monk, and to tell Swami so tomorrow—I doubt if I shall—but to stay here, at any rate, till Brahmananda's next birthday. Where would I go after that? I don't know. Just "out." Sex, of course. But it's much much more than that. I have to explore every corner of the cage before I can assure myself that it's as big as the universe.

April 18. Talked to Swami after breakfast and told him about yesterday. I forget already just exactly what he said. It was the way he said it that matters:

No, it didn't make any difference if I left this place; it would always be my home. God wasn't specially here. Acts aren't important in themselves. It's no good promising not to do things. "That's your Christian training," said Swami, smiling, and he added, "Can you imagine me as a Christian monk? I would never have been a monk if I hadn't met Brahmananda."

May 14. Sudhira goes down to the hospital every afternoon, to nurse a friend who has just had an operation. The other day, a nurse came into the room and whispered to Sudhira that they were in a fix; a woman had been brought in dying, and there was no bed for her—they'd wheeled her into one of the waiting rooms and screened it off; and now the staff was so shorthanded that there was no nurse to spare. Would Sudhira go and be with her so she wouldn't have to die alone? Of course, Sudhira was delighted. The woman took about twenty minutes to die. No chaplain appeared, so Sudhira repeated her mantram all the time. "And just before she died, she opened her eyes and gave me such a funny look; as though the whole thing was a huge joke between us two."

June 7. First news coming in about the D-day invasion of France. I keep wondering if Heinz is alive and if he's fighting there; and what is happening to so many other friends, English and American, who may be part of it.

A letter from Vernon. He now definitely suggests that he shall come West and live with or near me and study with Swami—though he doesn't want to join up at the Center—not, at any rate, for the present.

(Vernon had gone back to New York at the end of 1941. We had met two or three times while I was working with the Quakers at Haverford, and had exchanged occasional letters since then.)

I went into the living room and Swami said, smiling, "You are worried about something, Chris." I mentioned the invasion, and Vernon—but not Alfred. However, as always after talking to him, I began to feel calmer.

June 12. 11 a.m. Have just finished three hours in the shrine, had breakfast. My sit was uneventful, lots of japam, avoided thinking much about Alfred, or worrying, or feeling mad at anyone. I yawned a great deal, and the salt from the tears has dried under my eyes. A dull gray morning. Have just smoked a cigarette, which I didn't mean to.

2 p.m. Have done the worship. Found I'd forgotten most of the ritual, but muddled through somehow. It's very distasteful to me, at present.

I feel bored, sullen, resentful. Envious of Denny, who told me the other night in a bar, "I've decided to hold on to the things I can see." Must I be the only one to follow this way of life? Well, that's where Vernon can help. If it works out.

Denny says he's sure I'll be out of here within six months.

3:30 p.m. Did half an hour in the shrine. Ate bread and honey, and peaches with sour cream. Outlook on life a little brighter, but still quite unconstructive. Swami is gay and excited, because they've found a big property on the Pacific Palisades which would do for the new Center. It costs $35,000; but this amount can probably be raised by selling off the outer lots to various members of the congregation who will want to build homes there.

5:15 p.m. Have spent another hour in the shrine. This much I have doped out: I would never leave the Center on Alfred's account.

10 p.m. Finished vespers. Ate a sardine supper. Put in a final fifteen minutes, to make up seven hours. I feel a kind of stolid forlorn satisfaction, nothing more. Terribly tired. I'm like a nursemaid who has been dragged around all day by a spoilt child, full of energy and whims and demands. The child is asleep at last, but he'll be awake at crack of dawn and raring to go. Oh God, I am so sick of him and his complaints and his damned love affair. He needs a sound whipping.

June 14. Got up at 4:15 and did three hours in the shrine. Merely in order to have it over with and be able to run away and play in Santa Monica.

Before breakfast, in the living room, Swami said, "Take away God, and what is left? Ashcans!"

June 15. At vespers, a sudden thought: a way of leaving this place without abandoning everything. Why couldn't Vernon and I live together somewhere in the neighborhood, not too much involved with the Center but keeping all the rules? I must have a stricter check on my life than Swami. I need someone like Vernon—someone who'd have a stake in my life; so that my failures would be his failures, too, and vice versa. This worked for a short time with Denny, in 1941; we really relied on each other. But Denny is now going along a different road. Vernon is the only person who really needs me, right now, and he's the only person I really need. I wonder if Swami would understand all this? He must. I'll make him, somehow.

We've just heard that the Pacific Palisades property is already sold.

Marcel Rodd, a local publisher, had started coming to see us, because he had agreed to publish our *Gita* translation.

June 20. Rodd is a pale little shrimp of a man, with great dark eyes full of boyish impudence. He's English, with Levantine blood. He and Swami meet, as it were, at a halfway house in the Middle East, bargaining and giggling Orientally, and understanding each other perfectly.

June 22. Woke yesterday morning with a scalding sore throat. Today I still have a temperature. It's much preferable to my mental fevers.

A long talk with Dr. K. He believes that everybody who tries to lead the religious life is sure to get sick; it's part of the process of renunciation, "dying to the world." If you persist, you snap out of it and your health improves. He sat on the bed, smiling and holding my pulse, and I began to feel better immediately.

June 30. I got back from Santa Monica yesterday, after spending four days with Alfred.

After breakfast, I went into Swami's study and told him everything—all about my relations with Alfred. "Now that you have come to Ramakrishna, you will be taken care of," he said. "I promise you that. Even if you eat mud, you will be all right."

I also told him about my plans for Vernon. I said we would want to live by ourselves but it could be just around the corner from Ivar Avenue. Swami agreed to everything, but I can see that he wants to get Vernon into the family, right from the start. He said, "I don't want you to leave here, Chris. I want you to stay with me as long as I'm alive. I think you'd be all right, even if you left here. But I want you . . . I think you have the makings of a saint."

I laughed. I was really staggered. "No," said Swami, "I mean it. You have devotion. You have the driving power. And you are sincere. What else is there?"

July 8. Told Swami I feel so frustrated whenever there are any rules I have to follow. He said that there aren't any rules; I'm just to do what I feel I have to do. I said I feel bothered by pujas. He said, "Well then, don't come to them."

He told me how tired he sometimes gets and how bad he feels when he seems to lose all control over people. The only way he can help them is by prayer, and sometimes it appears not to work. They go haywire—he calls it "hay-weird." He recommends japam, and talking about God continually, to everybody, in whatever terms each one will accept. Actually, I do do this quite a lot, with nearly all my friends, and it's surprisingly easy and natural. You can express the basic ideas of Vedanta in terms of art, or science, or politics, or sex. In fact, one need never talk about anything else—though one does.

Denny, that sourest of all critics, refuses to be impressed when I tell him about Swami's tolerance and open-mindedness. According to him, Swami is bound to accept me on any terms, because I'm so useful to the Vedanta Society as a translator and editor. I get very angry when he talks like this, and I think it's utterly unjust to Swami. But the fact remains that he is much less lenient toward most of the others. Maybe he realizes what a lot of karmas I dragged into this place with me out of the past.

(Once, fishing for a compliment, I asked Swami why he so seldom scolded me. He answered, "I don't scold for the big faults." He gave no sign of awareness that this statement had crushing implications. I was so taken aback by it that I didn't question him further, either then or at any later time. Was his answer based on a misunderstanding of my question? I shall never know, now.)

July 10. *My day of silence. Asit and I had late breakfast together, after my first session in the shrine room. Yogini came in and asked me questions, which I answered with nods, head shakes, written sentences on a scribbling pad. As usual, this developed into a game. Asit said, "If you shek your haid so vylently, you will injoor it." I wrote, "That's one thing you need never be afraid of," and handed it to Yogini, who replied, "I take aspirin sometimes." I record this conversation because it's typical of the nicer aspect of my life in the family.*

The proofs of the Gita arrived. In the afternoon, Marcel Rodd called, so Swami had to release me from my silence to discuss business. Rodd was much amused. I could see him thinking that religious people are all alike; God is forgotten as soon as there's any money involved.

July 11. *Drove out with Swami, Sister, and Dr. M. for a property hunt on the Palos Verdes headland. It was so* beautiful there that I felt more depressed than usual. The dreadful hungry boredom of Alfred's absence. Without him, the oleanders and the sunlight and the shining ocean were in vain.

At first, the house agent was very cagey; no, they had hardly anything, times were so uncertain, it would be too expensive, etc. etc. Then he took Dr. M. aside and murmured something, and Dr. M. shook his head decisively. At which the agent's manner instantly changed. Well, come to think of it, there was one excellent lot, a real bargain, just what we were looking for . . . Later, Dr. M. explained to us what we'd already guessed—that the agent had thought Swami was a Negro. An East Indian, according to their standards, is altogether different, almost a white man. Sister was even more outraged than Swami at the idea of our having our Center in a restricted area.

(I remember one more property hunt which isn't recorded in my diary. Swami and I went to look at a site we had been told of, on a hill overlooking the Arroyo Seco, near Pasadena. The land had some empty, partially roofless buildings on it. These were obviously being used by teenagers for their orgies. Bottles were scattered about, with, here and there, a pair of torn panties or a used condom. The walls were covered with graffiti—the largest of them announcing in huge letters: JACK HAS SYPHILIS. Swami didn't appear to notice any of these details specifically, but his face showed a certain uneasiness. After a few moments, he turned to me and said seriously, without the least trace of irony: "You know, Chris, I don't think this place has a good atmosphere.")

After several postponements, Vernon arrived from New York on August 12. He spent the first week in one of the rooms at Brahmananda Cottage. Then he moved to a tiny apartment near the Center which I'd rented; I was planning to share it with him later.

But now something quite unforeseen happened. A wealthy old man, who had been a disciple of Swami for some while already, made a gift to the Vedanta Society of a house he owned at Montecito, near Santa Barbara, together with enough money to pay its property taxes.

August 28. Swami has decided that this shall be the new Center we've been looking for. For the present, Amiya is to be in charge there, and other members of the family will take it in turns to go up and stay. Swami will commute back and forth. After the war is over, the Society will move up there and extra buildings will be added.

Swami has invited Vernon to live at Montecito. There's a garden house he can have, which stands apart from the main house. Vernon seems pleased with the idea and wants to go as soon as possible. I don't know what to think. I didn't want him to plunge into the family so quickly—but then, I didn't altogether realize how sold he is on Vedanta. And, after all, why hesitate? We have to try it.

I'll probably spend a lot of time at the Montecito house myself. We went on the 20th, to look at it. It's very beautiful there. The house stands high up the mountain slope, on the edge of the national-forest land. You look over the bay with its islands; a much finer view than any around Santa Monica. It's still quite wild country, with deer and coyotes and rattlesnakes and even some mountain lions. The other homes in this area are mostly large estates; you don't feel the presence of neighbors. It's not expanding like Los Angeles. The war seems hardly to have touched it.

Vernon has exactly the right attitude toward the Center; sees the funny side of it, and yet realizes the necessity of the funny side, and the significance behind it. His being here seems to lighten up the whole place and every minute of the time. I no longer want to rush away to Santa Monica. And the Alfred situation has practically ceased to exist.

Vernon's popular with the family already. Swami says, "Who could help loving him?" Amiya coos over him. Sarada is romantic about his looks. He wrestles with Webster and teases Asit.

The other day, Chris Wood came to visit us. After he left, Swami exclaimed, "What a <u>good</u> man!"

This comment of Swami's made a particularly strong impression on me, because I had grown so accustomed to the shrugs and head shakings of Gerald's Christian friends over Chris's open homosexuality. It wasn't that they disliked Chris—though shy, he was always polite to them—but not one of them would have described him as "good." How *could* he be good? He was immoral. When Swami called Chris "good," the word had to be understood in relation to his statement: "Purity is telling the truth." Chris was certainly "pure" and therefore "good" in this sense. He was remarkable for his frankness and truthfulness, about himself and about everybody else. You couldn't imagine him pretending to feel or think anything that he didn't. You might say that his sex life was a function of his truthfulness. It *had* to be open and a scandal.

As happens in many long and intimate relationships,

Gerald and Chris had become locked into opposite and complementary roles. In their case, these roles were absurdly symbolic; Gerald played the Saint and Chris the Sinner. The Saint prayed for the Sinner and the Sinner cooperated by continuing to sin. However, Chris was essentially a believer—or at least a would-be believer—not an unbeliever, as his role demanded. Even if he had wished to join the community of believers at Trabuco, he could only have done so by changing his role and becoming the Repentant Sinner. This was unthinkable. Chris could never have acted out such a lie against his nature. Besides, by changing roles, he would have upset the balance of his relationship with Gerald, whom he loved. The same thing would have happened, in a different way, if he had become Swami's disciple.

What Chris did do, at this time, was surprising enough, because it was a breach of his usual reticence about his deeper feelings. He wrote a review of *The Gospel of Sri Ramakrishna*. (*The Gospel of Sri Ramakrishna* is a compilation by Mahendranath Gupta ["M."] of conversations between Ramakrishna and his disciples and devotees. A new translation by Swami Nikhilananda, head of one of the two New York Vedanta Centers, had been published in 1942.)

Chris's review begins:

"The Gospel of Sri Ramakrishna? It's awfully long. What's it all about? It certainly weighs enough! And what a strange-looking man!" "It's a fascinating piece of biography," I answered, "quite extraordinarily honest. And as for its being long, the truth about anyone is never dull. Try it; I don't think you'll be disappointed." And, I added to myself, maybe you'll get something

more than pleasure out of it . . . Which made me wonder what I, also an outsider, had got out of it. But, of course, there are really no outsiders. For, the more I think about Ramakrishna and his disciples, the more I am aware of a growing conviction that, sooner or later, by some route or other, this is the way we all must go.

And it ends:

And when at last, ceasing to reason, one stills one's mind, there is something more. There steals over one a strange nostalgia, an almost-memory of something once known, long since forgotten. And one wonders, all too well aware of the answer, what has one in place of that which is lost? Vanity, illusion; just nothing.

Chris had shown me this, as he sometimes showed me his stories, with a characteristic air of self-deprecation. I had persuaded him to let Swami see it, and Swami had at once insisted that it must be published in our magazine. This was probably why Chris had been invited to visit us at the Center, which he very rarely did.

August 29. A stupefyingly hot day. I sat under the acacia, on the front lawn, correcting the magazine proofs. Vernon came out of the temple and told me that he'd had the best meditation of his whole life. It makes me so wonderfully happy, having him here.

So now another attempt begins, to live this life the way it ought to be lived. I have Swami. I have Vernon. I have this place. I have some experience behind me and some acquired confidence. If I fail, I will have no alibi whatsoever.

I doubt if there is anybody in the whole world who,

from my point of view, is luckier than I am right at this moment.

September 9. Vernon started to grow a beard. Swami told him to shave it off. "This is not Trabuco," he said.

Swami told me that when he joined the monastery all his friends were amazed: "They thought I was just a dandy-boy. I parted my hair and wore rings and a gold chain. I liked to play practical jokes. I was known as the best-dressed boy in Calcutta."

He said that when I go up to Montecito he wants me to make a great deal of japam. "When once you are established in that, you can go anywhere. It is all the same."

September 10. Vernon left for Montecito today. In rather a dither, because lots of people have gone up there—Swami habitually invites twice as many people as there are beds. Vernon's first night won't be spent in the garden house, or, if it is, he won't be sleeping alone there. If he can't have any privacy, he's ready to leave.

I've got to explain this to Swami and I can, because I understand just how Vernon feels—I've been through it myself. Vernon was also upset because of a visit to his friends in Santa Monica, who told him that mysticism isn't right for him. This makes me furious. We'll have enough trouble without outside interference.

September 18. For a long time now, a fight has been going on between Swami and the draft board, over Asit —Selective Service wanting to put him in the Army, Swami saying they shan't—because Asit is not only a visitor in this country but a member of a subject race which isn't eligible for U.S. citizenship (though, of course, Asit could become a citizen if he wants to, as soon as he's been inducted and has spent a short period of time as a soldier). An additional argument is that the British themselves don't conscript Indians. Swami has taken the matter up with the American Civil Liberties people and there will be a court case. But, while that is pending, they have advised Swami and Asit not to resist induction.

Finally, today, Asit was inducted. Before he left for the induction center, this hundred-percent Westernized future movie director became a traditional Hindu and prostrated before Swami on the temple steps, making the gesture of taking the dust from Swami's feet and touching it to his own forehead. (This was only pantomime, of course, since Swami's shoes were flashing with polish.) Meanwhile, Swami blessed him. It was startlingly beautiful.

(The tone of the above entry suggests that this was the first time I had personally witnessed such a salutation—it is called a *pranam*. In those days, I don't think that any of us ever prostrated before Swami. Sister might perhaps have done so while the two of them were together at the Belur Math, where this would have been normal behavior. Many years were to pass before pranams became usual at the Center.)

Partly, no doubt, because of Asit's case, partly because of the inevitable wartime suspicions which attach themselves to aliens, we found ourselves under official observation. When one of us would ask another if any new students had shown up at a lecture, it became an in-joke to answer: "Oh no, it was very quiet—just the family and the F.B.I."

And then Swami got an overt visit from two self-identified agents, neatly dressed and smiling. Swami wasn't in the least intimidated; indeed, he seems to have enjoyed himself. I wasn't present. According to him, their dialogue went more or less as follows:

Swami: Gentlemen, what can I do for you?

Agent: Swami, we've been given to understand that you speak against England and the British rule in India.

Swami: Yes, I do. I want the British kicked out of India.

Agent (laughing): Well, we kicked them out of this country.

Swami: Then why do you question me?

Agent (a shade less friendly): Could it be, Swami, that you are getting money from Germany, or Japan perhaps, to make this propaganda?

Swami: Do you think they are fools, that they would give me money for something I do freely?

Agent: Could it be, then, that you are collecting money for your countrymen here to go back home and fight the British?

Swami: Listen! If I knew any Hindu boy who had to be *paid* before he would fight the British, I'd throw him out of this house!

Thus the interview ended in laughter and reassuring handshakes. The agents didn't visit us again, and our lectures no longer seemed to be monitored—or, if they still were, it wasn't by such obvious flatfoots as before. Later some highly respectable members of Swami's congregation got in touch with the F.B.I. and vouched for his good character.

September 20. Swami and I visited a Mr. Williams who is responsible for deciding cases of objection to military service on religious grounds. We were trying to get a 4-D classification for Webster.

Mr. Williams received us in a very bare office downtown; we had to sit on piles of fishing tackle. Taking it in turns, and sometimes contradicting each other, we made an extremely garbled statement of the aims of Vedanta philosophy. Ordinarily, I would never dream of contradicting Swami in the presence of strangers, but I was convinced that I knew better than he did what words to use in talking to a novice like Mr. Williams —and, after all, Webster's future as a monk was at stake.

Mr. Williams sat silent, apparently not understanding a word. But when we'd finished, he said, smiling, "What you've just told me isn't as unfamiliar to me as you may think, gentlemen," and he produced from his desk a volume of Ramakrishna's sayings.

(Webster got his 4-D classification, but not until the war was just about to end.)

September 22. Asit has shown up already, delighted with Fort MacArthur and his uniform. The girls pamper their little warrior and goggle at his stories. He won't be sent any place else until after the court hearing, and the lawyer is sure he'll win it and be let out.

(Asit did win his case. He was discharged from the Army on January 3, 1945. He left quite unwillingly, because he had enjoyed himself so much. His officers, not to mention his many buddies among the enlisted men, appear to have been unanimously on his side and to have taken a sporting interest in the result. The judge himself was Irish and frankly anti-British in his attitude. While Asit was still in the Army, he was invited to give a lecture on the Indian political situation; this was attended by several hundred men, and received with enthusiasm.)

Twelve

September 25, 1944. Swami, George, Sarada, and I
drove to Montecito this morning. At present, there is
nothing to report. It's just another move. I have a dear
little room with a light nicely fixed over the desk, and
now all I have to do is finish Prater Violet and get together a book of selected articles from our magazine and
write an introduction to it—and pray. Meanwhile, something will develop between Vernon and myself, for good
or bad. No use worrying.

Amiya is girlishly happy here. She plans a family
within the family—herself, Vernon, me. She's prepared
to make us comfortable, like an affectionate aunt. This
is her home now. It is not my home. Perhaps no place
ever will be again. There's nothing tragic in that. To
learn to be alone and at home inside myself—that's what
I'm here for.

September 26. Vernon is depressed. I asked him if he
wants to leave. He said that he felt "an obligation" to

me. I feel as if all our troubles are starting, just as they started before.

October 6. Vernon away in Los Angeles, seeing the dentist. I'm alone here with Amiya. Realize how fond of her I am. It's so beautiful here. So calm and still. The grounds are three quarters wild, with thick jungly undergrowth, and a creek, and huge rocks you can climb onto and look out over the valley. At night we hear the howling of the coyotes and the quick uncanny trotting of the deer; the deer come right down through the garden, nibbling everything which isn't fenced in. It is cold and we build huge log fires and sit talking about England and Vedanta and the members of the family. It is very snug.

October 10. Swami is up here again. Today he gave a class, and Krishnamurti came to it. He and Swami had never met before.

(Swami had always been prejudiced against Krishnamurti, because of Mrs. Besant's publicity-making on his behalf, long ago, in India. As a youth, Swami had been outraged when she announced that Krishnamurti was an avatar. Later she used to annoy Brahmananda by trying to involve him with the Theosophical Movement. As a monk, Swami had had standing orders not to admit her to the monastery when Brahmananda was there.)

However, the meeting today was a huge success. Krishnamurti sat quietly and modestly at the back of the class. And when Swami was through, he came over and they greeted each other with the deepest respect, bowing again and again with folded palms. And then they had a long chat, becoming very gay and Indian, and laughing like schoolboys.

Some of Krishnamurti's followers, who had sneaked in, knowing in advance that he was coming here—which we didn't—stood eyeing us a bit suspiciously. But within fifteen minutes we had begun to fraternize. So a small but useful bridge was built.

It now became increasingly obvious that everything was going wrong between Vernon and me. My first mistake had certainly been to let him join the family so quickly. In his letters, he had made it clear that he needed time to observe life at the Center from the outside and decide whether it was the right life for him. I had agreed, and had therefore planned that we should live together on our own for a while. But when Vernon arrived and Swami immediately took control of him—as I had guessed that Swami would—I didn't even try to prevent it; because, I suppose, that was what I really wanted. No wonder if Vernon had felt trapped.

By nature, he was a loner. It had been hard enough for him, when we had lived together before; he was only able to bear it by spending large amounts of time away from me. It was even harder for him to live in a group, although it was easy for him to charm each member individually.

No doubt, he had taken it for granted that we should now be simply brothers, in a monastic sense. What he wanted from me was disinterested helpfulness; no more than that. I was to help him get accustomed to his new life. This I was willing and eager to do. But I had other ideas of my own.

I was still strongly attracted to Vernon sexually. Therefore, I wanted to use him to neutralize my sex drive. As long as I had him with me and knew that he was getting no sex, I didn't so much mind not getting any myself. (This dog-in-the-manger approach to chastity is perhaps not uncommon in monasteries and convents.) I also had a fantasy—too secret to be clearheadedly examined— of a sublimated love affair between us. We would be monks for each other's sake; this would be our way of loving each other.

I believed that Vernon guessed, more or less, what it was I wanted and that it scared and repelled him. I know that he felt I was using emotional blackmail on him to make him remain with me, instead of letting him come to his own decision. That was what he had meant by referring to an "obligation." After a few weeks, he did speak out and tell me he wished I would go back to the Hollywood Center and leave him at Montecito. I left him, but I didn't go direct to the Center. I needed the calm of a neutral environment, so I went to visit Chris Wood in Laguna.

(Vernon left Montecito later that winter and settled down in Los Angeles to a secular life. After this, we began meeting again, as ordinary, affectionate friends.)

November 25. Am writing this in the downstairs bedroom, waiting for Chris to come and say it's time to go swimming. The weather has been glorious all week.

As always, Chris is a refuge. His friendship has no strings attached, and, at the same time, you know you can't lean on him. He simply offers you a place to stay and his company, if you want it, within certain hours. He respects your privacy absolutely. When you do confide in him, he never makes you feel you have given yourself away.

I expect to go back to the Hollywood Center next Monday or Tuesday, to stay for some while. I've got to start trying to get a movie job. I need money badly. Yesterday I finished the final polishing of Prater Violet.

There is no sense in running away from the Center at present. I've got to learn to live with the family without becoming involved in it. Avoid gossip. Avoid their feuds. Concentrate on what is essential—contact with Swami, and prayer. Associate with people you can really help in one way or another, and not with those whose curiosity is always offering you a basin for your tears.

November 30. Have been back at the Center for two days. Swami asked me how I was feeling and I told him a little, not much, about Vernon. This evening, in the shrine, I saw the various alternatives so clearly that they frightened me. Can I possibly face the prospect of living here indefinitely? Or of growing old messily, by myself?

Am starting to see Alfred again. An awful lot of my guilt about this is simply fear of appearances. I shouldn't feel guilty if I weren't living at the Center. That being true, my guilt is spurious.

Swami says that the only refuge is in God. What a terrible thought that is—and yet it's also reassuring and absolutely obvious. Shall I ever get it properly through my head?

December 5. Down to Santa Monica to see Denny. He was very sweet and sympathetic. He suggested, as so often before, that I should come and live with him here, or that we'd go East together and he'd study at Columbia. But I can't walk out on Swami right now. And Denny himself is so unsettled. I could never rely on him.

Swami was still up, sitting by the fire, when I got home. "You will live long," he told me—and explained that he'd been thinking about me just as I walked in, and that the Hindus believe this is an omen of longevity. Suddenly I felt such peace. There he sits, while I roam around. After all, there is really no problem, no difficulty. Why do I tie myself in all these knots?

December 16. Just back from the beach. Denny found a sea gull with a broken wing and amputated it, which made the bird more comfortable but didn't solve its problem. I followed it up the beach and saw how the other gulls pecked at it, and how it couldn't fly or swim and would almost certainly starve. So I killed it. This made me feel horrible all day. I asked Swami, did I do right? And he said no, one shouldn't interfere with the karma of any creature. This doesn't quite convince me, however. What else could I have done? Taken the sea gull home, I suppose, and made a pet of it. But this wasn't practical, with Dhruva around.

December 31. Sure, I ought to stop seeing Alfred or leave the Center or both. But, sooner or later—probably quite soon—Alfred will go to New York. Sooner or later, I shall get a movie job or start another book. Meanwhile, nothing prevents me from doing the one thing that's important—make japam.

Everything else, including your scruples about your conduct, is vanity, in the last analysis. Never mind what other people think of you. Never mind what you think of yourself. Stop trying to tidy up your life. Stop making vows—you'll only break them. No more tears, I beg. Come on, St. Augustine—amuse us. And let's make this a <u>happy</u> new year.

In 1945, Vivekananda's birthday was celebrated on January 5. (Like Easter, the Hindu holy days fall on different dates from year to year, because they are fixed in relation to phases of the moon.) On the morning of the birthday, Sister would bring coffee, bacon, and eggs on a tray into the shrine room. She would pour the coffee for Vivekananda and later she would light him a cigarette, leaving it to burn itself out in an ashtray. Meanwhile, the *Katha Upanishad* would be read aloud, because that had been his favorite scripture. What gave this ceremony its special feeling of intimacy and personal contact was the fact that Sister actually had served breakfast to Vivekananda in her own home, while he was visiting California at the beginning of the century.

Though my diary doesn't say so, I think this was the year that Swami first let me read the *Katha Upanishad* at the breakfast ceremony. In later years, this became my only opportunity to take an active part in ritual worship at the Center, and I nearly always did the reading if I was in Los Angeles.

Early in January, a writer for *Time* magazine came to interview us. *Time*'s editors had decided to run a piece about Swami and the Vedanta Society and me, with reference to the publication of our *Gita* translation. Swami was delighted. I had misgivings but agreed that this would at least be a far-reaching advertisement for the *Gita* itself—which, in those days, was practically unknown to the American magazine-reading public, despite its many previous translations into English.

The piece appeared in the February 12 issue of *Time*. My misgivings were justified:

Ten years ago Christopher Isherwood was one of the most promising of younger English novelists, and a member of the radical, pacifist literary set sometimes known as "the Auden circle." Now, thinking seriously of becoming a swami (religious teacher), he is studying in a Hindu temple in Hollywood, Calif. . . . Much-traveled Author Isherwood's early novel, *The Last of Mr. Norris*, was a grisly, eyewitness account of British pro-Nazis in Berlin. His *Journey to a War* (with verse commentary by W. H. Auden) was a stark, unromanticized look at embattled China. Now this rebellious son of a British lieutenant colonel lives monastically with three other men and eight women in a small house adjoining the alabaster temple of the Vedanta Society of Southern California. He shares his income and the housework with his fellow students, and daily ponders the teachings of his master, Swami Prabhavananda . . . Three times each day Isherwood repairs to the temple, sits cross-legged between grey-green walls on which are hung pictures of Krishna, Jesus, Buddha, Confucius, other great religious teachers. The swami sits bareheaded, wearing a long, bright yellow robe that sweeps the floor. He too sits cross-legged, pulls a shawl around him, and for ten minutes meditates in silence. Then in a ringing bass he chants a Sanskrit invocation, repeats it in English, ending with the words, "Peace, Peace, Peace!" This dispassionate ceremony is the ritual of a mystical order of which slight, agreeable, cigaret-smoking Swami Prabhavananda is the Los Angeles leader . . .

The mistakes made by the writer—no more and no fewer than were to be expected—all became household jokes. There was the "alabaster" temple, the "small house" in which four men and eight women live "monastically," the robe which "sweeps the floor," the "dispassionate" ceremony (whatever that might mean) which lasts just over ten minutes, three times a day.

Swami joined in our laughter, but he was perfectly

satisfied with what had been written. He didn't take offense at the three adjectives used to describe him— "slight," "agreeable," "cigaret-smoking"—which I read as a condescending put-down. He found it no more than my due that the writer had featured me as the star of the Vedanta Society. The publicity didn't repel him, it made him prouder of me. On such occasions he was truly a father.

Personally, I felt humiliated, but in a way which I couldn't fairly blame on *Time*. If I had indeed been wholeheartedly dedicated to my life in religion, I would have treated this brief flare-up of notoriety with indifference—yes, even to that photograph the magazine had printed of Swami and me on the temple steps, captioned *In their world, tranquillity!* To be made to look ridiculous is one of the milder ordeals which any sincere believer in any unfashionable cause must face. But here was I, being introduced to the American public as an austere and devoted monk when, in fact, I was probably about to desert the Center and was already indulging in unmonastic activities during my off-hours at the beach and elsewhere.

Also included in the *Time* article was a statement that:

> Larry, the dissatisfied young hero of Somerset Maugham's current best-selling novel, *The Razor's Edge*, whose search for faith ended in Vedanta, is said to be modeled on Isherwood.

I have no proof that anyone on the *Time* staff had actually started this rumor, but *Time*'s reference to it gave it a wide circulation and I began at once to get letters asking me if it was true. I wrote a letter for publication in *Time*, declaring that it wasn't—though, of course, I couldn't be certain of this, since novelists may be inspired by the most improbable models. Maugham soon published his own denial, however. My identification with Larry has persisted, nevertheless, through the years, and is still occasionally alluded to by gossip-mongers.

I have already mentioned, in an extract from my 1943 diary, that I had written to Maugham about the exact meaning of a verse in the *Katha Upanishad*. This verse compares the path to enlightenment to the edge of a razor, and I had explained that the image of the razor is used to describe a path which is both very painful and very narrow. Therefore, one should not say, as many translators do, that the path is "difficult to cross." Nothing is easier than to step across a path, or a razor, from one side to the other. What is difficult is to *tread* the razor's edge, and the path to enlightenment.

For some reason, Maugham chose to ignore this bit of advice. When *The Razor's Edge* was published in 1944, its epigraph read:

> The sharp edge of a razor is difficult to pass over;
> Thus the wise say the path to Salvation is hard.

To Swami and me, it seemed that "pass over" is nearly if not quite as ambiguous as "cross."

On February 21, I started work at Warner Brothers Studios. I was assigned to several films, one after another. My period of employment ran right through the summer, with only short layoffs, and didn't end until the end of September.

This return to screenwriting was the beginning of the

last phase of my stay at the Center. Up to that point, I had been a monastic, despite my backslidings. Now I became a screenwriter who happened to be living in a monastery. My daily discipline was no longer to meditate, make japam, and wash dishes, but to conform to studio hours and produce an adequate number of script pages. (Meditation on workdays became limited to the early morning; japam to odd moments between conferences with the producer and dictation to my secretary.) Certainly, my extra-monastic life was now less frivolous than before, since I was associating with fellow workers instead of playmates. But I still managed to find time for quite a lot of play.

In June 1945, Maugham came to Hollywood to stay with George Cukor and write a script for the film of *The Razor's Edge*. Cukor had said he would direct it. There were meetings between Swami and Maugham and Cukor because Maugham wanted Swami to tell him exactly what spiritual instructions Shri Ganesha, the holy man in his novel, would have given to Larry. So Swami wrote them out for Maugham, as concisely as he could.

But Cukor was unable to direct the picture, after all. And Maugham's screenplay, although completed, was not going to be used. Another director took over, with a different script, written by Lamar Trotti. However, Swami was still enthusiastic about the project and wanted to do anything he could to help it forward. He told me to write to Trotti and offer him our services as technical advisers, making it clear that we wanted no money, no official status, and no screen credit; it was to be a private relationship between him and ourselves. Trotti never answered our letter, no doubt because he feared that he might compromise himself by doing so.

I, with my experience of studio politics, could understand his silence. Nevertheless, it was a pity. We might have helped him make the religious scenes less sanctimonious and more authentic than they are in the finished film.

I have an impression, rather than a memory, of a social evening at Cukor's house to which Swami and I were invited. My impression is of Swami's appearance and behavior in these surroundings. Some famous ladies of the screen were present, but this didn't mean that Swami was being upstaged or neglected. They all knew who he was, what his connection was with Maugham and Cukor and therefore why he had the right to be present. They could, indeed, regard him almost as a minor colleague in show business. Swami himself seemed quite relaxed in their presence and was easily moved to giggles and rabbit-toothed smiles. The evening had a surface of perfect polish.

What, then, was odd and comic about it? Nothing—except from my own point of view. To me it seemed that these ladies were aware of something in Swami which they found mysteriously disconcerting. They themselves occupied a good deal of ego space. Admittedly, they did this with charm and skill; if their ego sheaths had been crinolines, they would never once have knocked over the furniture. Swami's ego, on the other hand, didn't seem to be occupying nearly *enough* space. Thus their distance perception was subtly distorted. They weren't sure where they were with him. Their own egos started making experimental adjustments to the psychic gap. They became extraordinarily sincere, simple, modest. They began to overact.

But this wasn't all of my fun. As I watched them, I remembered that, in the days when Swami was starting his life as a monk, actresses in Bengal were still being regarded as socially equivalent to prostitutes. For this very reason, whenever one of them came to visit Brahmananda for spiritual instruction, he would receive her with special graciousness and hospitality. And he taught his disciples that every woman, actress and prostitute included, was to be revered as an embodiment of the Divine Mother. Was Swami mindful of Maharaj's teaching at this moment? And how would these ladies react if he told them about it? Quite possibly, they would be delighted and exclaim, "Why, isn't that the cutest thing you ever heard!"

I don't remember that Swami made any objection to my going back to film work. Perhaps he felt that, as long as I continued to sleep, most nights, under the roof of Brahmananda Cottage, there was still some hope of my suddenly deciding that I had a monastic vocation, after all.

What I actually needed at that time was either complete freedom or much stricter monastic discipline. Life at the Hollywood Center or at Montecito was so permissive and bohemian that its few rules were merely an irritation. Only monastics as dedicated as George could remain in such a situation without weakening. It wasn't until the early nineteen-fifties that Swami began making the rules stricter—partly because, by then, the number of monastics had increased.

If such a tightening up of discipline had been introduced in 1945, I might just possibly have decided to stay on and try to make a fresh start, renouncing my film work and my outside friends. Although I was really fond of some of them, I had begun to find their tolerance humiliating. They weren't in the least shocked by the inconsistency of my life as a demi-monk; they were amused by it. To them, it seemed "human"—that is to say, it excused them from feeling awed and rebuked by my religious beliefs.

When I ask myself, shouldn't I have left the Center much sooner than I did, I find that I can't say yes. It now seems to me that my humiliation and my guilt feelings were unimportant. By staying on, I was getting that much more exposure to Swami, which was all that mattered. Every day I spent near him was a day gained. And that I had lost the respect of many outside observers was, on the whole, good—or at worst it was a thousand times better than if I had fooled anybody into thinking me holy.

Thirteen

When I did finally move out of the Center, at the end of August 1945, it was for a reason which had nothing to do with the Vedanta Society. I had recently met a young man with whom I wanted to settle down and live in what I hoped could become a lasting relationship. His name was William Caskey. He had been born in Kentucky, of mixed Irish and Cherokee Indian ancestry. I always thought of him as being predominantly Irish, but that was perhaps because I found his Irish characteristics easier to recognize, having once lived in Ireland. Caskey himself felt that the Indian predominated.

What is much more important, in relation to this narrative, is that his mother's family were all Irish Catholics and that two of his great-uncles, to whom he was very much devoted, were priests. So he had had a thorough Catholic upbringing throughout his early life.

Nevertheless, at the age of sixteen, he had decided to stop going to confession. His attitude could be stated as follows: I won't go to confession because, if I do, I must tell the priest that I have had "carnal knowledge" of other men, and that I repent and resolve to sin no more. Which would be a lie. I have not repented and I have not resolved to sin no more; and the lie would be a much worse sin than the sex. These stinking hypocritical church people tell lies like that most of the time, when they confess. I believe in God a whole lot more than they do. Even the Church can't stop me from believing in Him. I will always believe in Him.

Caskey's faith, combined with his indifference to the fact that he was living in sin, seemed to give him a special kind of strength. I couldn't altogether understand his attitude, not having had his upbringing, but I could sincerely respect it, and my respect reinforced the bond between us. We were both believers. On the rare occasions when we found ourselves inside a Catholic church —this was usually while we were sightseeing in some foreign country—it came naturally to us to kneel down together and pray.

I never discussed Vedanta with him, knowing that he must find its view of sin hopelessly unserious. Caskey could hardly have tried to bring me around to his way of thinking, since this would have meant persuading me that I, too, was living in sin. Anyhow, he rather belittled converts. If you hadn't been born a Catholic, he said, you couldn't know what it was all about. Faith was established in infancy.

Caskey met Swami a few times and relations between them were polite. Swami must have known intuitively that Caskey was firm in his own beliefs. Caskey never criticized Swami to me in any way. This didn't mean, however, that either of us felt shy of making inter-creedal jokes. Once, when I had been to a puja, I brought back one of the cakes which the ladies of the congregation used to bake, to be offered to the Lord and later eaten at the lunch which followed. There was always an oversupply of these and I had been urged to take this one home with me. Next time we had a party, Caskey served the cake to our guests, telling them, with his satirical Southern drawl, "Do try some of this—it's just *delicious*—Chris brought it from Heaven."

My home life with Caskey was lively, noisy, drunken, sometimes full of laughter, sometimes quarrelsome, with head-on clashes of temperament. Caskey cooked well and loved to entertain. My own contribution to this was chiefly dishwashing—the only activity which linked me to my Quaker and Vedanta days. I couldn't regard anything we were doing as evil. It could sometimes have been called shocking, but that was only in the language of others, whose business it wasn't. I was simply glad to be living out in the open at last, with no appearances to be kept up and no need for pretenses.

Now and then, during hangovers, listening to Sinatra or some other spellbinder on the record player, I had moments of dull misery or a stabbing sense of alienation from what was present in the Hollywood shrine. But this pain was also perversely pleasurable, just because it was a genuine feeling. So often, when I was living up at the Center, I had been unable to feel anything at all.

Swami was always pleased to see me when I visited him. There were never any reproaches. I supposed he was biding his time, waiting for me to work off my bad karma, remaining certain that I was in the Lord's hand and could come to no serious spiritual harm. Still, I was anxious to prove my continuing loyalty to him. So I volunteered to help him with another translation. This was Shankara's *Crest-Jewel of Discrimination*.

The *Crest-Jewel* presented a much less difficult problem than the *Gita;* no variations of prose and verse were required. All I had to do was render Swami's already almost adequate English into a clear and suitable prose style, which could be used throughout the book.

At the beginning of the *Crest-Jewel,* Shankara states the case for the monastic life with brutal frankness:

> Only through God's grace may we obtain those three rarest advantages—human birth, the longing for liberation, and discipleship to an illumined teacher.
>
> Nevertheless, there are those who somehow manage to obtain this rare human birth, together with bodily and mental strength, and an understanding of the scriptures—and yet are so deluded that they do not struggle for liberation. Such men are suicides. They clutch at the unreal and destroy themselves.
>
> For what greater fool can there be than the man who has obtained this rare human birth together with bodily and mental strength and yet fails, through delusion, to realize his own highest good?

While I was working on such passages, it was easy to tell myself that I was unworthy of my task. Puritanism tempted the ego to assert itself in the role of Outcast Sinner, just when I should have been ignoring it completely and getting on with the job. This wasn't a question of being worthy or unworthy but of having the necessary literary skill; I had it, so what was there to worry about? It is arguable that, in certain cases, a spiritual teacher may lose credibility because his way of life contradicts what he teaches. But here it was Shankara, the impeccable, who was doing the teaching; I was merely his scribe.

My progress through the *Crest-Jewel* was slow. I didn't finish it until the end of 1946. It was published in 1947.

In January 1947, I took off by plane on my first postwar visit to England. I hadn't seen my mother or my brother, Richard, in eight years. This trip was clearly necessary and could be justified to everybody, including Swami, as a family duty. However, when it was over, I didn't return to California. Caskey was waiting for me in New York, where we had decided to try living for a while. It wasn't long before New York had convinced us both that it wasn't for us. But, meanwhile, I had had an offer from my publishers to write a travel book for them about South America. This appealed to us as an adventure and also because it would give Caskey a chance to practice his profession, photography. Our journey began in September 1947 and continued throughout the following winter and spring. From Buenos Aires we sailed for France, stayed a week in Paris, and then crossed to England.

While in Paris in April 1948, we saw Denny Fouts for the first time in about two years. My meeting with him is described in *Down There on a Visit* more or less as it actually took place, except that Caskey had to be left out because he wasn't a character in the novel. Denny was then smoking opium whenever he could afford to. When he couldn't, he had to content himself with a kind of tea brewed from the dross out of his opium pipe; from this he got small pleasure and violent stomach cramps. He didn't give us the impression of being depressed or debauched or down-at-heel, however. He was dressed with extreme elegance when he came to have dinner with us at a restaurant—or rather, to watch us eat. He did so with an air of controlled distaste, as though our addiction to solid food were a far more squalid vice than his. Now and then, his manner became a trifle vague, but his wit was as sharp as ever.

There is one memory which I want to recall here, although it is also recorded in *Down There on a Visit*. Arriving at Denny's apartment one day, we were introduced to some young French friends of his. They began what sounded like a parody of Frenchified intellectual conversation. One of them made a sneering reference to those dupes who believe in a life after death. What I can still hear as I write this is the withering tone in which Denny silenced him, exclaiming, "You little *fool!*" Denny's scorn was quite uncannily impressive. It was as if he *knew*.

He died that same year on December 16, almost instantly, of a heart attack, in Rome.

I saw Swami shortly after my return to Los Angeles in July 1948, but we didn't meet often during the rest of that year. I was busy at M-G-M, helping write a film based on Dostoevsky's *The Gambler*. Also, I had started writing *The Condor and the Cows*, the book which describes our South American journey.

During the fall, Swami added to my work load with a project of his own—to translate and write a commentary on the yoga aphorisms of Patanjali. Although they are usually called aphorisms in the English translations, their Sanskrit name *sutras* is more descriptive, because *sutra* means, literally, "thread." Composed in a period when there were no books, these terse sentences were designed to be easily memorized; they form only the bare connective thread of a philosophical exposition. Here are Patanjali's first four sutras:

This is the beginning of instruction in yoga.
Yoga is the control of thought waves in the mind.
Then man abides in his real nature.
At other times, man remains identified with the
   thought waves.

It will be seen that a great deal of explanation has
already become necessary here. In ancient times, a
teacher would repeat each sutra from memory and would
then explain it in his own way. Often, these explanations
would be memorized by his students and passed down
to later generations. Thus a large and growing body of
commentary attached itself to the original work. Vivekananda himself had made a commentary on Patanjali
while he was lecturing in the United States, and Swami
quoted from this extensively.

When I started work, my intention was simply to
polish Swami's commentary and perhaps revise its phras-
ing, here and there. But comment inspires comment.
Additional explanations and illustrations kept occurring
to me and being slipped into the text. Furthermore, I
found myself writing for an audience of my own, those
of my friends who knew almost nothing about Vedanta
and needed to have Patanjali explained to them in
Occidental terms. Through all this, I had the support
of Swami's approval. Still, I am more aware now than
I was then that our editorial "we" had to represent two
audibly different tones of voice, the Bengali and the
British.

(Our Patanjali was published in 1953. The publishers
had asked us for a special title, to distinguish it from
other translations of the sutras, and in an uninspired
moment I had suggested *How to Know God,* which was
enthusiastically accepted. The title now makes me think

of all those books which tell you *how to* fix the plumbing, plant a vegetable garden, cook on a barbecue, etc., and embarrasses me so much that I avoid saying it aloud, if I possibly can.)

November 6. Master, be with me specially at such times. Help me to remember you constantly and let me feel your presence. You aren't shocked by the camping of the publicans and the screaming of the sinners. You didn't condemn—you danced with the drunkards.

This was written after a party which my diary describes as a "massacre." It had left me with an unusually bad hangover and, no doubt, a sinkful of dishwashing to be done. Such a situation was apt to arouse my puritan resentment against the life I was allowing myself to lead. Only, this time, it seems that my reaction was more positive. If we *had* to have such parties, why not mentally invite Ramakrishna to join us? He couldn't refuse.

Ramakrishna had been known to get out of a carriage to dance with drunkards on the street. The sight of their reeling inspired him because it made him think of the way a holy man reels in ecstasy. He danced with his friend G. C. Ghosh, a famous dramatist and actor, when Ghosh was drunk, and encouraged him to go on drinking. Ghosh took advantage of Ramakrishna's permissiveness and visited him at all hours of the night, sometimes on the way home from a whorehouse.

Ghosh became a kind of patron saint for me—I felt closer to him than to any other member of Ramakrishna's circle—but I wasn't worthy to be his disciple. I failed to go the whole hog, as he had, either in debauchery or devotion. Ghosh dared to reveal himself shamelessly to Ramakrishna, thereby making a sacrifice of his own self-esteem and self-will and submitting totally to Ramakrishna's guidance. That was his greatness. I am sorry, now, that, throughout my long relationship with Swami, I never once came into his presence drunk. Something wonderful might have happened.

On March 1, 1949, I went up to the Center to take part in Ramakrishna's birthday puja. Webster was there. He had left the Center not long after I had. I think he was already married, or engaged to be.

At first he was a little awkward and on the defensive with me. Then we settled down into the mood of old alumni, and joked about the new building schemes— the temple is to have enlarged wings. The old place certainly has changed. Nearly all the girls are now up at Montecito, and there are several new monks here. George took flash-bulb photos throughout the puja. This bothered some people, but it's his privilege, granted by Swami.

They have recently bought another house, the one that stands behind 1946. There is a room in it which Swami says is for me. It rather scares me, the way he waits. Shall I ever find myself back there? It seems impossible—and yet—

While Swami was in Arizona the other day, as the guest of some devotees, he was taken to Taliesin West, where he met Frank Lloyd Wright. Swami—who had never heard of Wright—and whose previous ideas of architecture were limited to domes and lots of gold— was greatly impressed. "Mr. Wright," he said, "you are not an architect, you are a philosopher." And he added that, at Taliesin, you felt yourself "not in a house but protected by Nature." I couldn't help laughing when Swami told me this, because the cunningest flatterer couldn't have buttered Wright up more completely than

Swami had, in his utter artlessness. Needless to say, Wright was enchanted.

July 26. Today I went to the Center to attend Sister's funeral—or rather, the part of it which took place in the temple. I think her family organized another ceremony elsewhere.

Sister died last week in Montecito. I saw her there on the 20th, I drove up for lunch. She had had pneumonia then, and an attack of uremia, but she seemed better that day. The dark plum-colored rash which had broken out in several places on her body was clearing. She apologized for it with her usual courtesy. She didn't want me to touch her hand, which was smeared with salve. She had known me as soon as I came into the room. "It's so nice to see old friends," she said. After a few minutes she drowsed off. Amiya and Swami told me that, much of the time, she thought she was back in Honolulu, where she lived during her youth. Swami also told me that she had had difficulty in urinating but was able to do so after he'd given her a drop of Ganges water. (How this would horrify some people I know!) I came away with a feeling that she was going to recover this time.

Today was a hot morning. I arrived at the temple in a bad mood, having been horrible and unkind to Caskey before I left the house. Some people arrived with flowers, which I hate at funerals and never bring if I can avoid it. There were women in various degrees of elegant mourning. Swami sat on the sofa in the living room. You couldn't exactly say his face looked tragic, but the brightness had left it and it was almost frighteningly austere.

He took my arm and led me into his bedroom, where he told me about Sister's death. Just before it happened, Swami found himself "in a high spiritual mood," and then they called him into her room, and at that moment the breath left her body with a faint puff, through the lips.

"She was a saint," Swami said. He believes that she passed into samadhi at the end. He said how, recently, she had told him that she never left the shrine until she had seen "a light." She thought this quite normal and supposed that everybody saw it. In fact, she was apologizing to Swami because, in her case, it often took quite a long time and made her late for meals and kept people waiting.

Came away in a calm happy "open" mood, and felt a real horror of my unkindness to Caskey and of any unkindness to anyone. Thinking of Sister, I remembered how I asked her, once, what Vivekananda had been like. She answered without hesitation, "Oh, he was like a great cat—so graceful."

By gradual degrees, Gerald Heard had become disinclined to go on living at Trabuco. No doubt, as he grew older—he was now sixty—he felt the strain of being the central figure in this group, and of all the talk and letter writing and planning that it involved. This year, he came to a decision: Trabuco ought to belong to an organization which could make more effective use of it. Gerald easily persuaded his fellow trustees to agree with him, as soon as he had made it clear that he himself was determined to retire. And so Trabuco, which had never been the property of an individual, was offered to another non-individual, the Vedanta Society.

It so happened that a number of young men had joined the Center during the past months. Swami sent several of them to live at Trabuco. It was officially opened as a Vedanta monastery on September 7.

In October, Swami left for India with George and three of the nuns. They returned in May 1950. I saw Swami fairly often after his return, but I have no record of our meetings. My diary keeping almost stopped, that year, because of misery-sloth induced by the Korean War and the gradual breakdown of my relationship with Caskey. We were both aware of this breakdown but wrongly blamed it on the pressures of life in Los Angeles, so we decided to move down to Laguna Beach. Once settled into a house there, we soon began to jar upon each other again. My few diary entries of 1951 are mostly self-scoldings—for giving way to feelings of help-lessness, for being "criminally unhappy," for trying to impose my will on Caskey under the guise of "reason." I now began to spend more and more time away from him, staying in Los Angeles.

August 22, 1951. Today I had lunch with Swami, who is at Trabuco. He urged me, more strongly than ever before, to come back and live with them. He said, "It must happen. I've wanted it and prayed for it so much." I answered evasively, as usual.

Gerald Heard and Chris Wood came to visit him later, and I returned with them to Laguna and had tea. I asked Gerald what he thought I should do about Trabuco. He said that I should obey Swami and go to live there. He said that he knew Swami was "deeply disturbed" about me, and that he was disturbed him-self. If I didn't do as Swami told me, "something ter-rible" might happen to me.

I asked, "What?" Gerald said that I might lose my faith entirely and cease to believe that God exists. He then became very mysterious, saying that he feared I was being followed by "something" which was trying to possess me, and even hinting that he had had a glimpse of it. I asked him to describe what it looked like. He gazed at me solemnly for a moment and then answered sternly, "No."

I was hugely impressed by the dramatic power with which Gerald delivered his warning, but I simply couldn't take it seriously. I felt that this was his literary self speaking—especially since he had just written an excellent supernatural thriller in which a man performs a black-magical ritual to destroy his enemy, and consequently gets haunted by a familiar spirit in the form of a fox. *The Black Fox* was the title of Gerald's novel.

It wasn't that I pooh-poohed the idea that one could be possessed by a familiar. I had a wholesome respect for the dangers of dabbling in black magic and would never have done so under any circumstances. What I didn't believe was that one could fall into its power without somehow cooperating. My recent life had been sex-absorbed and drunken and angry, but certainly not devilish; I was sure I had never done anything to deserve the attentions of a black fox. As for losing my faith, the opposite was true. In my present dilemma, it was actually getting stronger. Indeed, I was beginning to think that it might drag me back to the Center, against my will.

August 23. This morning, on a sudden impulse, I drove to Trabuco and saw Swami and talked to him about the possibility of coming to live up there, or in Hollywood. I was careful not to commit myself but of course Swami now takes it for granted that I'm coming.

He said that both Gerald and Aldous had come to him and told him things about the way I am living, and asked him to remonstrate with me. Swami had answered, "Why don't you pray for him?"

I was touched and delighted by Swami's reaction, which I interpreted as a rebuke to Gerald and Aldous. Wasn't he telling them, in effect, "You'd do better to love Chris more and criticize him less"? That was what I wanted him to have meant. It did annoy me that the two of them had spoken to Swami behind my back— and yet, what else could I have expected? They regarded me as an irresponsible child. You don't interfere with the doings of other people's children, you go to the parent. When I asked Swami what it was that they had told him, he said vaguely that I'd been seen "in some bad place"—the nature of the place didn't seem to interest him. It could only have been a homosexual bar. But who could have seen me there? Obviously neither Gerald nor Aldous in person. No doubt it was some miserable demi-devotee with a foot in both worlds; just like myself, six years ago. He must have feared that I'd recognized *him* at that bar, and relieved his own guilt by reporting me and my improper behavior.

I found it much easier to forgive Aldous for his interference than Gerald. Aldous didn't know any better, he was essentially a square. Happily, my resentment against Gerald was to disappear before long, because of a profound change he made in his own outlook.

August 29. I have to admit that I'm hardly meditating at all under my present living conditions, and that I would do far more at Trabuco. But Trabuco is what I shrink from. I dread the boredom of the place and the isolation. I shouldn't be a good companion for the boys. And I remember all the difficulties of my life at the Hollywood Center.

What I now dimly begin to see is that there must be no more categorical relationships, as far as I'm concerned.

I believe that's what went wrong between Caskey and me, and the Center and me—trying to ensure permanence by getting yourself involved, that's no good. No good saying, "Now I'm married" or "Now I'm a monk," and therefore I'm committed.

Without some awareness of God and some movement of the will toward Him, everything else is madness and nonsense. It's far better to feel alienated from God than to feel nothing. I shrink from "the spiritual life" because I immediately visualize the circumstances which usually surround it—the intense-eyed seekers coming to ask questions after lectures, the puttering at the pujas, the dreadfully harmless table humor. But all this is aesthetic snobbery—and unnecessary. If you don't like gymnasiums, don't go to them. You can exercise anywhere. Yes, but mind you do exercise.

An appalling confession: during the past years, I've very very seldom prayed for Caskey.

I don't remember breaking the news to Swami that I wasn't going to rejoin the monastery, after all. Probably I let things drift and said nothing. And soon I was excused from giving him an immediate answer by an unexpected development in my worldly life. John van Druten had decided to make a play (*I Am a Camera*) out of certain parts of my novel *Goodbye to Berlin*. In the fall of 1951, I left California for New York, to sit in on the play's rehearsals. Later I visited England and Germany and Bermuda, remaining away from Los Angeles until April 1952.

While in New York, I stayed for a time with Auden. We had met often during my earlier trips East, but that had nearly always been in the presence of other people. Now we were alone together in his apartment and able to have long, intimate talks, as in the old days.

We talked a great deal about Wystan's Christian beliefs without getting into any arguments. And I showed him entries in my diary describing my life at the Vedanta Center. He shook his head over them, regretfully: "All this heathen mumbo jumbo—I'm sorry, my dear, but it just *won't do*." Then, in the abrupt, dismissive tone which he used when making an unwilling admission, he added: "Your Swami's quite obviously a saint, of course."

Fourteen

May 12, 1952. At Trabuco. I've been here since the 4th and plan to stay till the 21st. The Patanjali aphorisms are practically finished.

Now I'm trying to finish part one of my novel before I leave here. I feel very calm and in a way unwilling to leave. But I don't for a moment seriously consider becoming a monk again. I don't consider anything except how to get my novel written. My only worries are financial—how much of my "Camera" royalties should be set aside for income tax?

J., one of the monks, describes this group as "six individualists all going different ways." Yet they are wonderfully harmonious with each other, and all likable. "Too many people around here," says J., "are scared of the Old Man" (meaning Swami) "or they've got him figured all wrong. He's the only person I ever met in my life I like everything about."

I try to fit in unobtrusively and not get in the way of their routine. Am not getting much—or indeed anything, consciously—out of the meditation periods. But

I often feel very happy. Hardly any trouble with sex, yet. I think that's mostly middle age. Anyhow, I certainly needed a rest!

I feel sympathy and liking for these boys, but their problems aren't very real to me, because their situation is so utterly different from mine. They are stuck here. They plod around in their heavy work boots, much of the day, doing outdoor chores. Life here is much more physical than it was at the Hollywood Center. The place demands to be constantly maintained and they are stuck with it, like soldiers with a war. I'm like a correspondent, visiting the front for a few days only.

The chores I do are voluntary and therefore pleasurable—pulling weeds out of the vines or raking the kitchen garden in the blazing sunshine. The hot courtyard with the dark-leaved fruit trees has a sort of secret stillness; one feels hidden away, miles from anywhere. At night we look through the telescope, at Saturn, or at the ranger station on the top of the mountain.

May 19. Shall be going back to Santa Monica the day after tomorrow. I've done wonders of work since I arrived here. Finished Patanjali, finished part one of my novel and made a promising start on part two, worked over some Vedic prayers Swami wanted translated, written lots of letters, and pulled up lots of weeds.

When I typed out the title page of the Patanjali this morning, I wrote "by Swami Prabhavananda and Christopher Isherwood," and Swami said, "Why put <u>and</u>, Chris? It separates us."

It's impossible to convey the sweetness and meaning with which he said this. All day long, he fairly shines with love. It was the same when he was here earlier, at the beginning of my stay, and told us: "If you have a friend and do good things for him for years and years, and then do one bad thing—he'll never forgive you. But if you do bad things to God for years and years, and only one good thing—that He never forgets." What strikes me, again and again, is his complete assurance, and his smiling, almost sly air of having a private source of information.

I asked Swami how it is that he can always end a meditation period so punctually. He said it's like being able to sleep and wake up at a certain time, no matter how deeply you become absorbed. The notion that meditation periods should be of varying length, according to mood, is "romantic," he said.

January 27, 1953. Have been here at Trabuco since January 9. (On the 6th, Caskey and I said goodbye and he left for San Francisco, hoping to get a job on a freighter and ship out to the Orient.)

Today I finished the rough draft of my novel. I am very grateful for this tremendous breakthrough. 88 pages in 18 days, which is about two and a half times my normal writing speed, maintained despite the interruptions of shrine sitting, kitchen chores, ditch digging, and planting trees. I feel as if my whole future as a writer— even my sanity—had been at stake. And yet I daresay I seemed quite cheerful and relaxed, to the others. Such struggles go on deep underground.

This has been the toughest of all my literary experiences. A sheer frontal attack on a laziness block so gross and solid that it seemed sentient and malevolent—the Devil as incarnate tamas, or Goethe's eternally no-saying Mephistopheles. What with having given up smoking, getting no drink and no sex, I was nearly crazy with tension. I actually said to Ramakrishna in the shrine: "If it's your will that I finish this thing, then help me."

The diary version of my prayer to Ramakrishna needs further explanation. I had had, since childhood, an instinctive dislike of petitionary prayer—those church appeals to the Boss God for rain, the good health of the Monarch, victory in war. Swami didn't totally condemn it, but to me there was a sort of impertinence in asking God for the fulfillment of any worldly need. How was I to know what I really needed? I felt this all the more strongly because I didn't doubt that such prayers are quite often answered—or, to put it in another way, that you can sometimes impose your self-will on circumstances which *appear* to be outside your control. When I prayed, it was nearly always for some kind of spiritual reassurance or strength, for faith or devotion.

This prayer to Ramakrishna was therefore a breach of my own rule. What made me break it? I must have been reacting to the pressure which Swami had already begun putting on me, to write a biography of Ramakrishna. He was thus creating a conflict of interest between his project and mine. So I appealed to Ramakrishna to decide the issue. I remember feeling at the time that this was a kind of sophisticated joke—camp about prayer, rather than prayer itself. But camp, according to my definition, must always have a basis of seriousness. Ramakrishna would understand this perfectly.

My prayer could have been better phrased as follows: "Don't let me feel guilty about trying to write this novel. Either convince me that I must drop it altogether, or else take away my writer's block, so I can finish my book quickly and get started on yours."

I have recorded this simply as a psychological experience, not as a proof that Ramakrishna answered my prayer. The unbeliever will maintain that prayer is just oneself talking to oneself, and the Vedantist will partly agree with him, saying that it is the Atman talking to the Atman, since all else is illusion, from an absolute standpoint. Looking back, I can no longer blame Mephistopheles—or whatever one chooses to call the force that blocks an act of creation—even though he did nearly cause me to have a nervous breakdown. Indeed, I feel I ought to be grateful to him. He at least tried to stop me finishing what turned out to be my worst novel: *The World in the Evening.*

That spring, I realized that I had fallen deeply in love with a boy whom I had known for only a short while, Don Bachardy. He was then eighteen years old. The thirty-year difference in our ages shocked some of those who knew us. I myself didn't feel guilty about this, but I did feel awed by the emotional intensity of our relationship, right from its beginning; the strange sense of a fated, mutual discovery. I knew that, this time, I had really committed myself. Don might leave me, but I couldn't possibly leave him, unless he ceased to need me. This sense of a responsibility which was almost fatherly made me anxious but full of joy.

Don's first meeting with Swami was on May 21; Swami came with George to visit us. Don now remembers that "his gestures seemed very precise and delicate, the length of his hands impressed me, they were like long delicate fins; I was able to observe him physically because he didn't try to impress you with his personality, the way most people do."

All I now remember is that Swami made some approving remark about the look in Don's face. Others had noticed this, but their comments merely referred to a vitality, a shining eagerness for experience, which often moves us when we see it in the young. Swami, as I well knew, was able to detect more intrinsic values; he was like a jeweler who can recognize at a glance the water of a diamond. From that moment, I felt that Don, and thus our relationship, was accepted by him.

Gerald, too, accepted and approved of Don. Indeed, he spoke of our relationship as if it were a daring pioneer research project of great scientific importance, urging me to keep a day-to-day record of it. He had now begun to discuss publicly the problems of "the intergrade," meaning the homosexual, and the role which homo-sexuals might play in social evolution. He had also made what was, for him, a truly revolutionary pronouncement: "One used to believe that tenderness is polar to lust. Now one realizes that that isn't necessarily true."

All this was only part of an astonishing and mysterious transformation. For Gerald's health had greatly im-proved, and he seemed less dyspeptic, less puritanical, warmer, merrier. He could now be persuaded to accept an occasional glass of sherry and would sometimes even eat meat. One happy result of this transformation was that he and I resumed our old friendship, with Don included in it.

These are two dreams which I had about Swami during 1953:

August 21. I was sharing a bed with Swami in a house which I knew to be a male whorehouse. (I knew this but I don't know how I knew it; there were no other people in the dream, and the room was an ordinary, quite respectable-looking bedroom.) Except that we were shar-ing a bed, our relations were as they always are. I was full of respect and consideration for him. We were just about to get up and I suggested that he should use the bathroom first. He didn't react to this. But he said, "I've got a new mantram for you, Chris. It is: 'Always dance.' " "What a strange mantram!" I said. Swami laughed: "Yes, it surprised me, too. But I found it in the scriptures."

December 16. This dream was a kind of companion piece to the other, for Swami and I were again in a bedroom. This time, I didn't know that we were in a whorehouse. My vague impression was that this was a hotel and that we were there because we were making a journey together. I was helping Swami get undressed to go to bed. I felt eager to attend to all his wants and was very respectful, as before. When I tried to help him put on his bathrobe, we found that it had somehow got entangled with mine—the sleeves of my robe were pulled down into his. Swami said, "Oh, so you have a bathrobe? I was going to give you mine." And I said, "But I can throw mine away."

The mood in both these dreams was joyful, but there was more fun in the first of them and more sentiment in the second. My bringing Swami into a whorehouse suggests to me a desire to introduce him to another part of my life, in which he had no share. (Actually, I had had very little experience of whorehouses myself; and that had been years earlier.) This dream whorehouse, where no boys are visible, seems symbolic, anyhow. Sharing a bed with Swami represents a situation of absolute chastity. Perhaps this was inspired by a memory of my sensations while using Swami's bedroom, when he was away from the Center, in 1943.

The dream mantram, "Always dance," makes me think of something which hadn't yet happened at the time of my dream; shortly before Maria Huxley's death,

in 1955, she told a woman friend, "Always wear lip-
stick." This was a remark which beautifully expressed
Maria's particular kind of courage—taking care to look
your best, even when you are sick and afraid of dying,
in order to spare the feelings of those who love you.
"Always dance" could have a similar meaning. But it
also seems to me to refer to Ramakrishna's dancing in
ecstasy. Since this is described throughout *The Gospel
of Sri Ramakrishna*, Swami could truly say that he had
"found it in the scriptures."

In the second dream, Swami's bathrobe, with the
sleeves of my bathrobe pulled down into its sleeves,
seems an image of the guru's involvement with his disciple. Hindus believe that it is risky to wear other
people's clothes or use their personal belongings. If you
do, you may to some extent inherit the consequences of
the former owner's thoughts and actions. But your guru
is an exception. His cast-off clothes and belongings cannot bring you anything but good.

The nuns at the Center had enthusiastically adopted
this belief. They would carry off, to keep or distribute,
almost anything which Swami had owned and now
didn't want. As the Vedanta Society grew, and Swami
got more and more birthday and other gifts, the turnover
became rapid, and devotees treasured mementos of
Swami which he had barely had time to use or even
touch.

Through the next two years, my diary keeping has many
lapses. Here are my only diary entries about Swami in
1955:

*March 2. After supper, Swami had a class in the living
room. He was asked what it was like to live with an*

illumined soul—specifically with Brahmananda and
Premananda. He answered, "What attracted me was
their wonderful common sense." Then he said how few
people bothered to come and see Ramakrishna while he
was alive, though most of them became ardent devotees
after he was dead. I couldn't help thinking that this ap-
plies to Swami and myself, nowadays, and I hoped he
wasn't thinking the same thing. Later, when we were
alone together in his room, he talked about U.

(This was an old lady who had just died, while staying
at the Center. In her youth, she had known Vivekananda and some of the other direct disciples.)

Swami recalled how terribly afraid she had been of dying.
"And then, when it happened, she didn't feel anything.
How very merciful they were to her!"

June 20. On Father's Day, Swami passed on to me a
shaving brush he'd just been given but didn't need, because he uses an electric razor. I gave him a bottle of
sherry, which had to be hidden from a party of visiting
Hindus, who were severely orthodox.

(Swami sometimes drank a glass or two before meals.
Alcohol was approved by his doctors as a relaxant, especially in view of the prostate trouble he suffered from
in later life. Swami wasn't being hypocritical when he
refrained from drinking in the presence of those who
would have been shocked by it; he simply tolerated their
prejudice, which he anyhow found unimportant.)

August 25. I called Swami and asked him for his blessing
on my birthday tomorrow. He said, "Live many years
and I'll watch you from heaven."

September 14. This evening I was up at the Center. Swami looked very well and happy. He said, "I get so bored with philosophy nowadays—even Shankara." Then he told me that this morning, in the shrine room, he had been intensely aware of the presence of Swamiji and Maharaj. "If there hadn't been anyone else there, I'd have bawled."

He says his favorite chapter in the Gita is chapter 12, on the Yoga of Devotion. He says, "I used to want visions and ecstasies—now I don't care. I only pray to love God. I don't care to lecture, now. But when I start talking, I enjoy myself. I enjoy talking about God." (I thought to myself: He's like a young man in love.)

Swami said, "Webster came to me the other day. He said to me, 'Swami, it's your fault that I left the Center. You should have used your power to stop me.' I asked him if he was meditating and making japam. He said, 'No. You must make me do it.' I was very touched. Such devotion!"

(On several other occasions, I had heard Swami rebuke devotees who took Webster's attitude and asked him, so to speak, to do their praying for them. He told them that they were just lazy. So I was all the more impressed by his belief in Webster's sincerity.)

In October 1955, Don and I left for Europe, to visit Italy, Switzerland, Germany, France, and England. We got back to Los Angeles in March 1956.

In my diary, I note that "Swami, with his usual persistence, brought up the question of the Ramakrishna book again." This means that I hadn't kept my part of the bargain made in the Trabuco shrine room three years earlier. Now that my novel was long since published and our traveling was over for the present, I had no more excuses to offer. I knew I must start writing *Ramakrishna and His Disciples* at once. Wanting to do this on an auspicious day, I picked April 1. This year, it was both All Fools' Day and Easter Sunday.

After our return from Europe, I began to see a good deal of one of the monks at the Hollywood Center. As John Yale, he had become a monastic probationer in 1950. We had met from time to time during the past six years, but not often, because of my various absences from Los Angeles and his journey to India in 1952–53, visiting the Ramakrishna monasteries there—this he later described in his book, *A Yankee and the Swamis*, published in 1961. By 1956, he had taken his first vows (brahmacharya) and been renamed Prema Chaitanya. (*Prema* means "ecstatic love of God." *Chaitanya*, "awakened consciousness," is always added to the other given name of a brahmachari of the Ramakrishna Order.)

Prema was then still in his thirties, slightly built but tough and energetic. He had dark hair and a pale handsome face which sometimes showed great inner suffering but was nevertheless youthful-looking. Before joining the Order, he had been a successful publisher in Chicago. Now he was working to build up the business of the bookshop at the Center, and doing this so efficiently that its mail-order earnings were becoming an important part of the Vedanta Society's assets. He also helped edit our magazine, which would begin printing my Ramakrishna book, chapter by chapter, as it got written. Thus Prema and I found ourselves in constant collaboration.

I often thought that, if Prema and I had arrived at the Center at the same time and begun our monastic life together, we might have been a real support to each other. Certainly we had much in common. We had both revolted against the moral precepts of our upbringing. We both had severe standards of efficiency and were apt to be impatient of the sloppy and the slapdash. We both suffered from self-will and the rage which it engenders. He was more desperate than I, and his desperation might have taught me his courage. I was more diplomatic than he, and might have saved him from offending many people by his outspokenness.

As things turned out, however, our relationship had its frictions. The Chris whom Prema met must have been a disappointment to him. No doubt he had expected a good deal from the part-author of the *Gita* translation which had renewed his religious faith when he had first read it, back in the nineteen-forties. But now I had become a worldling, no longer subject to monastic discipline. My visits to Swami were like those of a Prodigal Son who returns home again and again, without the least intention of staying, and is always uncritically welcomed by a Father who scolds every other member of the family for the smallest backsliding. I know that Prema was drawn to me, as I was to him, but I must have seemed a creature of self-indulgence and self-advertisement, with the easy modesty of the sufficiently flattered and a religion which was like a hedged bet on both worlds. Prema often envied me and sometimes hated me. He confessed this with touching frankness.

April 14, 1956. With Swami, George, and Prema to a meeting at a women's club, where Swami had to speak for twenty minutes to open a prayer-discussion group. Swami in a gray suit with a pearl-gray tie. He must always seem, at first sight, so much less "religious" than the sort of people who introduce him on these occa-

sions; more like a doctor or even a bank manager than a minister. The stage was hung with blue velvet curtains; on one side, the flag. The audience chiefly composed of women in very small hats, many of them with folded-back veils in which tiny spangles sparkled.

June 15. This afternoon, Swami came to tea, along with George and Prema. Don was pleased because I told him that serving a meal to a swami would probably save him 500 rebirths. After they had left, he drank the remains of Swami's tea as prasad. I think that reading my 1939–44 diary has made him much more interested in everything to do with Vedanta.

June 22. Don and I went to tea at the Center. Swami said to Don, as we were leaving, "Come again—every time Chris comes."

July 15. Swami called today, much worried because Maugham had sent him an essay on the Maharshi, and all the philosophy in it was wrong! Now we have to concoct a tactful reply.

(The Maharshi, a famous holy man, had died only a few years before this. Maugham had met him during a trip to India in 1936. I can't remember what mistakes Maugham made in expounding the Maharshi's philosophy. Our letter, pointing them out, must have been sufficiently tactful, for Maugham replied gratefully and made the suggested alterations in his essay "The Saint." This was published, with four others, in *Points of View*, in 1959.)

October 25. This morning, I went to see Swami. He was in his most loving mood. He seemed entirely relaxed by love, as people are relaxed by a few drinks. He just beamed.

We were talking about the possible number of inhabited worlds. Swami said, "And, only think, the God who made those thousands of worlds comes to earth as a man!" Something about the way he said this—his wonder and his absolute belief, I suppose—made my skin raise goosepimples. I said, "How terrifying!" and that was exactly how I felt. It's quite impossible to convey in words the effect made on you by a situation like this—because what matters isn't what is said but the speaker himself, actually present before you and giving you, in some otherwise quite ordinary sentence, a glimpse of <u>what he is</u>.

He told me that one of his ambitions is to found a boarding school, one half for boys, the other for girls, where "they would be given the ideal"—first on the high-school level, later on the university level. He remarked that boys always seem more restless than girls. They always feel that they ought to do something or get something. Swami would tell them, "You have to <u>be</u> something."

He repeated what he has so often told me, that he feels in all his work responsible to Brahmananda. When he initiates disciples, he hands them over to Brahmananda or to Holy Mother. He would like to stop giving lectures, but if he tries to shirk any duty, he finds that he loses touch with Brahmananda: "I can't find him; then I know he is displeased."

Going to see Swami is like opening a window in my life. I have to keep doing this, or my life gets stuffy. It doesn't matter what we talk about. He said, "Come again soon. I like seeing you, Chris," and I told him I think about him all the time and have conversations with him in my mind. I was moved, as we parted, and felt shy.

November 8. Went to see Swami—today being the 16th anniversary of my initiation (and the 10th anniversary of my becoming a U.S. citizen!). Swami said that drugs could never change your life or give you the feeling of love and peace which you got from spiritual visions. Drugs only made you marvel—and then later you lost your faith.

In May 1953, having volunteered to be a subject for the psychiatric researches of Dr. Humphry Osmond, Aldous Huxley had taken four tenths of a gram of mescaline. Early the next year, he had published *The Doors of Perception*, an account of his experiences under the drug. Since then, Aldous and Gerald had been meeting occasionally with a few friends, either to take mescaline or lysergic acid or to talk about the insights they had obtained from them. It should be emphasized that the talking was far in excess of the taking; these were all prudent people of high intellectual seriousness, not thrill seekers on a spree.

At the height of the psychedelic-drug craze in the nineteen-sixties, it wasn't unusual to hear a taker claim casually that he or she had been in samadhi. It was generally accepted that all spiritual states could be drug-induced. To Swami, this was a deadly heresy, and he regarded Aldous and Gerald as its originators. Actually, their statements on the question varied slightly from time to time and left their hearers or readers with differing impressions.

Swami himself had had only one experience with any kind of hallucinogen; while he was still a young monk in India, he had been given by his fellow monks, as a practical joke, a liquid prepared from hemp. Not knowing what this was, Swami had drunk a lot of it and had had disagreeable psychic visions followed by a long period of spiritual dryness, during which he had lost his faith altogether. My diary account of his story continues:

I asked him, hadn't he considered leaving the monastery at that time? "NO!"—Swami can say that word with more emphasis than anyone I have ever known—"Why should I do that? Because I had stopped believing in God, that did not mean that I believed in the world."

But I wasn't ready to accept Swami's condemnation without experimenting for myself. I had asked both Aldous and Gerald to let me join in a drug session and had got evasive answers. Then I was told, by a third party, that they had agreed I was too unstable emotionally to be a suitable subject. I was indignant, and at once decided to try mescaline on my own. In 1955, it was still legal. I had bought some tablets while Don and I were in New York, about to sail for Europe.

On our way there, while stopping off in Tangier, we had had an unexpected opportunity to try hashish. Puffing at kif cigarettes and gobbling majoun with the overeagerness of beginners, we launched ourselves into a nightmare adventure. Don became paranoid; I discovered claustrophobia. Looking back, twenty-four hours later, I had felt that this had brought Don and me even closer together; it was like a shared physical danger. I had reacted to it by making japam. But I might equally well have done that if we had been on a small boat in a storm. The adventure itself couldn't be described as spiritual.

About four months after this, in London, I took one

of the mescaline tablets, alone; we had agreed that Don should remain an objective observer of my behavior. In general, the effects were very much as I had heard them described. I felt exhilarated. My senses, particularly my sight, seemed extraordinarily keen. Certain patches of color were almost scandalously vivid. Faces on the street looked like caricatures of themselves, each one boldly displaying its owner's dominant characteristic—anxiety, vanity, aggression, laziness, extravagance, love.

I told Don that we must take a taxi to the Catholic cathedral in Westminster, "to see if God is there." God wasn't. His absence was so utter that it made me laugh. So we went on to Westminster Abbey. Here the situation appeared even more comic to me. I had to go into a dark corner and stay there until I could control my giggles.

The Abbey's old rock-ribbed carcass was greatly shrunken; I felt I was inside a dead dried-up whale. And it was full of ridiculous statues—the one of Sir Cloudesley Shovell was especially pleasing. No God there. Nothing alive at all. Even the poppies around the tomb of the Unknown Soldier were artificial.

I had taken mescaline twice more after this, later in 1956, with almost exactly the same effects. I still didn't feel sure enough of the nature of the experience to be able to agree wholeheartedly either with Swami or with Aldous and Gerald. I therefore said as little as possible whenever the subject was being discussed by either party.

During November 1956, a young man whom Swami and I both knew was arrested and charged with sexual solicitation in a men's washroom. Swami's reaction was: "Oh,

Chris, if only he hadn't got caught! Why didn't he go to some bar?"

This was one of the times when Swami's unworldly worldliness made me laugh out loud.

November 22. Have just returned from seeing Swami. He talked about grace—how Maharaj had told them that there are some people who just get it. "God can't be bought." Even if you do all the japam and spiritual disciplines, you still can't command enlightenment. It's always given by grace.

Swami's younger brother went into samadhi while being initiated by Swami Saradananda. Then, as he grew older, he became an extremely avaricious lawyer. But, no matter what he does, he is liberated. On his death-bed, he'll "remember."

Fifteen

January 23, 1957. Swami took us to the little house in South Pasadena (309 Monterey Road) where Vivekananda stayed for a few weeks in 1900. Went upstairs to his bedroom, which has been made into a shrine since the Vedanta Society took the house over. Sat there with Swami, while the other guests chattered loudly downstairs. Swami meditated and I tried to concentrate on his meditation. What a privilege—to be with him in Vivekananda's presence! Felt a keen elation. I was so safe with him. I tried to hold this feeling. I want some of it for when I'm dying. How could I be afraid then, if I felt he was with me?

On February 12, I discovered a small tumor on the side of my lower abdomen. It hadn't been there the previous night when I went to bed. Even on first examining it, the doctor didn't think it was malignant, though he said it must be removed at once, to make sure. So I went through three days of dread, this being my first cancer scare. What really shocked me was how suddenly such a growth can appear.

During the waiting period, I saw Swami. Without telling him about the tumor, I got him talking on the subject of death.

He said he now isn't afraid of dying at all—though of course he would prefer to avoid pain. This life seems to him "all shadows." He was very convincing, and I believed in his belief. But there is one problem which he doesn't have—the extra pain I would feel in parting from Don, knowing that he isn't a devotee. I certainly don't want to go to the plane of existence, the loka, where the devotees of Ramakrishna are said to go, unless I could believe he'd be following me there.

(The tumor did prove to be non-malignant.)

February 21. I feel a new or renewed relationship to Swami. This has been growing for months. It's as if he were exposing me to stronger and stronger waves of his love—yet, all the while, making almost no personal demands on me. I saw him last night—still, as he said, "floating a little," after an operation he had had on a cyst. He was like a small adorable animal with ruffled fur as he sat on his bed telling us about the early days in the monastery in India. I don't feel he is altogether a person any longer.

March 3. This evening, we drove up to the Center in time to catch the end of the vespers of the Ramakrishna puja and be touched by Swami with the tray of relics. It was Don's own idea that he should come with me and do this and I was very happy that he suggested it. (When we went to vespers at the Brahmananda puja on February 1, he didn't come forward to be touched—because, I suppose, he didn't want to commit himself and perhaps get in too deep.)

April 10. I've just been up to the Center. Swami told me that he dreamt he was handing out copies of my book on Ramakrishna to crowds of people, and he was saying, "Chris's book!" I was there, too, in his dream.

Swami is very excited about the book and wildly over-optimistic. He says it will be "a turning point in the growth of the Society."

And now for the first time I dimly get a new conception of the book. I want to introduce some autobiographical material, telling how I myself got to know about Ramakrishna. I mentioned this to Swami this evening. He said, "However you write it will be all right."

June 12. To see Swami. When I put out my hand to shake his, he first made me bend down and gave me his blessing. He seldom does this. He told me, "Whenever you think of God, He thinks of you."

August 23. Swami told me that George is going to India to take the vows of sannyas sometime next spring. That got us talking about him. How, from being a comic figure, he has developed during these past fifteen years. He's still cantankerous and obstinate, but he's so devoted and so full of love that Swami feels he is turning into "a great soul."

September 13. Not to be sly—this is the essence of a revelation Prema feels he's had, as the result of cooking for Swami at a cabin camp up in the Sierras. Prema says he used to be ashamed of Swami because he sounded off and yelled at people and banged the table; but now he sees that it's wonderful not to be afraid to show one's feelings. "We must be bold," Prema said. "We mustn't be conservative."

He told me that Swami spent most of his time shut up in his cabin, and that his mood seemed continuously indrawn.

September 18. Saw Swami for the first time since he got back from the Sierras. I remarked that Prema had told me he had spent most of his time in his cabin, and he said, "Yes, I was having such a wonderful time with the Lord."

It is a measure of my psychological double vision that I can both accept this statement as literally true and marvel that such a statement, made by anybody, could ever be literally true.

I realize, more and more, that Swami is my only link with spiritual life. But that's like a San Franciscan saying that the Golden Gate Bridge is his only link with Marin County. What more could I ask for?

I was very much moved as we sat together and Swami told me that he wants to have this joy not only occasionally but always. "Then I can pass it on to you all."

"It's all Maharaj," he said. "Everything he told me is coming true. I didn't understand him at the time. Now I begin to know what he was talking about."

Swami keeps repeating that Maharaj matters most to him—more than Ramakrishna, because Swami actually knew Maharaj. "And that's how I feel about you," I said. "Ah, but, Chris, I am like a little pebble against the Himalayas." "I have absolute confidence in you, Swami," I said, with tears in my eyes but still aware how funny it sounded.

September 25. Swami told me about Swami Sankarananda, who is now president of the Ramakrishna Order.
He used to be Brahmananda's secretary. Sankarananda
became officious in the performance of his duties and
took it upon himself to decide which visitors should be
allowed to meet Brahmananda and which should not.
When Brahmananda found out what was happening, he
got very angry. He sent Sankarananda away to live in
another monastery and refused to see him for years. In
fact, Brahmananda waited until he himself was dying
before he allowed Sankarananda to come back, and forgave him.

I have accepted the idea that Brahmananda's scoldings, even when they were unjustified, could be spiritually beneficial. But his behavior, in this instance, really
puzzles me. Swami defends it by saying that it gave
Sankarananda an opportunity to show his greatness of
character by remaining in the Order and not bearing
Brahmananda any ill will. He also says that Brahmananda
lent people strength to endure his displeasure. However,
Swami does admit that he was shocked, at that time, and
even protested to Brahmananda against his seeming
cruelty. So this is maybe one of the things Swami was
referring to the other day—the things he has only come
to understand lately, about Maharaj.

On October 8, Don and I began a journey which would
take us right around the world. We flew to Japan, spending two weeks there, then on to Hong Kong, from which
we took a boat to Singapore and Bali and back to Singapore. Then we flew to Bangkok, with a side trip to
Angkor. Then, on November 30, we flew from Bangkok
to Calcutta.

Visiting Calcutta and its neighborhood was the reason for our whole journey, from Swami's point of view. I had told him that, before I wrote the final draft of my biography, I wanted to see the places associated with Ramakrishna. There are not many of them—the villages of Kamarpukur (his birthplace) and Jayrambati (the birthplace of Holy Mother), which are about three miles apart from each other and seventy from the city, and also a few buildings within the Calcutta area, notably the temple at Dakshineswar, where Ramakrishna spent nearly all of his adult life.

I arrived in Calcutta suffering from the ill effects of some bug picked up in Bangkok. This made the necessary sightseeing depressing for both of us, although it was well organized by some of the swamis of the Order, chiefly Vitashokananda. After four days we were invited by them to leave our grand but dirty hotel and move into the simple clean guesthouse of the Belur Math. While we were there, we briefly met Sankarananda, now a massive stately courteous old man whose health was failing.

On December 9, we flew from Calcutta to London, and on January 12, 1958, from London to New York. We got back to Los Angeles on January 30.

On December 11, 1957, while we were staying in London, I had had a dream about Brahmananda.

The first part of my dream had no particular location. I was somewhere talking to someone in monastic robes whom I knew to be Brahmananda. I say "knew" rather than "recognized," because I had no clear image of his physical features—although they were so familiar to me when I was awake, because of all the photographs I had seen.

Brahmananda said to me that he couldn't understand why Ramakrishna had traveled from one place to another, since he was able to see God anywhere. I went away and thought this remark over. Then I decided to go back and ask Brahmananda why *he* had traveled around so much—far more, actually, than Ramakrishna had.

When I returned to put my question, Brahmananda was seated on a platform; this was about six feet high, with trees growing behind it. Both the platform and the trees were somewhat Japanese in appearance. (Remembering them after waking, I thought that I might have borrowed them from the scenery of the Kyoto temples, which Don and I had recently visited.)

As I approached the platform, Brahmananda prostrated before me. And I prostrated before him, shedding tears and thinking of my unworthiness but also feeling a tremendous joy. Although my forehead was bowed down to the ground below the platform and the platform was so high, I felt Brahmananda's hands touching the back of my head in blessing—which would have been physically impossible for him. (This may have signified that the power of a blessing cannot be limited by distance.)

I suppose that the astonishment and joy caused by Brahmananda's prostration and blessing made me forget about my question. Anyhow, I didn't ask it. As I got up and walked away from the platform, there were suddenly other people around me. One of them asked, "Did Maharaj tell you anything you may tell *us*?" This was said with deep respect. I knew that Brahmananda's behavior toward me had made them regard me as someone of importance. I shook my head, still shedding tears but now beginning to feel vain and take credit to myself for the grace which had been shown me. Then I woke up.

During my dream, it had seemed to me that I understood why Brahmananda prostrated before me. I had interpreted his action by relating it to a scene in Dostoevsky's *The Brothers Karamazov*, in which the saintly Father Zosima bows down at Dmitri Karamazov's feet. Zosima later explains that he had bowed down to the great suffering which he saw was in store for Dmitri.

However, when I was awake again and was considering the dream, I realized that this interpretation couldn't be correct. Zosima's reaction, produced by Dostoevsky's own obsession with suffering and guilt, would be quite foreign to Brahmananda's way of thinking as a Vedantist. Even if my karma was as bad as Dmitri's, Brahmananda would still regard me as an embodiment of the Atman, not as a *jiva*, an individual soul living in ignorance of its divine nature. I now interpreted Brahmananda's prostration as a reminder—the Atman in himself was bowing down to the Atman in me in order to remind me of what I truly was. Brahmananda, unlike Zosima, had not only bowed down but also blessed me as an individual soul, thus reassuring me that he loved and accepted me even with all my present imperfections.

Although my dream had had a dreamlike setting, my change of attitude in it, from humble thankfulness to smug self-congratulation, had been psychologically lifelike. I had been very much my ordinary self throughout it, despite its extraordinary happenings. Thus it had had some of the quality of a normal experience.

I now realized that I had never, before this, felt strongly drawn to Maharaj. That was because I had misunderstood his nature, finding him awesome and remote. Vivekananda's humorous, aggressive, sparkling personality attracted me much more because he seemed more human—that is, more of an individual. But what my dream experience had given me was a moment's awareness of a love which was larger than human. For the first time, I began to understand what Swami meant when he said that Maharaj had *become* love. That, perhaps, was why I had been conscious of him in my dream as a presence, rather than as an outwardly recognizable person.

When I described all this to Swami, he assured me that my dream had actually been a vision. He was speaking from his own experience in stating that you could have a vision either when awake or when asleep; both kinds were equally valid.

"It was a great grace," he told me solemnly. On another occasion, speaking to Prema, he interpreted this vision as having been a sign from Maharaj that I was the proper person to write the Ramakrishna biography. How like Swami that was! When he had set his heart on something, it *had* to have the Lord's blessing.

March 13, 1958. Swami told me that the people at Belur Math had written that George had been utterly transformed by sannyas in a single day—but they didn't say how. George himself had written: "Three days ago, I became a Brahmin. Two days ago, I became a ghost— one always becomes what one fears! Yesterday I became Krishnananda." There is a majestic note of impersonality in this last sentence. It's like when you say, in the ritual worship, "I am He."

(George was referring to different stages of his preparation to take the vows of sannyas. The sannyasin has to renounce all caste distinctions. Since you can't renounce what you haven't got, George had first to be admitted into the highest caste, that of the Brahmins. Taking sannyas is regarded as a spiritual rebirth. Since you can't be reborn as long as you are still alive, George had first to think of himself as having died and become a ghost.)

March 28. Swami said he has only recently discovered that God's grace is actually in the mantram. Maharaj had told him that this was so.

April 24. Swami says that visions don't matter—only devotion matters. He told me to "remember the Lord."

May 9. Swami said that enlightenment is not loss of individuality but enlargement of individuality, because you realize that you're everything.

June 26. Swami told me that he feels the presence of the Lord almost continuously; he no longer has to make much of an effort. When he wakes up in the night— which he has to do, two or three times, to go to the toilet, because of his prostate trouble—he feels the presence. Sometimes it is Ramakrishna, sometimes Holy Mother, Maharaj, or Swamiji. I asked if it made any difference that he had known Maharaj and seen Holy Mother during their lifetimes, but not the others. No, he said, they were all equally real.

He says he never prays directly for problems to be solved. He only asks for more devotion to the Lord.

August 22. Unwillingly, I have to admit to myself that the whole introductory section of Ramakrishna and His Disciples—telling how I personally came to know about him—is irrelevant. I've written seventy pages and it's not that they're bad; they just don't belong in this book. I can probably use them, one of these days, somewhere else.

(The Vedanta Society's press published a revised version of this material in 1963, as a pamphlet called *An Approach to Vedanta*.)

August 31. Swami told me on the phone that a well-known actress came to him and asked if she should go to India. Swami said, "Why? You won't get anything out of India unless you have reached something inside yourself." He then asked her if she had been meditating according to his instructions. When she told him no, he "got all excited" and told her not to come back until she had done so for a month. So then she got out of her chair and sat on the floor at Swami's feet and said, "Teach me once again." So he did, and she went away —on probation!

November 19. Tonight I went up to the Center. Suddenly I was so glad to be sitting on the floor beside Swami's chair—like his dog, without saying a word. After supper, I read them the revised first chapter of the Ramakrishna book.

December 11. Swami told me that he'd had "a terrible time" that morning, in the shrine room: "I mean, a good terrible time." He had been overpowered by the knowledge that "there is abundant grace." He had cried so much that he had had to leave the temple. He said, what was the use of reasoning and philosophy, when all that mattered was love of God.

Early in January 1959, while I was having supper with Swami, he mentioned the apartment house which the Vedanta Society was about to have built, as an income property. Several devotees were planning to move into it. He urged me and Don to take one of the apartments.

To have done this would have been almost the same as moving into the Center itself, right across the street. We should have become involved in all its activities, to the gradual exclusion of our own. No doubt, Swami would soon have got into the habit of sending for me at all hours, just as he would send for one of the monks or nuns, whenever he was troubled by an anxiety or inspired by a new project . . . No, the apartment house was out of the question for us, and I never considered it seriously, though I had to pretend to him for a while that I was doing so.

Swami's suggestion was obviously his first move in another back-to-the-monastery campaign. This time, my relationship with Don was under attack. When monk- or nun-making was possible, one had to accept the fact that Swami, being Swami, would do his best to break up any worldly relationship, however fond he might be of the individuals involved in it.

Though I knew better than to try to persuade Don, I did, of course, hope that he might eventually become Swami's disciple. I longed to share that part of my life with him. But, in that case, Swami would have to accept us as a pair of householder devotees. I couldn't imagine myself becoming a monk again under any circumstances, as long as I had Don. If Don were to decide to become a monk, I suppose I might have followed him back into the Order—even though I knew that this would be a separation; a more painful one, perhaps, than death or desertion. Swami would keep us living apart from each other in different centers. He had already "put asunder" several married couples who wished to become monastics, sending the wife to Montecito and the husband to

Trabuco. The old permissive days of the single Holly-wood household were long since over.

April 29, 1959. Swami told us he believes that he, as an old man during his last incarnation, met Brahmananda as a young man. This was during the eighteen-eighties, on the bank of the river Narmada, where they were both practicing austerities.

I don't think I had ever heard Swami say this before— as he grew older, he revealed more and more of his past life. If I had heard this earlier, I should have remembered it as a possible explanation of Maharaj's otherwise mysterious question, when he and Abanindra first met: "Haven't I seen you before?"

Swami's statement also relates to a story which is printed in his book about Brahmananda, *The Eternal Companion*:

> I was sitting cross-legged in front of Maharaj with his feet resting on my knees. This was the position in which I often used to massage his feet. Then something happened to me which I cannot explain, though I feel certain that it was Maharaj's doing. I found myself in a condition in which I was talking and talking, forgetting my usual restraint; it seemed to me that I spoke freely and even eloquently for a long time, but I do not remember what I said. Maharaj listened and said nothing.
>
> Suddenly I returned to normal consciousness and became aware of Maharaj leaning toward me and asking with an amused smile, "What did you say?" I then realized that I had addressed him as "tumi" (the familiar form of "you," which is used in speaking to equals and

friends). I hastened to correct myself, repeating the sentence—I have forgotten what it was—but using "apani" (the respectful form of "you," by which we addressed him). At this, he seemed to lose all interest in the conversation and sat upright again.

I can only assume that Maharaj wanted to corroborate his own intuitive knowledge of my past lives and that he therefore put me into this unusual state of consciousness in which I was able to tell him what he wanted to know.

(The Hindus believe that memory of our past lives is stored in the mind and can be evoked by oneself or by another person. If Swami had been an old man at the time of this previous meeting with Brahmananda, it would have been natural for him to address the young Brahmananda familiarly.)

In the middle of that summer, one of the monks at Trabuco decided that he wanted to leave the Order and marry a woman he had met. He had been in the monastery for years and the monastic life had seemed to be his true and contentedly accepted vocation.

Swami had been known to get violently upset in such situations, shedding tears and lying awake for nights on end. On first hearing about the woman, he had exclaimed, "I'd like to poison her!" Later, however, he became calm and seemed almost indifferent—which rather hurt the monk's feelings. This intrigued me. When I questioned Swami, he showed a curious objectivity, as he often did when discussing his own reactions. "I couldn't pray for him, Chris. I don't know why. I only said that the Lord must do his will. I prayed three whole nights for ———," naming another monastic who had left the Order.

Swami's view was: Why did the monk have to marry this woman right away? Why didn't he go off with her somewhere and have an affair? Then he would probably get tired of her and want to come back to the Order. Swami was quite ready to take the monk back, as long as he wasn't married; but if he did rejoin the Order, Swami said, he would be sent to one of the Ramakrishna monasteries in India for a while, before returning to Trabuco. The monk finally got married, however.

Lest readers think that Swami's attitude to the woman betrayed male chauvinism, I should mention that on another occasion, when one of the nuns wanted to marry a man, Swami's attitude to him was equally ruthless.

On September 22, 1959, Swami left for India with five nuns who had just taken their final vows, thus becoming our first *pravrajikas*, female swamis. Swami returned three months later.

During 1960, my diary records almost nothing of interest about Swami or the Vedanta centers.

On September 17, I had a visit from one of the newer monks at Trabuco. He was obviously uncertain whether he wanted to go on living there or not and hoped to get some reassurance from me. Could I give it to him? *Should* I give it to him? I had been in this situation several times before, and it was always tricky.

He asked me about my time up at the Center in the nineteen-forties, why I joined and why I left. I tried to avoid presenting myself to him as a model he could identify with—pointing out that I didn't start off by deciding to become a monk, that I was drawn into the

Center because of Swami's desire to have me as a collaborator on his Gita translation, that when I decided to leave there was no dramatic break, that I have continued to see Swami and be his collaborator ever since.

"So really," he asked, "it's much the same now as if you'd stayed on there being a monk?" But I couldn't let him think that. So I owned that there had been a "jazzy" (the words I sometimes pick!) period in my life after I'd left, and that, indeed, people had come to Swami and told him I was going to the dogs—and that Swami had charmingly shut them up . . . So then I got the conversation off onto Swami and how marvelously he has changed since I've known him—proving that the spiritual life does bring its reward . . . I hope he was satisfied.

(Apparently he wasn't, since he left the Order not long after this.)

December 26. Swami's birthday lunch. Swami radiant, all in white. "You don't have to tell me that you love me," he said to us, after the girls had sung the gooey second verse of the Happy Birthday song.

February 17, 1961. Today was the Ramakrishna puja, so I went to vespers. There were lots of people, and Swami unwisely decided to save time—he thought it would take too long for each one of us to come up into the shrine room, be touched by the relics, offer a flower, and leave again. So, instead, he came down out of the shrine room with the tray of relics and moved around among us, touching us with it as we sat on the floor of the temple. This arrangement would have worked if each person had got up and left the temple after being touched. Only, a lot of them didn't. Prema said he believed that one individual was dead drunk, but I think it was sheer affectation; some like to pretend to themselves that the touch of the relics has put them into a trance. Thus an absurd traffic jam was created and Swami became confused. So several were touched twice and others not at all.

March 2. Yesterday I called the Center and told them that I wouldn't be coming there for supper, as I usually do on Wednesdays—this was because I wanted to get on with my work. A bit later, Swami called me and said, "I'm lonely for you, Chris." It wasn't that he was nagging at me to come. He just felt like saying this, so he picked up the phone and said it. There are no strings attached to his love, therefore it is never embarrassed. The ordinary so-called lover is out to get something from his beloved, therefore he is afraid of going too far and becoming tiresome.

Don spent nearly all of that year in London, studying art at the Slade School. In April, I went over there to be with him. I returned in October.

In November, I went to stay at Trabuco with Swami and with Swami Ritajananda, who was leaving soon to take charge of the Vedanta Society at Gretz, just outside Paris.

As we sat in the cloister, with that marvelous still-empty prospect of lion-golden hills opening away to the line of the sea, I said to Swami: "You're really <u>certain</u> that God exists?"

He laughed: "Of course! If he doesn't exist, then I don't exist."

"And do you feel he gives you strength to bear misfortune?"

"I don't think of it like that. I just know he will take care of me. It's rather hard to explain. Whatever happens, it will be all right."

I asked him when he began to feel certain that God existed.

"When I met Maharaj. Then I knew that one could know God. He even made it seem easy . . . And now I feel God's presence every day. But it's only very seldom that I see him."

Later, after Ritajananda had joined us, Swami said, "Stay here, Chris, and I'll give you sannyas. You shall have a special dispensation from the Pope." He said this laughingly, but I had a feeling that he really meant it —otherwise, he surely wouldn't have said it in Ritajananda's presence.

I said, "Swami, that would be a mistake worthy of Vivekananda himself."

(This was an allusion to the fact that Vivekananda had sometimes given sannyas to Western disciples who were—judging from their subsequent behavior—quite unworthy of it.)

Swami says that the Hindu astrologers predict the world will come to an end next February 2nd. However, the astrologers themselves are praying that it shan't happen. I objected—rather cleverly, I thought—that Ramakrishna has predicted another incarnation for himself on earth, and that this contradicts any such prophecy. Swami agreed.

November 8. Yesterday evening, I got back from Trabuco and went up to the Hollywood Center to attend
the Kali puja, just to please Swami. I never feel I have
any personal part in it. It belongs, quite naturally, to
the women, and how they dress up for it, in their saris!
One of them had let her hair down, falling loose over
her shoulders but, oh, so elegantly arranged. Well, it's
their party . . . Meanwhile, I sat outside the shrine room
in a corner and gossiped cozily in whispers with one of
the monks from Trabuco, as we waited for Swami to
asperse us with Ganges water. This he did vigorously,
as if he were ridding a room of flies with DDT.

(This reminds me of another, earlier occasion, at a
puja also being held at night, when Swami was about
to asperse the assembled devotees. Suddenly he burst
out laughing and exclaimed, "You look so funny, sitting
there!" His laughter—in which, after a moment's shock,
we all joined—shattered the gravity of this ancient
ritual, making it now and new.)

Sixteen

Don and I were in New York during December and January; he had a show of his portrait drawings there. He stayed on for a while, after its opening, to do more portraits on commission. I got back to Los Angeles on January 27, because I wanted to take part in Vivekananda's breakfast puja.

January 28, 1962. Prema met me and drove me to the Center. I spent the night in one of the apartments of their apartment house. This morning, just before six, I saw Swami, and then we all went into the shrine for the breakfast ritual. I read the Katha Upanishad—vain, I have to admit, of my rendition.

The *Katha Upanishad* begins by telling a story which introduces its philosophical message:

Vajasrabasa is making a sacrifice, to win God's favor. At the same time, being miserly, he is trying to cheat God by offering up his worst cattle, the old, the barren, the blind, and the lame. Nachiketa, one of his sons, sees this and is shocked and disgusted. He asks his father scornfully, "To whom will you offer *me*?" And he repeats this question until Vajasrabasa gets angry and tells him, "I offer you to Death."

Nachiketa, who is ardently spiritual, "like a flame of fire," but also, one feels, a bit of a prig, answers that Vajasrabasa must not go back on his words, even though they were spoken in anger. Nachiketa is ready to die, and he sets out at once for the house of the King of Death.

But, after this noble exit, there is a comic anticlimax. Death is not at home. Nachiketa has to wait three days for his return.

The King of Death is a character whom Bernard Shaw might have put into a play. Outwardly, he is a figure of majesty and terror; inwardly, he is disillusioned and therefore wise. He knows now that he was foolish to have wished to become King of Death, since his power is not eternal.

When Death arrives home, he is scolded by his servants. They tell him that he has insulted this Brahmin youth by keeping him waiting. Death, as a mere householder of a lower caste, must show hospitality to every Brahmin, or he will lose the merit of his good karma. So Death approaches Nachiketa with courteous apologies and offers him three boons, in compensation for the three days he has waited.

The first two boons which Nachiketa asks are immediately granted. Then, for his third boon, Nachiketa requires an answer to the question: When a man dies, does he continue to exist, or doesn't he?

The King of Death is secretly delighted. This question shows him that Nachiketa is a serious seeker after knowledge. However, wanting to be certain of Nachiketa's seriousness, Death slyly tests him further by raising objections. Even the gods, he says, were once puzzled by this mystery. The truth of it is subtle and hard to understand. Why doesn't Nachiketa ask for something else—sons and grandsons, a hundred years of life, cattle, elephants, horses, gold, a huge kingdom, heavenly maidens such as are ordinarily not to be had by mortals, together with their bright chariots and their musical instruments?

But Nachiketa rejects all these, saying that no one who has met Death face to face, as he himself has, could desire such things, knowing them all to be perishable and therefore worthless.

Whereupon Death, convinced that he has found a worthy pupil, begins to teach Nachiketa the truth about immortality . . .

Reading this story aloud in the shrine room, I consciously did my utmost to entertain our invisible guest as he sat at his breakfast. Now and then, I would raise my eyes to the shrine and address him directly. I hammed up the passages of drama and comedy, trying to make him weep or chuckle . . . You were showing off, I would later accuse myself; is *that* what you call worship? I was offering Vivekananda what I do best, I would reply; and if I don't enjoy my own performance, how can I expect *him* to?

Then I had breakfast with Swami. He has been pestered by another of these madwomen—they're one of his chief occupational hazards. She broke into his room recently, in the middle of the night, and later wrote letters accusing him of forcing her into samadhi against her will, and of teaching her masturbation by remote control. Swami can never help laughing when he talks about such situations, but they scare him when they happen.

He gave me mahaprasad, a grain of rice from the Jagannath Temple at Puri. Ramakrishna said that this prasad is like Ganges water, "Brahman made visible."

Swami has a whole store of these grains and takes one first thing in the morning, every day.

May 24. The madwoman has been sending Swami more anonymous letters, with torn-up photos of Ramakrishna or Swami in them, and the question, "Is the farce still going on?"

June 2. Don said this morning that he would like to have a mantram and wished Swami would give him one. It's the first time Don has ever said this.

June 7. Yesterday evening, Don came up with me to the Center, talked to Swami alone, and told him he wanted a mantram. Swami seems to have been pleased and surprised—as well he might be, since Don has known him for nearly ten years without asking for one! He gave Don some instructions about meditating and told him he'd initiate him next December.

(The mantram Swami gave Don must have been a provisional one, not the personal, permanent mantram which he would be given at the time of his initiation.)

Swami is being threatened again by the madwoman. So the boys have fixed a buzzer system between his room and the monastery. If she arrives in the middle of the night and starts to smash in Swami's door, he merely has to flip the switch and the monastery is alerted like a fire station. The boys can be over in eighteen seconds —they have rehearsed it!

July 9. Don left for New York this evening, to draw various people. While waiting for his plane at the airport, we talked about the mantram Swami gave him. He

said that repeating it has made a tremendous difference
to him already. He also said he was afraid that making
japam might take over his life. He was afraid he might
get in deeper than he was ready to get, and be unable
to think about anything but finding God. I said well,
that was something we neither of us could do anything
about, if it was going to happen. My attitude wasn't due
to pious resignation. I just don't believe it will happen,
so I have no idea how I should react if it did. I suppose
I should be both miserable and delighted.

That autumn, the swami in charge of one of the other
Vedanta centers died. A woman member of his congregation had gradually, through the years, established herself as a power figure. Now she seemed to be threatening
to take control of the Center. Its other members, we
heard, were all under her influence and would do nothing
to oppose her.

A few days later, while I was visiting Swami, several
women devotees were discussing the situation in his
presence. One of these women was particularly vehe-
ment. She kept telling Swami that he ought to get on a
plane and go and deal with the power woman in person,
but that he was afraid to. It was a strangely ugly scene,
reminding me of the women in Icelandic sagas who taunt
their men into going out to kill someone. The woman
who was speaking seemed to turn into the woman she
was attacking.

This was one of the rare occasions on which Swami
appeared to me to be intimidated and temporarily helpless. Yet I didn't feel disturbed. Such glimpses of his
weaknesses and faults helped me to see him doubly—
as Abanindra Nath Ghosh and as the receptacle of "this
thing," the Eternal. If I had felt that it was Abanindra

who was getting more and more spiritual, I should have been shocked by his accompanying weaknesses. But no, I told myself, that isn't what's happening, at all. Abanindra, with his weaknesses *and* his virtues, is fading away, while "this thing," which has always been present within him, is becoming more and more evident.

During October, Swami somehow got to hear about a book, not yet published, which described its author's unsuccessful search for a suitable spiritual teacher, either living or dead. Ramakrishna was among the candidates. The author had at first felt attracted by Ramakrishna's personality but had decided against him on the ground that he was (I quote) a homosexual who had had to struggle hard to overcome his lust for his young disciple later to be known as Vivekananda.

Swami was outraged. He met with the author, who was persuaded or intimidated into deleting this passage from the manuscript. I could understand Swami's indignation, although, as a homosexual, I couldn't altogether share it. Certainly, the author's statement about Ramakrishna and Vivekananda was irresponsible and unsupported by any convincing evidence. Still, it didn't shock me so much that I was unable to examine it, and my reactions to it, calmly.

It is on record that Ramakrishna said he had been troubled by lust on at least one occasion and had overcome it through prayer. However, he didn't say that his lust had had any particular human object, so it may have been simply an upsurge of sexual desire. Swami used to tell us that it was necessary for Ramakrishna to experience all the temptations which a human being can feel.

Did I then believe that Ramakrishna could have felt

lust for Vivekananda? How could I possibly say with any assurance what a Ramakrishna could or couldn't have felt? Such a being sometimes behaves in a way which we can't explain, because his motivations are quite different from ours. When one of Ramakrishna's disciples was asked why Christ blasted the barren fig tree, he answered, "First become a Christ, and then you'll know why he did that." Only the wretched little puritan, with his fixed rules of conduct and catalogue of sins, is certain that he can understand, and judge, everybody's motives, including God's.

The one assumption I thought I could safely make was this: Since we know from the records that Ramakrishna always spoke and acted with complete childlike frankness, it seems probable that, if he *had* felt lust for anyone of either sex, he would have immediately run to confess his lust to the individual concerned, and then told everyone else in the neighborhood about it. Which would mean that, if such a situation had indeed ever arisen, it must have been known of and concealed by Ramakrishna's biographers.

It didn't surprise me that someone reading about Ramakrishna for the first time should be disconcerted by the extremely emotional way in which he expressed his love for his young male disciples—and that such a reader should also fail to realize that Ramakrishna's kind of love feels no inhibitions because it makes no demands. Most of us are familiar only with the kind of love—be it parental or romantic—which does demand something in return. So we suspect Ramakrishna's love of having ulterior homosexual motives.

There is another excuse for accusing Ramakrishna of homosexuality; he sometimes dressed in woman's clothes. As a boy, he did this for a joke; he was a talented impersonator and mimic. As an adult, he wished to experi-

ence every sort of religious mood, including the mood of
a female devotee of Krishna. He used to say that one
"should make the outside the same as the inside"; and
so, when he took part in certain pujas, he wore woman's
clothes, with ornaments and a wig, to complement his
devotional mood. This naturally scandalized the conventionally pious. Ramakrishna regarded the distinction
between the sexes as a part of *maya*, the cosmic illusion;
therefore, he can't have thought of himself as being
exclusively masculine or feminine. In daily life, he didn't
appear effeminate, and when he dressed as a woman he
changed so completely that his friends often couldn't
recognize him.

I was well aware of these facts and yet, when talking
to fellow homosexuals, I would often put it that Ramakrishna "got into drag." This expressed my need to think
of him as someone who was, at least to some extent, one
of us. I couldn't honestly claim him as a homosexual,
even a sublimated one, much as I would have liked to be
able to do so.

I wished that I could have discussed these matters in
Ramakrishna and His Disciples. But that was out of the
question. For my book had now become an official project of the Ramakrishna Order. Each chapter was sent
off to India as soon as it was finished, to be submitted
to the approval of Swami Madhavananda, the present
head of the Order. (Sankarananda had recently died.)
Many of Madhavananda's comments and corrections
were helpful. But, every so often, I was made aware that
there were limits to his permissiveness.

On October 20, 1962, the Chinese attacked Ladakh in
Kashmir and the North East Frontier Agency, gaining
much territory claimed by India.

November 1. Nehru has dismissed Krishna Menon as defense minister, holding him responsible for India's unpreparedness for the Chinese invasion. Swami said of Menon, "He should have been lynched!" Swami is very chauvinistic about the crisis. He would like India to ally herself with the West.

November 14. Just back from spending three days at Trabuco. While there, Swami said to me, "Just think, you might have been a swami by this time." But then he added, as he has never done before: "But perhaps you are more useful like this."

November 22. Saw Gerald yesterday. We talked about morality. How nowadays people tend to think of religion as being only a set of ethical standards. I said I don't go to Swami for ethics, but for spiritual reassurance: "Does God really exist? Can you promise me that he does?" I feel this so strongly that I can quite imagine doing something of which I know Swami disapproves— but which I believe to be right for me—and then going and telling him about it. That simply isn't very important. Advice on how to act—my goodness, if you want that, you can get it from a best friend, a doctor, a bank manager.

Swami has reverted to his caste psychology. After all, he does belong to the Kshatriya, the warrior caste. Not only are the Chinese to be run out of the whole area; he demands Tibet! I think he'll be really disappointed if this truce leads to peace . . . Well, there you are, that's the other side of the coin. I disagree with Swami's attitude, utterly. I'm still a hard-line pacifist. If he were someone else, I'd say it was disgusting to see a minister of religion—and at his age—demanding bloodshed. But

Swami is Swami, so it doesn't matter. It's not what our relationship is all about.

Charles Laughton was at the Cedars of Lebanon Hospital, dying of cancer. One of my visits to him was on November 29:

He was sleepy and in pain but quite lucid. He said, "The preoccupation is with death, isn't it?" What he really wanted to ask, though he didn't put it directly, was whether or not I approved of his having seen a priest. I told him I certainly did. He said he would like to see another priest, a better one, but he didn't make it clear in what way better. I tried to tell him tactfully that it didn't really matter if he got to see another priest or not. He should speak to God, ask for help. Because God is there. "I know," Charles said.

He kept dozing off and I was holding his hand and praying to Ramakrishna to help Charles through his suffering and dying. I even said what I have never said before, "Do it for Brahmananda's sake, for Vivekananda's sake, for Prabhavananda's sake," and this was "put into my mouth," it seemed.

All mixed up with the praying, which moved me and caused me to shed tears, were the caperings of the ego, whispering, "Look, look, look at me. I'm praying for Charles Laughton!" And then the ego said, "How wonderful if he would die, quite peacefully, right now at this moment!"

It is most important not to make these confessions about the ego as though they were horrifying. They are not—and it is mere vanity to pretend that the ego doesn't come along with you every step of the way; it is there like your sinus, and its intrusions are no more shocking than sneezing.

The really important question is: Why should I pray for Charles? Shouldn't I let him do it? Wasn't I like an agent, trying to muscle in on a deal?

December 8. Swami, when asked about prayer, said that it is good both for you and for the person you pray for; and he added: "You see, when you are speaking to God like that, there are not two people, there is only one." He also said that all you needed was faith that the prayer would be answered. You didn't have to be a saint. If you had faith, then it would be answered. He said this with that absolute compelling confidence of his.

December 18. Don's initiation day. It imposed the usual states of aversion and boredom on him; the long, boring puja first, the devout congregation, the reek of Sunday religion. The initiation of Don and of several other devotees took place immediately after the puja. He didn't stop for the end of the homa fire, or for lunch. And now —as I did, all those years ago—he has forgotten his mantram and must go back and check it with Swami!

Never mind. The deed is done, and of his own free will. That's all that matters for the time being—maybe for years to come. It will catch up with him.

December 26. We went to Swami's birthday party and Swami wrote Don's mantram down for him. Don hates to destroy the paper it was written on, but Swami told him to.

Swami looked absolutely radiant. He told us that his best birthday present had been "a visit from Maharaj." He had woken at five this morning, gone to the bathroom, got back into bed, and had then had a (seemingly) long visitation dream of Maharaj, sometime before seven o'clock. He couldn't say if it had taken place here or in India. He had been dressing Maharaj. The wearing cloth was crumpled. He was impressed by the beauty of Maharaj's skin; it was golden and shining.

I never knew before that Swami quite often suffers from feelings of sickness, after initiating people. "But I didn't feel anything bad that day," he told us, referring to Don's initiation day. "They must have been all good people."

January 3, 1963. The nuns at Montecito have been getting threatening phone calls: "You bitch. Tell your Swami to get out of this country in twenty-four hours, or we'll burn the temple!" The nuns have called in the police, who take the matter quite seriously and have even been patrolling the area by plane. Swami, telling this story, said, "You beech."

January 29. The Brahmananda puja two days ago appears to have been an extraordinary occasion. Prema says that Swami seemed to be filled with power: "He kept blessing people and you felt he could really do it!"

February 1. Swami has a new project which excites him: to get some young swamis from India, train them at Trabuco, and then send them as assistants to the various American centers. I realize that he doesn't want to produce American swamis to head American centers. He thinks that American congregations wouldn't take them seriously. He does believe, however, that American swamis could do valuable work in India.

February 20. Swami retold the story of how he met Brahmananda and of the various stages of his involvement with him. This included one episode which, he says, he has never told anybody else. In the days before he became a monk and was still a student in his late teens, he once went to see Brahmananda at someone's house. (Balaram's?) When he arrived, he suddenly felt a strong desire to go over and sit on Brahmananda's lap. This made him ashamed, so he ran out of the room without even speaking to Brahmananda.

February 28. Last night, Swami warned us strongly against making japam while you are feeling resentment against anyone. He even thinks it could harm that person, after the manner of black magic.

March 6. Somebody gave Swami Montgomery Hyde's *The Three Trials of Oscar Wilde*. Swami commented, after reading it, "Poor man!" And to Prema, he said, "All lust is the same."

(I was surprised that anyone would have given Swami such a book. But Swami's reading had certainly become increasingly liberal in scope as he grew older. His early period—during which he regarded all novels as "a trash" —had come to an end (or so I seem to remember) when someone persuaded him to try *The Brothers Karamazov*. Swami loved it, particularly the part about Father Zosima, and thereafter began to read all kinds of novels indiscriminately, hoping for another such experience. "The trouble is, Swami," I told him, "you started off with the best one.")

June 2–5. Some notes made while staying at Trabuco:
Light rain falling. The noisy frogs in the lily pond in front of Swamiji's statue. The dog got skunk secretion all

over him and lay outside the shrine and you could smell him even when you were inside it.

Watching Swami huddled in his chadar before the shrine, with the bald patch at the back of his head, I thought: He's been doing this all his life. He isn't kidding.

Swami said that he had "the intense thought that I am the Self in all beings, so how can one harm anyone? It's a wonderful life, if you can feel like that . . . I say, Oh Lord, don't test me!" (Swami later explained that he meant he didn't want to suffer.)

Pope John XXIII—whom Swami has always greatly admired—has just died, after terrible sufferings. Swami said that this was perhaps because it was his last life; bad karmas are sometimes burnt up by suffering.

Swami told me: "Pray for devotion and knowledge. Say Not I but Thou." But he added that it was no use praying that God's will be done, because God's will will be done, anyway.

His three big spiritual experiences:

A vision of the Impersonal God, at Puri. He lost outer consciousness and was aware of nothing but light and a voice saying in English, God, God, God. He couldn't see the images or the people worshiping. A brother swami, Sujji Maharaj, grabbed one of his arms and told a priest to hold the other one. Later Swami asked him, "How did you know what was happening to me?" He answered, "Because I've lived with Maharaj."

Then, in his bedroom in Sister's old house in Hollywood, he saw Holy Mother "very powerful." After this, he was dazed for three days.

Then, once, in the temple, he saw Swamiji, with Ramakrishna, Holy Mother, and Maharaj more dimly behind *him. Swami took this vision to be a special reassurance that Swamiji wasn't angry with him—shortly before this, he had had a letter from Ashokananda of the San Francisco Center, accusing him and me of having insulted Vivekananda.*

(The alleged insult was contained in my introduction to *Vedanta for the Western World,* a selection of articles from our magazine, *Vedanta and the West.* Ashokananda must have read this introduction when it first appeared in the magazine itself, early in 1945, several months before the book was published.

In the passage to which Ashokananda objected, I began by describing Vivekananda's extraordinary strength of intellect, character, and will. Then I suggested that, if he had never visited Dakshineswar and met Ramakrishna, "he might well have become one of India's foremost politicians."

Admittedly, the word "politicians" was unwisely chosen; it is so often used in a derogatory sense. The kind of politician I had in mind was Gandhi.

I think Ashokananda also objected to the idea that Vivekananda could ever, under any circumstances, have followed a way of life other than the monastic. Vivekananda used to recall how, as a child, he had pictured himself "as foremost among the great men of the world," but also "as having renounced everything in the world." He would add, "I always ended by choosing the latter— I knew that this was the only path by which a man could achieve true happiness." So Ashokananda was right, from his point of view. And I was ready to admit that I hadn't expressed myself clearly. What I had actually been trying to point out was that Vivekananda's great qualifications for worldly success made his choice of the monastic life all the more impressive.

Swami was enormously disturbed by Ashokananda's accusation, which he took to mean that we had insulted Swamiji *intentionally*. Even though he knew that this was nonsense and even though his vision of Swamiji had reassured him that Swamiji wasn't offended, he would brood on the accusation from time to time, throughout the rest of his life.

Meanwhile, peace was made with Ashokananda—outwardly, at least. And for the book, the offending phrase was altered to: ". . . one of India's foremost national leaders.")

June 23. Swami was impressed because Queen Elizabeth and Prince Philip had gone to Victoria Station to welcome Radhakrishnan, the president of India. I told him I didn't find this at all impressive; it was only a matter of protocol. But Swami disagreed: "A few years ago, they'd have just said he was a native." In Swami's eyes, Elizabeth and Philip have a kind of reflected glory, despite their dowdy harmlessness, because they are related to India's Mother-Tyrant, Victoria!

A boy who comes to the readings at the Center on Wednesdays said that a man at the place where he works had told him a hard-luck story and so he had given the man ten bucks, and then the man had spent it on liquor. "Did I do wrong?" the boy asked, very earnestly. Swami much amused.

August 16. Don found me the perfect title for my novelette—A Single Man—a couple of weeks ago. Today I was revising the description of Ramakrishna's cremation. I wanted to convey an image of the Ganges waters flowing past the cremation ghat, offering no reassurance, no sense of security to Ramakrishna's mourners. Don thought a little and said, "How about the <u>inconstant</u>

waters?" "Wonderful! What made you think of that?" "Romeo and Juliet."

1963 was the centenary of Vivekananda's birth. Since he was born in January, the celebrations had begun then and were continuing throughout the year. Their final event was to take place in Calcutta, from the last days of 1963 through the beginning of January 1964. This was a so-called Parliament of Religions, to which foreign devotees of Vivekananda and swamis of the Order from centers abroad had been invited.

Swami had long since started a relentless campaign of gentle hints that I should come with him to India and speak at the Parliament. I had answered evasively. But, on September 25, he had succeeded in making me say yes. Having done so, I was immediately horrified. I wrote in my diary:

A passionate psychosomatic revolt is brewing in me against the Indian trip. I am almost capable of dying at Belur Math, out of sheer spite.

On November 4, I again found myself inside the Cedars of Lebanon Hospital, nearly a year after I had seen Laughton there for the last time. Now I was visiting Huxley. I knew already that he, too, had cancer and that it was spreading rapidly.

Aldous was in obvious discomfort, but there was nothing poignant or desperate in his manner, and he clearly didn't want to talk about death. Not talking about it made me embarrassed, however, and I touched on subject after subject, at random. Each time I did so, Aldous commented acutely, or remembered an appropriate quotation. I came away with the picture of a great noble vessel sinking quietly into the deep; many of its delicate marvelous mechanisms still in perfect order, all its lights still shining.

Seventeen

December 16, 1963. Don is in New York. Woke up in a big flap this morning; travel dread gripping me. So I have started taking Librium in advance.

December 18–19. About fifty people came to the airport to see us off. The parting was like a funeral which is so boring and hammy that you are glad to be one of the corpses. Anything rather than have to go home with the other mourners afterwards!

We got onto the plane at last and it took off. Swami said, "To think that all this is Brahman and nobody realizes it!" I sat squeezed between him and George; the Japan Air Lines seats are as tight-packed as ever. Despite my holy environment, I couldn't help dwelling on yesterday afternoon's delicious sex adventure. I even did so rather defiantly.

After Honolulu, the long long flight northwestward, passing the dateline between the 18th and 19th through the almost infinitely extended afternoon. Tried to read

Cather's Song of the Lark, but could concentrate only on *Esquire* articles—Calder Willingham's reply to Mailer, Mailer's threats to write a novel, Vidal on *Tarzan of the Apes*.

Swami ordered a drink and pressed me to take one. I refused, feeling priggish but knowing that this trip will be even worse for me if I don't keep it dry. Swami refused a steak. He has always maintained his beef taboo but never imposes it on us. He and George ate stuffed chicken instead. My steak was perfect. We got to Tokyo at about 6:30 p.m.

Swami spent most of December 20 in bed, having slept badly. George and I wandered around Tokyo. This was certainly the longest stretch of time in our lives that we had been alone together and in a non-religious atmosphere—unless one could call Tokyo's commercial Christmas display religious. (In an English-language magazine published in Japan, I found a joke drawing: a Japanese child and his mother are looking into a shop window full of Christmas decorations, all of them strictly Western in style, and the child is asking: "Do the Americans have Christmas, too?") The magic of Japanese window dressing made everything on sale seem toy-like, including the photographic and audio equipment. George himself became a child, overcome by temptation. Chuckling as though he were doing something naughty, he bought a camera and a tape recorder. This made us suddenly intimates and fellow conspirators—since George already had a camera with him and would be too ashamed of this extravagance to confess it to Swami.

On the twenty-first, Swami woke with pains and a slight fever. He feared a recurrence of his kidney trouble and said he would like to fly straight back to Los Angeles, if only there weren't all those people awaiting us in India who would be disappointed. His indecision didn't make me at all uneasy; I felt an equal readiness to go back, to go forward, to stay where I was. I might have mistaken my mood for resignation to God's will, if I hadn't recognized it as the indifference caused by Librium. If this is how so-called ordinary unimaginative people feel when they travel, I thought, well—good for *them!*

Inevitably, Swami decided that we must fly on to Calcutta. We arrived there after many unforeseen delays—which, normally, would have driven me frantic— in the dead of night. But the welcoming party of monks was still at the airport, waiting. Swami and George (who instantaneously became Krishnananda) had flower garlands hung around their necks. I was happy to see Prema and Arup (another of our Hollywood brahmacharis), who had arrived in India ahead of us. They were to take sannyas at the Math early in January.

By the time that we had got through the passport control and customs, and into the cars which would bring us to Belur Math, I was aware that the Librium had lost its power. I felt a magic begin to work as we drove through the dark lanes and streets. I smelled and felt the strange perfumed softness of India; the perfume is dust and charcoal smoke. A booth, brilliantly alight and noisy, in which a kirtan was being held. The darkness around it full of phantom people.

December 22. Belur Math is far more delightful than I'd remembered it. The light is so soft. In the afternoon, the monastery grounds along the riverbank are crowded with visitors. The people just sit on the grass or peer into the shrines; they don't seem to annoy the worshipers. A small black cow walks by and various groups shoo it away; they are not a bit respectful. Prema loves it all, says he never wants to go back to California.

Swami, seated in the room which Sankarananda had when we saw him in 1957, is like the Head of the Order —more kingly, gracious, and assured than any of the other swamis. He doesn't seem different here; he isn't adapting himself to India, just making himself at home in it . . . He showed us the exact spot where he first met Brahmananda, on the upper balcony of the building he is now staying in. As Swami stood there, describing their meeting in all its often-repeated details, it seemed uncannily actual.

I am staying at the new guesthouse, just outside the monastery compound—I don't think it existed when Don and I were here. Also at the guesthouse are a few other devotees from the States. Swami and Nikhilananda from New York come and have their meals with us. Nikhilananda, like Swami, was an anti-British terrorist in his teens and has the distinction of having been imprisoned in a British concentration camp. Now he is quite a despot. He bullies his Western disciples ruthlessly. He can't bully me because I belong to Swami. I greatly respect and rather like him. He talks obsessively and critically about the weaknesses of the Indian character, which are, according to him, fatalism, love of chatter, and indifference to social abuses. Swami says wistfully to me, "I can't make conversation." He is a little bit jealous, afraid that Nikhilananda will impress me.

December 23. When I came here in 1957, I only made a pranam once, to Sankarananda; I didn't bow down to any of the other swamis. This was because I didn't want to embarrass Don—my bowing down would have called attention to his refraining from doing so, and he couldn't bow down because, in those days, he wasn't a devotee.

During this visit, I am playing it very broad. I bow down even to the most junior swamis. This is partly clowning, partly aggression—and how it embarrasses many of them! A few retaliate—I have to take a standing jump backwards, to avoid having them do it to me.

December 24. We drove into Calcutta, where I made a reservation on the BOAC flight to Rome for January 7. That seems centuries away. Swami changed into Western clothes to come with me—I think because he didn't want people to know he was a swami and keep making pranams. He looked dapper and ridiculously non-Hindu. He very seldom dresses so formally at home.

Crowds and crowds and crowds. This is what a vast area of the world must be like, now—the part one prefers to forget; squalor, overpopulation, near-starvation. Old trucks, bullock carts, rickshaws, little closed cabs such as Ramakrishna used to ride in. Holy men smeared all over with ashes. And the skinny wandering bulls.

Arup is sick with the shakes.

This evening, after vespers, we had a Christmas Eve puja for Jesus. They built up an altar on a side aisle of the temple, with shelves of fruit and cake, surmounted by a picture of the Virgin and Child.

I had been told to read the birth of Jesus from Luke and the Sermon on the Mount from Matthew. Was much disconcerted when I found that they had given me a Roman Catholic Bible—it was the first copy I'd ever looked into. I had to sight-read unfamiliar phrases, such as "our supersubstantial bread," or else substitute phrases from the King James version, which I guessed that the monks here would know better.

All those dark faces listening to this mock-Hindu paleface! I knew exactly how I ought to be feeling, but I didn't feel anything at all. The ceremony wasn't in the least embarrassing, however. They sang a couple of songs to "Sri Isa" in Bengali, which had the merit of lifting Jesus right out of the West and putting him back in Asia, where he belongs. George recorded it all on his new Japanese recorder.

December 25. How nice it is to wake here, on my refreshingly hard bed under the mosquito net! Waking up is helped by the rude crows, and a bird which emits liquid tropical whistles, and the factory sirens and riverboat hooters and the noise of trains crossing the Vivekananda Bridge, and then finally the great smashing clash of buckets and pans as the help starts to get ready for breakfast, which we eat at seven-thirty. A purely British meal: porridge, cold scrambled eggs, marmalade, strong black tea, hard toast. The art of preparing this must have been passed down from one generation to the next, since the British left.

Arup is still shaky. Swami is very concerned because, he says, if you aren't perfectly well, you are not allowed to take sannyas. One of the hazards of the ceremony is that you have to bathe in the Ganges, and in the middle of the night, too. Telling me this, Swami drops his voice, as though he were describing some obscene rite of sexual initiation performed by a primitive tribe, instead of the most ordinary of Hindu holy acts.

Poor Arup, when I went in to visit him, seemed isolated and a bit humiliated by his illness, which I suspect is nothing but psychosomatically expressed India horror. Prema has almost forced him into this role by grabbing the role of India lover. The greatest possible demonstration of India love is not to get sick here.

All over the Math grounds, they are putting up pandals, canvas tent halls with a bamboo framework, for speeches and mass meals on the day of the Vivekananda birthday puja, January 6th.

December 26. Prema has taken hundreds of photographs, from which we are to choose illustrations for the Ramakrishna book. We spent the morning looking through them. Prema, with his usual crushing frankness, remarked that he has been rereading the book and doesn't think it's really "great." I agreed with him, of course, and added that I could probably give a much more vivid impression of Ramakrishna when talking to a sympathetic stranger in a bar, after several drinks. There is that in me which will never write its best to order. Deep down, I have always resented the censorship of the Math.

Meanwhile, thank God for the greatness of Willa Cather. I am relishing every single page of *The Song of the Lark*.

December 27. This afternoon, I talked at the Ramakrishna Mission College. They had fixed up their gymnasium for the occasion; the stage seemed partly a shrine, partly an Oriental parlor. On the back wall a thing like a monster valentine, enclosing Vivekananda's portrait. Downstage were a draped couch and a draped table with a stick of incense burning on it, right under the noses of us speakers, as we sat on the couch, garlanded by the students, like gods. (Luckily, we were allowed to take the garlands off before speaking; they were terribly hot.)

I was fairly good, I guess. Not that I said anything much, but it came through without hesitation and loud. Then Swami was asked to answer questions. He was all silver and gold—silver hair and gold skin with a silvery *light on it, and the blending yellow of his robe.* He told the boys that their college would be a success only when it produced at least a dozen monks a year. He was adorable—smiling and teasing and yet quite serious. Many of the students had their arms around each other as they listened. They were slim pliant-waisted youths with dark melancholy mocking eyes and smiling white teeth; many wore mustaches. Afterwards we were served gray sweetened milk-tea and oranges and cookies. There were also glasses of water. Swami, who is determined I shan't be poisoned on this visit, said quite loudly, "Don't drink that, Chris."

December 28. This morning, one of the papers prints an interview with me, which begins: "Why did distinguished writer Christopher Isherwood become such a strong admirer of Swami Vivekananda—to the extent of banging his fist on the table in raptures, as he did in Calcutta on Friday?"

Today Swami, George, Prema, and I had lunch with the swamis in the monastery dining room, sitting on the floor. You eat with your right hand, mustn't use your left. I finally had to sit on mine, because it kept flying up to my mouth to help the right.

Now and then, one or another of the swamis would start a chant. I noticed particularly one sturdy old swami because he chanted with such enthusiasm. I could easily picture him as a young boy, just entering the monastery; he hadn't really changed at all. He had taken his vows unquestioningly and never faltered. Such a comical old man, his nose nearly meeting his chin. And all he has done with his life has been to take Ramakrishna's teachings absolutely literally. With the result that he has no children, no money, no fame, and isn't afraid of anything in this world or the next.

Later Prema lectured at the college, on the Vedanta Society of Southern California, showing slides made from his own photographs. Seen in this setting, they seemed exotic because they gave you such an exaggerated impression of American luxury and cleanliness. Even the freeway looked well swept, and the Hollywood shrine room appeared so sleek with polish, so well carpeted, that it was more like a hotel bedroom. The very flowers and trees had an air of wealth . . . I didn't feel that the students quite understood any of these pictures. Surely they must find them unnatural, almost sinister?

Then we were shown a documentary film of the procession which inaugurated the Vivekananda centenary celebrations, last winter—a straggling confusion of military cadets, banners, floats, cows, musicians, political speakers. Vivekananda appeared again and again—as a giant photograph, as a cardboard cutout borne aloft, as a plaster statue on a truck; absurd and yet imposing. And this all the students understood and applauded.

December 29. Swami, George, and I have moved into Calcutta. During the sitting of the Parliament of Religions, we are to stay at the International House of the Ramakrishna Institute of Culture, because it is much nearer to the place where the Parliament is being held. The International House is grand and well planned, but its floors are grimy with fallen dirt, like floors in New York.

That day, a Dr. Roy, whom we had just met, offered to get us a negative of one of the photographs taken on August 16, 1886, showing Ramakrishna's corpse lying on a cot, surrounded by his disciples, before being carried to the cremation ghat. Prema and I had already seen this and wanted to publish it in *Ramakrishna and His Disciples.*

Hitherto, the Math had been against displaying any of these photographs of the corpse, feeling that this would be in bad taste. When one of them was included among the illustrations to *The Gospel of Sri Rama-krishna,* its lower third had been cut off, so that only the mourners were visible, gazing down at what you couldn't see.

We objected to this censorship because it suggested that something repulsive had had to be concealed— which was not true. The corpse certainly hasn't been prettified and posed, as it would have been by Western morticians. It lies openmouthed, showing its teeth, look-ing totally discarded. But the general effect isn't shock-ing, merely a simple statement of the fact of death. Swami agreed with our point of view, adding that many representations of the crucified Christ with his bleeding wounds *are* repulsive, yet they are shown openly in churches. Thanks to Swami's persuasiveness, we got the Math's permission to publish.

The inaugural session of the Parliament of Religions began at 3:30 p.m. and went on for three hours. Not one of the speakers bothered to project his voice; they droned through their written addresses as if they were saying mass. There was an audience of about eight thousand people and I doubt if eight hundred of them really understood English. They sat there with—no, one can't call it patience—with animal passivity.

I got a rosette to wear, to show that I was a delegate of the Parliament; orange, with blue and purple ribbons, enclosing a soulful portrait of Swamiji which is in-scribed: "Every soul is potentially divine."

Then I went on with Swami to the Star Theatre, where Girish Ghosh used to act in and direct his own plays. Swami wanted me to see the old paintings of Ramakrishna and Girish which still hang there, backstage. The backstage part of the theatre is probably very much as they knew it; the rest has been modernized.

A performance was about to begin. Actors and actresses paused to bow to the paintings before going on stage. We went out front and watched the play for a while. I would gladly have stayed longer, if Swami hadn't wanted to get back to the Institute of Culture. Without understanding a word, I felt I could never tire of the actors' intonations and gestures, their delight in their own vitality. Bengalis seem born for the drama. I felt I was getting glimpses of the kind of fun Ramakrishna and Girish had together, during one of Girish's drunken visits.

As night falls, a hideous smoky fog closes down— from all the charcoal pots on the streets and the soft coal fires in the houses. In my room, even though it is air-conditioned, I began to wonder seriously if I shouldn't be choked in my sleep.

December 30. Swami didn't sleep much. He complains of the smoke but won't go back to the Math. Looking out the window at dawn, I saw bent figures in wispy smoke-colored garments moving silently about like emanations of the smoke, as they lit fires to create more smoke.

At the Parliament, Prema spoke on "Vivekananda through the eyes of an American," very well. Here he is obliged to wear the white robe of the brahmachari, which turns him into a (to me) disconcertingly austere figure who seems older than the Prema I know. We laughed about this, later.

When it was my turn to speak, I tried to pretend to myself that the whole audience could understand me. And I found myself instinctively working to strengthen this illusion by using the great keynote names over and over again—Ramakrishna, Vivekananda, Brahmananda, and even Gandhi. These produced automatic applause, as I had known they would. I began my speech by saying that I wished them to regard me as an Englishman, not an American—thus offering them a tribute to Vivekananda by a descendant of their oppressors.

One of the youngest swamis accompanied me back to the Institute, having fiercely repelled the journalists and bossed a way through the crowd for me, to the car. He was bubbling with indignation because the interpreter who was there to render the gist of our speeches into Bengali hadn't done so but had made comments of his own. The swami added that many people in the audience did understand English and that they would certainly have booed the interpreter if they hadn't been intimidated by the pictures of Ramakrishna and Vivekananda which hung behind the platform. These turned the hall into a sacred place, in which you had to behave yourself.

December 31. Just before going to bed, I started to get the gripes. I shivered a lot and couldn't sleep all night. Lying awake in the dark, I was swept by gusts of furious resentment—against India, against the senior swamis of the Math (not the younger ones), against Swami himself, even. I resolved to tell him that I refuse, ever again, to appear in the temple or anywhere else and talk about God.

Part of this resolve is quite valid. I do honestly think that, when I give these God lectures, it is Sunday Religion in the worst sense. As long as I quite unashamedly

get drunk, have promiscuous sex, and write books like
A Single Man, I simply cannot appear before people as
a sort of lay monk. Whenever I do, my life becomes divided and untruthful—or rather, the only truth left is in
my drunkenness, my sex, and my art. (There are, of
course, dozens of audiences which would be ready to accept the drink, sex, and art. To these I could also talk
about God without falseness. They might be embarrassed but they would listen. Such audiences are not to be
found within the Vedanta Society, however.)

This morning, a party of us went out to Narendrapur,
where the Ramakrishna Mission has a huge project, a
sort of Boys Town which includes schools, clinics, and
a farm. It is impressively efficient. We have been told
that the government favors the Mission because it is one
of the very few social-service agencies in which there is
no graft.

The hot sun made me feel sick, but it was lovely to be
out in the clean country air. I came back to the Institute
and lay down. One of the swamis soon appeared at my
door, wanting me to take on a chore—probably to un-
snarl the English in which some of the delegates'
speeches are written; I have done this a couple of times
already. I would perhaps have said yes if he had asked
me nicely, but he prodded me so peremptorily that I
acted dazed-sick until he went away frustrated.

January 1, 1964. A good omen. The first person to visit
my room was a young brahmachari named Sashi Kanto.
He had come to wish me a happy new year. He says his
name means "Moon Beauty" or "Husband of the
Moon." He is from somewhere near Bombay—a big
boy, bulky and yet graceful in his cocoon of white
muslin. The cropped hair and the little topknot which
he wears as a brahmachari suit the charm of his long

sensitive nose and dark soft velvet eyes. He seems incapable of anything but love. Such languishing looks, delicate hand touches, and flashing glances are only possible for the absolutely innocent. Every day, he washes Swami's and George's gerua robes, regarding the opportunity to do them this service as a great grace.

I am still resolved to tell Swami that I won't give any more religious talks after I leave India. But I'll offer to give two talks about this trip, one in Hollywood and one at the Montecito convent, and also two readings on other Sundays before he returns to California.

Dr. Biswas, who is the son-in-law of Swami's sister, came to give me a checkup. While he was examining me, I asked—to make conversation: "Are you in general practice, Doctor?" "No," he replied matter-of-factly. "I specialize in leprosy." His hands were touching my skin as he said this. It was silly of me, but I felt an involuntary recoil and had to cover it by expressing great interest. He said there is a lot of leprosy still around and no law compels lepers to report for treatment; many are ashamed to do this. People of all classes get it—usually during childhood, from lepers who are nursing them.

After lunch today, Swami told a lady, one of the Swiss delegates, to stop wearing hats. She had on a weird contraption, like a slipped turban. She explained that she wore hats at the meetings out of respect for our holy surroundings. Swami answered that that was merely an idea of St. Paul's; it doesn't apply in India. He advised her to wear gerua on her head if she felt she had to wear something. But later she appeared hatless, with a ribbon around her hair, and looked very nice.

I have been given another badge; the same design, but this one has the motto: "Mother, make me a man."

This afternoon, I presided at a session of the Parliament; each of us has to assume the office of president once. My speech was chiefly about Girish Ghosh and the ways in which I identify myself with him. One sentence was, approximately: "I wouldn't dare to claim to have one quarter of Girish's devotion, I would not even claim to have half as much artistic talent as Girish had—or half his capacity for drinking." This did <u>not</u> get a laugh. Nor did they laugh when I told the story about one of the swamis in San Francisco being asked: "Swami, how is it possible that these ladies who have been your disciples for many years are all such awful people?" To which the Swami replied, "If they had not come to Ramakrishna, they would all be murderesses."

Just as I reached the end of my speech, I was handed a piece of paper with the message: "Continue for fifteen minutes." This was because they had just realized that the next speaker wasn't going to show up. I ignored it and stopped, irritated by their thick-skinned bossiness.

January 2. Last night, when I was in the bathroom brushing my teeth, a young swami appeared whom I've been seeing quite a lot of—the same one who was angry with the interpreter. He is a dramatically handsome boy, with almost black eyes, very dark skin, tigerish white teeth. He had decided to come and talk to me, whether I liked it or not. So we talked for more than three hours.

He began by telling me about his relations with a senior swami whose personal attendant he had been. His eyes blazed with remembered passion and also with satisfaction at his own hypersensitivity, as he described how —after waiting on this swami faithfully and faultlessly for months—he made one little slip, forgot to get some medicine the swami had ordered. Next day, he was told that the swami had been very annoyed. So he became furious and went into the swami's presence spoiling for a fight. But the swami somehow conveyed to him by a

glance how much he loved him. So all was well. This
motif of a loverlike need for reassurance kept recurring
in our conversation. You are equally ready to leave your
guru and the monastery forever or to fall at his feet in
tears. Such scenes could obviously become as necessary
to one as playing Russian roulette. They would have to
be repeated continually.

His family consisted of freethinking intellectuals.
They would all have been horrified to hear that he had
made up his mind to be a monk. He became converted
by reading the works of Vivekananda, and decided to
join the monastery in Madras.

He left home without telling anybody, in the middle
of the night. He thought he had planned everything perfectly in advance, but there was a last-minute hitch. He
very nearly missed his train because, at that late hour, he
had great difficulty in finding anyone to carry his suitcase
to the station for him. It was unthinkable for this upper-
class boy to carry his own suitcase in public—even
though he was on his way to a place where he would
renounce his class, his family, and all his possessions! He
quite saw, now, how funny this was.

He delights in being a swami. In what other station in
life, he asks, would a young man be treated with such respect by his elders? Famous men and women actually
take the dust of your feet! I find such silliness endearing.
How wonderful to be so innocent! He told me encourag-
ingly that I shall become far better known for my book
on Ramakrishna than for any of my novels. Incidentally,
he thinks that Romain Rolland's book on Ramakrishna
is supreme; all I can hope for is to be second best.

This morning, Swami, George, and I drove to Brahmananda's birthplace, Sikra Kulingram. It is a tiny village out on the flat paddy fields of the Ganges delta,
enclosed by large lush trees. A shrine has been built on

the actual spot—as nearly as could be determined—where Brahmananda was born. And there is a guesthouse, where we were to stay the night.

During the drive I felt awful—partly upset stomach and headache but chiefly mere rage, expressing itself in that battle cry of the ego, They shan't push me around!

When we arrived, we were told that George and I would have to share a room in the guesthouse. Did I resent this? No, I'm certain I didn't. I immediately said that I had a headache and wanted to lie down. What the ego really wanted was time to figure out what to say to Swami. It knew it was going to make some kind of a scene, and this needed to be rehearsed.

As soon as I had finished rehearsing, I got up again and began walking around, feeling better already. It was quite warm, with a brilliant blue sky. The leaves were flashingly green. Dark smiling children sat among them, half hidden in the shadows.

I found Swami talking to one of the other swamis— one whom I temporarily hate, as my chief pusher-around. I took Swami aside and told him I was feeling sick and wanted to have the car take me back to Belur Math at once. Swami seemed bewildered. He said gently yes, of course, but wouldn't I have lunch first? His bewilderment frustrated me for a moment. I had expected that he would cue me into my scene by asking some leading question. I should have remembered that that isn't his way. I had to go on under my own steam, feeling myself beginning to lose pressure already.

"Swami—it isn't just that I'm sick. I feel awful about everything . . . I've made up my mind: I can't ever talk about God and Religion in public again. It's impossible. I've been feeling like this for a long time . . . I suppose I've wanted to spare your feelings, but that's not right, either. Why shouldn't I tell you how I really feel? After all, you are my guru. You have to be responsible for me, anyway . . . It's the same thing, really, that I used to think when I was living at the Center, in the old days: the Ramakrishna Math is coming between me and God. I can't belong to any kind of institution—because I'm not respectable—"

At this, Swami laughed, more bewildered than ever: "But, Chris, how can you say that? You're almost too good. You are so frank, so good, you never tell any lie."

"I can't stand up on Sundays in nice clothes and talk about God. I feel like a prostitute. I've felt like that after all of these meetings of the Parliament, whenever I've spoken . . . I knew this would happen. I should never have agreed to come to India. After I'd promised you I'd come, I used to wake up every morning and dread it—"

"Oh, Chris, I'm sorry. I shouldn't have asked you—"

"You know, the first time I prostrated before you, that was a great moment in my life. It really meant something tremendous to me, to want to bow down before another human being . . . And, here, I've been making pranams to everybody—even to people I've quite a low opinion of. And that takes all the significance out of doing it—"

This was outrageously disingenuous, because the pranams I referred to were only playacting, anyway. I couldn't have said it if Swami had been able to look into my eyes. But he wasn't. I was wearing sunglasses.

All this time, we were walking up and down in the sunshine, along a path between the ranks of bushes, with George somewhere in the middle distance and the swamis on the porch of the guesthouse, and the hidden children watching. It seemed to me that they all knew a drama was being enacted.

Swami looked at me with hurt eyes. He said, "I don't want to lose you, Chris." His utter dismay was enough to break my heart. And yet I knew that he, too, had begun to playact—to call my bluff. He knew perfectly well it was unthinkable that I should leave him under any circumstances. I told him so. He went on looking dismayed.

I felt guilty, but not very. There had been some truth of feeling in my outburst, even if it was negative feeling. I knew that it was far better to have spoken than not to have spoken.

The other swamis took the news that I was going back to the Math with slightly cynical impassivity. George gave me a strangely understanding grin.

We had a silent embarrassed lunch at which I ate only rice. Then the driver took me back to Calcutta in a cloud of red dust. Having had its tantrum, my ego relaxed. India seemed suddenly charming. I felt no impatience when our car was stalled behind trucks full of vegetables in the village of De Ganga, where there was a roadside market. I almost loved the dark-skinned countrypeople, shouting at each other in angry voices without anger. And I was so happy to get back to my room at the Math guesthouse.

When I told Prema everything that had happened, he was amused but showed no surprise. His lack of surprise made me suspect that he may have been through a similar scene with Swami, himself.

January 3. Went to the Cultural Institute; Swami was lying in bed there, with a cough, very rumpled and sad. He had become sick at Sikra Kulingram. The country dust was officially blamed for this, but I had a strong impression—later confirmed by Prema—that I was responsible. Swami is quite capable of getting sick in order to work on someone's feelings; though I doubt if he realizes this about himself—it is purely instinctive behavior. All I could do was to be extra-solicitous and, at the same time, remain absolutely firm in my decision.

Of course, by making this decision, I have blackmailed myself into carrying out my duties with twice as much zeal, as long as I am here. Since Swami was sick, I had to represent him at an official tea party for about fifty culture enthusiasts. After tea, the swami in charge made all of them shush and then asked me questions, which I had to answer in a voice loud enough to be heard by everyone. He tried hard to maneuver me into saying that I disapprove of the dirtiness of modern literature. I politely avoided doing so.

January 4. Today Prema and Arup got their heads shaved, in preparation for sannyas. Now they are in a dilemma; they hate exposing their baldness, yet they would like to get their skulls suntanned, to be less conspicuous. The shaven Bengali monks, with their brown skins, look perfectly natural.

Prema tells me he feels this shaving was a crossing of the Rubicon; now he is one hundred percent committed. He and Arup have already been issued their gerua robes, neatly folded, ready to be put on at the prescribed moment, during the sannyas ritual.

Preparations for the Vivekananda birthday celebration are now nearly complete. There is an arch over the entrance gate, tented entrances to the shrines, hung with glass chandeliers, and a pavilion containing all the books about Vivekananda in every language.

To Javadpur University, to give a question-and-answer talk to the students. This I enjoyed because I didn't have to be holy. They wanted to hear a lot about Huxley. The professor who introduced me is writing a book on Yeats. He and his wife had reproductions of Van Gogh and

Rouault in their apartment, and a copy of Burroughs's *Naked Lunch.*

At supper, Prema and Arup were eating as much as they could, because their fast begins tomorrow morning. Prema says that no one should take sannyas until the ego has been "smashed." He feels that his conflicts with some of the nuns at the Hollywood Center were really blessings—a form of disciplining by Mother Kali.

January 5. Until today, I've had diarrhea, but this morning's stool is thicker. I feel nothing but the dull senseless urge to get the hell out of here. Such is my longing for escape that I'm not even nervous about the flight; a sinister sign. Masturbated this morning, not because I really wanted to, just out of meanness. I'm mean and sullen.

This afternoon, Swami moved back into his room at the Math. He has a swelling on the side of his face which he is trying to reduce with hot compresses.

January 6. A terrific wailing and drumming of instruments burst forth at about 4:30 a.m., announcing the Big Day. Prema calls this "snake-charming music."

Found Swami concerned about his face. He told Prema, "I want to leave the body in India," so Prema is worried. Arup fell asleep—which is strictly against the rules, during the sannyas fast—and dreamed of pork chops.

The Math grounds were crowded all day. Thousands of devotees were fed from leaf plates. Loudspeakers shouted. Kirtan singers wailed. A line of people waited on the staircase to bow down in Swamiji's room. Nikhilananda was in a very good humor at breakfast this morning. He said, "This is the country of self-destruction."

In the afternoon there was a meeting at which Swami

presided and spoke, despite his ill health. I spoke, too. When we got back to Swami's room, he held out his hand and asked me to massage it. I did my best, telling him that I'd never massaged a hand before. He answered gaily, "Why can't you do something for Swami you never did before?"

He was in his "baby" mood. He kept dozing off but wanted us to stay in the room with him. Was he perhaps in a high spiritual state and giving us the privilege of serving the "It" which had taken him over? In that building, with Vivekananda and Brahmananda so powerfully present, this explanation didn't seem farfetched.

January 7. Woke with a sore throat to the noise of snakecharming music over the loudspeakers. But this poor old snake couldn't rise. However, I did get up at 7:30 and went out to look for the newly made swamis. I found Arup first. He is now Swami Anamananda; Anama means the Nameless One. He looks marvelous in his gerua; the color brings out the blueness of his eyes and the paleness of his skin. He was embarrassed but delighted when I prostrated. Then some other people ran up to him and bowed down. He raised his hand in blessing, so benevolently, like the ancient abbot of a monastery, and murmured, "Bless you."

I walked with him, and presently Prema came by, in a group of other new swamis on their way to beg alms. (You have to do this for three days after taking sannyas; but it's no big problem because there are pious families which have notified the Math in advance that they are ready to feed you, so you know just where to go.)

Prema is Swami Vidyatmananda. Vidya means Knowledge; Vidya-Atman means the Soul of Knowledge. However, since Vidya means knowledge-in-its-essence—that is, spiritual knowledge—there is really no distinction between the two terms. Prema could just as well have been called Vidyananda, except that there is another swami with that name.

I ran over to him and prostrated and he hugged me warmly. The onlookers were pleased, I felt, to see us Westerners playing the scene according to their rules.

Later, I went into Swami's room. Like nearly all the other swamis, he had been present at the sannyas ceremony during the dead hours of last night. He was being massaged by a young monk. He said, "You see—I massaged Maharaj, so now I get massage!"

Then Prema came back from begging alms, carrying some food in a begging bag. According to custom, he had to offer it first to Swami, as his guru. I took some, too. It was soupy and tepid. I nearly gagged on it and I noticed that Swami took very little, although he remarked, "This food must be very pure!"

Then Swami Gokulananda of the Ramakrishna Mission College came in with two of his students. Swami began telling the boys about Maharaj: "I tried to think lustful thoughts in Maharaj's presence, and I couldn't. I tried deliberately, and I couldn't . . . But such an experience will not be possible again until the Lord comes back to earth."

Then, having softened them up, Swami repeated the demand he made the other day, that the college must produce more monks. "Run away from here," he told one of the boys. Then, turning to Gokulananda: "Swami, buy him a railway ticket to Madras. He can join our monastery there. Otherwise, he will get married to a little girl." Then, to the boy, in an affectionately teasing tone: "Yes, you will get married! And afterwards you will say, 'I couldn't help it; when I wanted to be a monk, my mother cried, so I got married.' " The boy laughed, embarrassed. Swami told him, "Write to me when you join the monastery—not before!"

After this, Gokulananda sent the boys away, because he wanted to talk to Swami alone. (It was Swami who originally persuaded him to join the Order.) So I left, too.

Going up the stairs to the balcony, I found that the Vivekananda Room was open. A swami was cleaning it, no doubt because of the mess made by yesterday's visitors. I prostrated and touched my forehead to the bed, praying the only prayer which seemed appropriate to my present mood: "Give me devotion—even against my will." Then I vent onto the balcony, took out my beads, and laid them for a moment on the floor, just where Brahmananda had stood when Swami first met him.

In the afternoon, I packed and then sat for a while with Swami. He is feeling much better, but the doctor wants him to have his lungs X-rayed in Madras. He will stay for a while at the monastery there. He suggested that I should change my plans and go with him, but he wasn't insistent about this. I felt he didn't even expect me to agree.

I also talked to Prema, who is very happy at the prospect of remaining in India for maybe a year and working on various projects for the Order. Arup will return to Hollywood soon. I'm sure India won't see him again.

Suddenly it was time to begin the official goodbyes. Leaving a monastery seems a much more casual affair than arriving at one. When you arrive, they are humanly pleased to see you. When you leave, they are philosophically resigned—it's the Lord's will; and all travel is anyhow only within maya, for how can we ever leave His presence?

George volunteered to come with me to the airport. This caused a delay, because a kirtan was in progress and he had left his tape recorder running on the musicians' platform. We waited for them to stop playing. They didn't. So he had the embarrassment of having to go up to the platform and take away the recorder in full view of the audience.

At the airport, George said to me with a grin: "I suppose you'll be writing that diary all night?"

Eighteen

I did write quite a lot that night—the plane was so cold
that I couldn't sleep anyway, and I wanted to add notes
to my diary while my memories of Belur Math were still
clear. I knew they would begin to fade next morning,
after I had landed in Rome and joined some American
friends there. Already, during the flight, there was one
distracting element: a party of Australians who had
started out with the plane from Sydney. Loud-voiced
muscular men who looked like cricketers in their open-
necked white shirts with rolled-up sleeves, they seemed
to me much more exotic than Indians—the Farthest
West invading the Far East.

Later, when talking about that night, I used to claim
jokingly that it was then I had first become aware that
Vivekananda—grateful, no doubt, for my help in cele-
brating his centenary—had given me a charming thank-
you present, an idea for a novel. A month after this,
my diary mentions that I am considering a novel about
Prema taking sannyas. However, I didn't start writing
this novel for another whole year and I didn't finish it

until 1966. It was published in 1967 as A *Meeting by the River*. The final version has almost nothing in it which relates specifically to Prema; but he was my invaluable adviser throughout its writing, particularly on the essential question: How does it feel to be a Westerner who is a Hindu monk?

Swami stayed in India more than a month longer than I did. During much of this time he was sick—which perhaps explains the mood in which he returned to Hollywood:

March 15, 1964. When I was up at the Center, one of the nuns remarked that someone had come into the bookshop and asked for a guidebook to the temples of India. So I said, why didn't they stock a guidebook to India? And Swami grinned and said, "No, Chris—I will not deliberately send anyone to his death."

He is full of such cracks at present, and behind them you feel a real resentment; he keeps declaring that he will never never return to India, that he couldn't meditate at all while he was there. And yet he also tells how he and George went with one of the Belur Math swamis to meditate in the shrine of the Divine Mother at Dakshineswar and how they all three became aware that the image was alive!

September 18. The day before yesterday, I went up to the Center and worked right through the proofs of Ramakrishna and His Disciples, incorporating all the corrections suggested by our various advisers. Now, aside from checking the captions under the photographs, the whole job is done and the rest is up to the publishers.

India had a last straw to throw on my back, after all this while. Someone from the committee of the Parliament of Religions wrote saying that one of my talks isn't ready for publication because it was never properly recorded. So they want me to rewrite it. No, *I told Swami. Whereupon, he said he would do it. Oh, the blackmail! Of course I had to say that, if he did it, I would revise it later.*

November 18. Swami told us: "Think about death—and then you'll know what to pray for."

American and British reviews of *Ramakrishna and His Disciples* began to appear in April 1965 and continued to do so throughout that summer. The majority of them were unfavorable. And I suspected some of the few favorable reviewers of being fellow believers rather than purely literary admirers.

One recurring objection to the book was that I, who had written such worldly novels, was its author. "It is still a bit difficult to regard Herr Issyvoo as a guru-fancier." Such critics had evidently expected that I would handle this subject, also, with irony or treat it as high camp. My matter-of-fact presentation of biographical source material disappointed and bored them: "A reverent but rather colorless guide . . . The whole book is written in this for-the-children manner . . . A second-rate fairy-story . . . Poker-faced solemnity while describing some of the antics of Ramakrishna . . . Describes this feverish history in a vein of utter credulity."

For Ramakrishna himself, there was some rather patronizing praise: "An extraordinary being . . . piety beyond dispute . . . devotion, happiness and good cheer . . . a gay and even humorous man." There was only one half-accusation of homosexuality: "A transvestite and something of a coquette."

My impression was that many of the reviewers—including even some who were themselves unbelievers—felt offended by the suggestion that Ramakrishna could have been an avatar, since this was a denial of the uniqueness of Jesus as Son of God. Few showed any respect for Ramakrishna's spiritual experiences, declaring them to be without relevance to the problems of life, "not so much unbelievable as purposeless," "ecstasy without ethics," mere escapism. His loss of outer consciousness while in the state of samadhi was dismissed as "a sign of weakness, not strength."

And then, from the English and the Eastern Americans alike, came those predictable sneers at Southern California—which, it was claimed, the cult of Ramakrishna had had no difficulty in penetrating, because it is "Christendom's soft underbelly." There was even a sneer at Swami, who was judged guilty by association with the book, since I had dedicated it to him: "I have always been slightly suspicious of Indian sects who choose to establish themselves in this, the 'crank belt' of Southern California. No doubt, on one level, such a decision is logical enough; this, after all, is the region in which the 'lolly' is to be found in rich profusion and I suppose that even the most saintly swami cannot afford completely to disregard the more mundane pressures of life."

November 17, 1965. Tonight Swami told me that he'd been astonished "to find some old tendencies" which caused him to feel caste prejudice. An official of the Indian government had come to see him and he had realized "by various indications" that the man must be an untouchable. Nevertheless, Swami had invited him to lunch, but had been "so relieved" when the invitation was refused.

Swami was so funny, telling me this. It wasn't the prejudice itself which seemed grotesque to me, only its subtleties—Swami hadn't in the least minded shaking hands with this man, but he hated having to eat with him at the same table. "You see, Chris, they eat carrions."

"But this man doesn't eat carrion, does he?" I asked.

Swami was really shocked: "Oh no! Of course not! He is an educated man. He is sent by the Indian government!"

December 21. At the class last Wednesday, we reached this passage in *The Gospel of Ramakrishna:* "As a devotee cannot live without God, so also God cannot live without His devotee . . . It is the Godhead that has become these two in order to enjoy Its own bliss." This obviously moved Swami very much, but he seemed unable to explain to us why. It must be something he has actually experienced for himself.

May 31, 1966. Yesterday I finished my third and final draft of *A Meeting by the River.* I've always known that I would have to show it to Swami—since he will be held responsible for me if the Belur Math takes offense at anything in the book. I have no great respect for the Math's opinion. But the thought of Swami reading the homosexual scenes makes me squirm inside. Why? I would never apologize for them, morally or artistically; they are an absolutely necessary part of the story. Furthermore, Swami has praised me for being myself and making no pretenses about the way I live my

life. Just the same, I squirm. Am taking him the manuscript tomorrow.

June 3. Swami rang up to say he'd finished my novel.
"As I finished reading the last scene there were two
tears running down my cheeks." What an angel he is!
He was obviously every bit as relieved as I was that he
didn't have to say it would offend Belur Math. He even
suggested that it could be sold at our bookshop, but I
felt that this was just his relief speaking, he knew quite
well that it couldn't. He did also say that any Calcutta
reader would know I was referring to the Belur Math,
because there is no other monastery like it on that part
of the Ganges.

On June 18, we had the customary Father's Day lunch
at the Center, honoring Swami as our father. This year,
some of the monks put on a musical show, with
Vedantically revamped lyrics of the songs from *My Fair
Lady*. One of the lyrics was about me: "Blimey, he's a
blinking limey and a real fine bloke."

I was embarrassed but also touched and pleased. I am
always aware of a relationship to the monastics here. I
am still a member of their family, even though I now
know very few of my relatives well. As for the non-
monastic respectable majority of the congregation, it is
only Swami's approval which forces them to accept me
and pretend to themselves that they haven't heard lurid
and no doubt fairly accurate rumors about my life. The
fact that I've written the Ramakrishna biography and
worked on the Gita and the Shankara and the Patanjali
translations must make my novels less, rather than more

excusable in their eyes—it isn't as if I didn't know any better!

July 16. Swami said that Maharaj had told him that morality is unimportant if you have devotion to God. "But of course we can't preach that," Swami added, with a giggle.

I said that that was all very fine, but I personally could feel no devotion at all. Swami said, "Anyone who says he has devotion or thinks he has devotion doesn't have it. People come to me every week and talk about their devotion to God. And I don't believe them."

September 1. Swami is in hospital, with visiting forbidden. The doctor admits that he has had a slight heart attack but doesn't seem alarmed. As always, it must be very hard to judge how sick Swami is, because he relaxes so completely toward any illness. If it wants him to be sick, okay, he'll be sick.

September 16. Saw Swami, at the convalescent hospital they have just moved him to. He says he is seeing Maharaj in his dreams, every morning early. Once they were sharing a bed. He also had an anxiety dream in which he was looking for Maharaj and couldn't find him, and meanwhile George ran over someone in the car and cut off his leg!

January 10, 1967. We had supper with Swami. He seemed much better. He told us that he has been going to the shrine in the mornings lately, which is something he hasn't done in a long while. "I was there one hour," he told us, with satisfaction—and both Don and I noticed the utter unselfconsciousness with which he talks about himself.

In February, problems arose. Swami had arranged for a junior swami (Asaktananda) to be sent over from India; he was due to arrive shortly. Swami planned to train Asaktananda as quickly as possible, so that he would be able to act as assistant to Vandanananda, our assistant swami, when Vandanananda became head of the Center after Swami's death.

Now, however, Vandanananda had just decided to leave Hollywood and return to India. So a second swami was needed, a senior. He would probably be hard to get; Belur Math didn't like parting with its senior swamis. And if this senior swami was allowed to come, he, too, would be a stranger to American ways and would also have to be trained—with extra tact, because of his seniority. Swami would have his hands full.

"Well, Swami," I told him, "this means that you'll have to live another ten years at least." He grunted humorously and protested, "Not *ten!*" But I did feel that he was accepting the obligation to stay with us for a while.

June 17. To the Center for Father's Day lunch. Usually, it's unpleasantly hot, but this year it was so cold that I was afraid Swami would get a chill, sitting outdoors. He had put on thick long underwear, he told me. He is looking wonderfully calm and happy these days and his health seems quite good, although he has to have a prostate operation in August.

In the middle of lunch he suddenly turned to me and said quietly but with great emphasis, "Give Don my love." *He took my arm and pressed it, as though he were actually shooting it full of love for me to pass on to Don by transfusion, later.*

In 1966, Gerald Heard had had a stroke which paralyzed his arm. He recovered from this and had talked about it to all of us with his usual amused scientific objectivity, showing no anxiety about his future. However, this stroke had been followed by others. And now Don and I could visit him only occasionally, when the doctor allowed it.

August 3. Gerald is very weak now and speaks in a faint voice, though his articulation is fairly good. Our presence at his bedside seemed to amuse him; I felt that we were part of a profound metaphysical joke; the joke was that we were within maya and therefore absurd, but, at the same time, absorbingly interesting to him. (I'm paraphrasing what I think he said, because I couldn't understand all the words.) He added, quite clearly, "It doesn't alter one's affection; indeed, it increases it." We both felt his affection, strongly.

He kept laughing, rather wildly and weirdly; I could imagine Ramakrishna laughing like that, describing a vision he was having. He is very thin and looks much smaller, but seems relaxed and perfectly contented. And yet—what awful toil dying so gradually must be!

November 2. Yesterday I talked to a devotee who was much concerned because Swami, when he appeared on Les Crane's television interview show on October 24, had publicly admitted that he has had the lower form of samadhi.

True, this admission can have meant nothing to the vast majority of the viewers. What worried the devotee wasn't that he felt Swami had been indiscreet or a show-off, but that he was afraid Swami might be planning to die soon. He recalled how cagey Swami used to be about mentioning his spiritual experiences to outsiders, and cited the example of Ramakrishna, who only revealed his nature fully at the end of his life.

I asked Swami about this, when I went up to see him later. He laughed, and then apologetically explained that he had felt obliged to speak of his experience in order to make a distinction between it and the experiences of takers of lysergic acid and other drugs. "But I didn't describe the experience itself," he added.

People who keep imputing deep intentions to Swami understand him very little, I feel. As Don says, "He works on automatic, most of the time." Of course, one may agree—in fact, I think one is forced to agree—that his sayings sometimes show an uncanny insight. But I don't think he is always aware of this—I mean, I don't think he chooses to be aware.

Some of the more sentimentally superstitious devotees love to find evidence of precognition and other extra-sensory faculties in Swami's most casual remarks. They coyly accuse him of having conveyed cryptic warnings to them about the conduct of their private lives, or even of foreknowing what the weather will be like two weeks ahead. I find this superstitiousness extraordinarily irritating—no doubt because I indulge in it myself, from time to time.

January 19, 1968. Swami telephoned this afternoon that Richard is dead, of a heart attack. It is such ages since I saw him that I didn't feel a great shock. And yet I remember him so vividly as he used to be, when we were both living at the Center, twenty-five years ago. Swami sounded very sad. I suppose part of his sadness is because he still thinks of Richard as a monk gone to waste.

Richard's funeral was on January 23, at Santa Barbara. I went up there for it and so did Webster, which seemed to please his parents very much.

Swami told me that Richard had been through a period of heavy drinking, which he had recently stopped. As soon as he stopped, he became noticeably changed and full of love. They found him dead in bed, lying as if relaxed in sleep, with his hair still neatly brushed; there were no indications of a death agony. The only odd thing was that two tears had trickled down his cheeks from the outer corners of his eyes. This, said Swami, might be a sign that Richard had died after an ecstatic spiritual experience; when you shed tears in ecstasy, they flow from the eyes' outer corners. It was very much in accordance with Swami's beliefs that Richard should thus "remember" his true nature and realize the truth of his guru's teachings, just before leaving the body.

March 16. *Swami has been quite seriously sick, but is being moved out of the intensive-care ward at Mount Sinai Hospital today or tomorrow.*

April 11. *Saw Swami yesterday evening. He said that he had expected to die, the first day of his illness. He had decided that, if he got better, he would spend much more time in meditation; that was what he wanted to do now.*

He looked absolutely marvelous, a little thinner in the face, but not at all sickly. His face seemed to shine with lack of anxiety.

August 12. Yesterday we saw Gerald. The last few times, he has scarcely been able to speak at all. But he still seems perfectly aware of everything said in his presence. I notice that one can always get a reaction out of him if one mentions Chris Wood—who of course visits him regularly. If I make fun of Chris a little, Gerald utters a noiseless laugh. It is Love's last faint signal.

October 23. Swami, in a wonderful exalted mood, said, speaking of Maharaj, "Chris—to think of it! I saw him!" His joy, the nowness of it, was so beautiful.

January 11, 1969. Got up at 5:30 and drove into Hollywood, to read at Swamiji's breakfast puja. After I'd read, I went in to see Swami, who is still officially sick but actually quite himself. There he was, lying in bed, snugly tucked in, with me prostrating before him. He looked out at me over the edge of the bed as though he were in a boat and I were swimming alongside. Then he made an effort and raised himself a little, acknowledging my prostration.

The puja had turned me on even more than usual—I think because of George, who had somehow filled the shrine room with joy. I wanted to talk about this to Swami—to ask him to make me feel like this all the time, instead of once a year—but I couldn't. However, as so often, he seemed to know what was in my mind, and said, "Just think, Chris, Swamiji himself appeared in that shrine!"

In March, the Mark Taper Forum of Los Angeles presented a stage adaptation of Bernard Shaw's story "The Adventures of the Black Girl in Her Search for God." This adaptation had been made by me, with the help of Lamont Johnson, who was to direct it. A party from the Center, including Swami, went to see it. This sort of irreverent joking about Jehovah and Jesus was very much to Swami's taste, so he loved the play. Would he have loved it if Krishna and Rama had been made fun of in the same manner? No.

May 31. Saw Swami this afternoon. He is in excellent health and spirits. He tells the same old stories, but every story is spiritually fresh each time. Today he told how Maharaj had come into the room, whispered in his ear the question Jesus asked Simon Peter: "Lovest thou me?" and then left the room again. This time, the story seemed extraordinarily spooky; it made my flesh creep and my eyes water. Swami wouldn't have needed to explain, even to an outsider, that Brahmananda hadn't meant, "me, Brahmananda." Swami's tone and manner made that obvious.

He told me also that he has come more and more to realize that Maharaj, Swamiji, Holy Mother, and Ramakrishna are "all the same." He said it was a long time before he could really feel the presence of Ramakrishna but that now this comes to him very strongly.

September 1. While Swami and I were alone together, he giggled and said, "It's a terrible profession, being a swami. Even I, in my old age—a woman wrote me and said, 'You are the star in my blue sky.' Imagine!"

October 21. A couple of weeks ago, when I came to see Swami, I took the dust of his feet. I don't often do this, it was a sudden impulse. Swami said quickly, "What's the matter, Chris—you aren't ill?" Which struck me as wildly funny. It sounded as if he thought that a sudden anxiety about my health had made me extra pious.

January 3, 1970. I saw Swami yesterday. He told me that, when the palpitations came over him while he was up at the Montecito convent, he had felt quite detached, as if his body belonged to someone else. "I felt a flustering in my chest and I was like an observer."

May 31. Swami called me on the phone because he wanted to read me a passage from a letter Vivekananda wrote to the Hale Sisters on July 31, 1894. He said, "I was reading it this morning and it made me cry."

"Stick to God! Who cares what comes to the body or to anything else! Through the terrors of evil say—my God, my love! Through the pangs of death say—my God, my love! Through all the evils under the sun say —my God, my love! Thou art here, I see Thee. Thou art with me, I feel Thee. I am Thine, take me. I am not of the world's but Thine, leave not then me. Do not go for glass beads, leaving the mine of diamonds. This life is a great chance. What, seekest thou the pleasures of the world! He is the fountain of all bliss. Seek for the highest, aim at that highest, and you shall reach the highest."

July 15. Swami told me how he was lying in bed, not long ago, in the middle of the night, and his little finger began to twitch and suddenly the thought came to him:

I have no control over this body, it is the Lord who controls it. And this made him ecstatically happy and he was awake for a long while, "having a wonderful time." He also told me that often while he is meditating he imagines that he is in the Ramakrishna loka: "They are all there and I am their servant."

August 17. Swami told me to try to make my mind a blank before meditating, and then to try to feel that I am in the presence of Ramakrishna, Holy Mother, Maharaj, and Swamiji. I asked, "Is it all right if I think of you there, too?" He said yes.

He also told me, as he has before, to say to myself that I am the Atman and that it doesn't really make any difference whether I am aware of this or not. I am the Atman, and that's that. This I do find helpful, because it makes all my fretting and fussing and fuming merely ridiculous.

September 20. My meditation is almost absurdly bad. Yet I am going through the motions regularly, twice a day, and isn't that something? And I am living with someone who also practices meditation, which is a great blessing and encouragement.

October 21. Swami has been ill again. I always feel that this is partly because his illness helps us to exert pressure on the Belur Math to send us another swami. Now his doctor has written them a letter and several of us have sent cables, saying how urgent this is.

(Belur Math did finally send a swami—not a senior but a junior, and not until June 1971. His name was Chetanananda.)

Whenever I see Swami nowadays, I take the dust of his feet on arriving and leaving. I do this because by doing it I make it easier for myself to think of him impersonally, as the Guru, when I'm meditating.

Once he said, "You don't have to do that every time." So I explained why I was doing it. This seemed to amuse him.

December 30. In one respect, I find Swami much more wonderful than those direct disciples who had all known Ramakrishna and were able to live together, sustaining each other in moments of doubt and weakness. I have always felt, since I first knew him, how hard it must be for him, here in this alien land, and I suppose I thought it possible that he wouldn't be able to bear it and would go back to India one day. But he's still here, an old man and all alone—for, however much we love him, we can none of us be really close companions. And yet, lo and behold, his faith has grown and grown and is its own reward. What else need any of us do but meditate on his achievement?

January 29, 1971. Went to Mount Sinai Hospital and saw Swami, so tiny and bird-legged and so beautiful with his silver hair. He was attended by two nurses, one Thai, the other Japanese. He said, "They are my daughters"; and already they seemed somehow to have become devotees, without quite knowing of what.

The earthquake of February 9 was felt even more violently in Hollywood than by us in Santa Monica. Swami told us that, when it started, he got out of bed, put on his robe, and went to stand in the doorway of his bathroom. As he did so, he remembered a text in

Sanskrit: "If Krishna saves, who can kill? If Krishna kills, who can save?"

February 21. I went to see Swami yesterday afternoon, having been told that I could, although he was feeling tired and his pulse was missing beats and he had slight asthma, which the doctor said was due to his heart condition.

I arrived early, so I went into the shrine room and sat up close in front of the shrine. I don't know when I did this last—not in years. It is quite different, and not nearly so satisfactory from my point of view, to sit at the side—as I do when I read at the Vivekananda breakfast pujas. I often try to imagine myself sitting alone in front of the shrine when I'm meditating here at home.

It began working almost at once and without my making any effort. I just kept reminding myself that it was before this shrine that Swami had had his visions and Sister used to see "the light" and George had been chanting for nearly thirty years. I exposed myself to it as though it were some kind of medical radiation and I were the patient, but I did try to include Don in the exposure. However, just when I imagined myself to be open to it, without any resistance, one of the nuns came into the shrine room and whispered apologetically that Swami was ready to see me. So I got up and left, telling myself that he is a human shrine, and therefore much more extraordinary, and that he contains relics too, his memories of Maharaj and the other disciples.

I found Swami looking surprisingly well. He described his latest treatment in great detail and with obvious relish, as he always does, and then told me that the doctor had asked him, "Are you depressed?" and that he'd answered, "Oh no, I'm never depressed!"

This may not be literally true; Swami certainly has his gloomy moods. But the beautifully amused smile with which he said it did express what I think he meant: once you have known a Maharaj, you may still get upset about trifles, but you can never again become really depressed, because real depression is losing your faith that life has meaning.

May 5. Swami told me that he had just initiated a woman he thought was slightly crazy. He did it because her husband begged him to, but he didn't like doing it. She smelled of garlic all over her body. (Could she have feared that Swami was a vampire, I wondered?) During the initiation, the figure of Krishna fell off the shrine and broke its pedestal, and Swami was so upset that he couldn't think of a mantram to give her—at least, not for a long while; and she couldn't make up her mind which chosen ideal to choose . . . This scene suggests to me the style of a new kind of religious farce.

May 11. At the end of the question period in the temple, Swami was asked, "Does the guru ever withdraw his love from a disciple?" The question sounded to me, and, I think, to most of us, subtly hostile and provocative. Swami answered, "I don't know yet."

The lazy good-humored tone of voice in which he said this was startlingly comic. It came out of his mouth so spontaneously, with such perfect timing, that everybody laughed and a lot of us clapped. It made me imagine a very relaxed Jesus, kidding and verbally sparring with Satan during the temptation in the wilderness.

August 4. We were talking about Hindus and Moslems, and Swami—to illustrate the fact that he had been on good terms with Moslems in his youth—told how, when he was on a train going to visit Maharaj, he sat down next to a Hindu priest. Suddenly the priest groped him, right up beside his crotch—Swami didn't use those words but he indicated the position of the priest's hand. "I felt very narvous," he said. "I didn't know what it was about." Sitting opposite to him were three Moslems. They saw what was happening and invited him to come over and sit with them, which he did. They also offered him food, which he didn't accept, although he appreciated their kind gesture.

(I couldn't help thinking that what this story really illustrated was the height of the social barrier between Hindus and Moslems, if such a drastic situation was needed to break it down!)

On August 14, early in the afternoon, Gerald Heard quietly stopped breathing. Michael Barrie, his devoted friend and secretary, was at his bedside. Later that day, Gerald's body was taken to the anatomy department of the medical school at the University of California, where it would be used for dissection or research and then cremated and buried without record. Gerald had made this arrangement many years previously and used to refer to it in conversation with his friends—some of whom, I believe, were slightly shocked.

Gerald's life had always seemed to me to have the aspect of an artistic performance, expressed in a language of metaphors and analogies. I now asked myself the question: Did his performance still seem valid, as true art must, in relation to the terminal mystery? I felt that it did—that our glimpses of him, undergoing this searching five-year test, had been powerfully reassuring. I believed that he had indeed been able to see his temporary state of dying in the context of what is both now and always "the real situation," and that therefore one of his favorite metaphors, "taking a look around the corner," had now become a description of his actual experience.

That day, I wrote in my diary:

I am only just beginning to realize that it has happened, at last. My chief feeling at this moment is that I would like to get on the air and tell the brute stodgy thick-skinned world that it has lost one of its few great magic mythmakers and revealers of life's wonder.

Swami said that Gerald had been able to come through this test so triumphantly because of the many hours he had spent in meditation. Michael Barrie had been tested, too. Toward the end, he had nursed Gerald single-handed, month after month, seldom leaving the house, being determined to spare him the one ordeal Gerald dreaded, a move into a hospital. Now Michael looked years older than his age, gray-faced and emaciated. Luckily, he still had enough stamina to make a recovery. Swami arranged for him to live at Trabuco. He stayed there several years.

September 22. Swami talked about grace and was so beautiful, so shining. He said that he didn't feel he had ever gone through any particular spiritual struggles; Maharaj had made everything easy for him. "All those visions I had, Chris, I never felt I had really earned them." As Swami said this, he positively shone with grace, he was the lucky one and his luck was adorable. When I left, I made an extra-long prostration until he said, "Get up now." Maybe he was embarrassed, feeling that I was worshiping him. And I was, but it wasn't <u>him</u>.

October 1. When Swami spoke of Maharaj last night, it was as if he had seen him only a few moments before. These weren't like the boyhood memories of an old man. I realized, more vividly than I usually can, what Swami means when he keeps saying that Maharaj is present with him.

Just before I left, he said in his unaffected childlike way that he was hungrier than he thought, and he phoned the kitchen and asked for a lamburger to be fixed for his supper. What seems childlike is that he never apologizes for showing appetite or otherwise taking pleasure in something "worldly," as "holy men" are expected to.

October 27. Saw Swami for five minutes—all that the doctor allows. He was sitting up in a chair in his room, having been told not to sit with his legs crossed, as that interferes with the circulation. (What can Americans know about Bengali circulation, I couldn't help thinking; Bengalis are practically born cross-legged.)

He seemed pleased to see me but was very quiet and withdrawn. Somehow he had an air of having been deserted. I asked him if he had had any spiritual experiences and he said, rather forlornly, "No—you see, Chris, I couldn't eat anything. When you don't eat you can't think. I realized for the first time what it means in the scriptures when it says that food is Brahman." He also told me that there were "gray waves" before his eyes when he looked at anything, because of his cataracts.

November 11. They are giving Swami tests to find out if his almost continual dizziness is due to bad circulation, or what. George and Len both sleep in his room, now —Len, as a former pharmacist's mate in the British

Navy, knows how to keep check on Swami's pulse at intervals, during the night. Swami complains that this overcrowding makes the room become "smelly." But he says that he can nearly always go to sleep by telling himself that Holy Mother's feet are touching his head.

January 5, 1972. Swami told me that he had made only one big mistake in his life. This was in Madras, while Maharaj was still alive. Maharaj was about to leave the monastery and go elsewhere. He instructed Swami to visit various places of pilgrimage and meditate there. When he had finished doing this, he added, "I shall miss you." This was when Swami feels he made his big mistake. He believes that he should have said, "I'm coming with you," and that, if he had said this, and insisted, Maharaj would have agreed.

In that case, they would have been together for more than a year—the rest of Maharaj's life. Swami believes that, during this period, Maharaj might well have taught him certain special spiritual disciplines which Maharaj had learned from Ramakrishna and had never taught to anyone. But, as it was, Maharaj left Madras without Swami and they never met again.

February 16. Yesterday we went to the vespers of the Ramakrishna puja. Swami was in the shrine room when we arrived. He looks much better, almost his old self. He had initiated someone that morning and someone else the morning before.

Asaktananda was doing the worship. Before he had finished, Swami stood up to leave the temple and return to his room. But then, on a sudden impulse, he stopped and began talking to all of us.

He told us how, immediately after he had joined the

monastery, he had been present at the Ramakrishna puja with Brahmananda, when Brahmananda had had a vision of Ramakrishna. There were musicians in the shrine room and Brahmananda had asked one of them to move his instrument a little, because it was touching the robe of the figure of Ramakrishna, which Brahmananda but nobody else could see.

Having had this vision, Brahmananda had declared that anybody, anywhere, who on that day took the name of Ramakrishna would be liberated. Swami ended by saying that he was sure that this was still true, and he made us chant Ramakrishna's name.

After we had been touched by the relics, we went to Swami's room. (Being touched by the relics raises a tricky question of protocol, if Don and I are both present. Since I am one of the oldest householder devotees, Asaktananda has taken to calling me up into the shrine room immediately after the male and female monastics have made their prostrations. Thus I save maybe as much as twenty minutes of hanging around, waiting my turn amidst the rest of the congregation. But this time saving is of no use if I then have to wait for Don, so I've persuaded him to follow right in my footsteps, just as married couples make their prostrations one after the other. No doubt this causes a lot of ill feeling. It must seem to anti-homosexuals that our relationship is thus receiving a sort of sanction by the Vedanta Society. But I refuse to be embarrassed.)

We found Swami on the telephone, trying with great difficulty to cut short a torrent of long-distance conversation from a well-wishing devotee. Don and I knelt and took the dust of his feet and he blessed us with his free hand, while still phoning. Then, as we sat on the floor in front of him, he insisted on our taking prasad—a big fat-making slice of rich cake each, and coffee for Don and tea for me, and then two tangerines each to take away with us.

March 8. This evening, when Don and I were in Swami's room, one of the senior nuns asked me to help them do something to discourage the personality cult of Swami, which, according to her, is getting more and more feverish and ridiculous. Since Swami has been isolated for quite long periods by his various illnesses, he has become a rarity—no longer someone whom everybody can easily get to meet. So now there are young girls who actually weep whenever they do see him, and people who stand around in the garden outside the door to his room, hoping they'll get a glimpse. When he's able to go out for a walk, quite a lot follow him in a procession.

Don told me later that he had agreed with what the nun said—also that he had felt Swami hadn't liked hearing it, although he hadn't made any kind of protest. My own feelings are mixed. On the one hand, I agree that the cult exists and that it has gotten much stronger lately. And even when I first came to the Center I was disgusted by the way some devotees gushed over Swami. It is true that a post-mortem cult of Swami might make it very difficult for whoever has to succeed him. And then again, as Don pointed out, this is, officially, a Vedanta Society first and foremost; the cult of Ramakrishna is only practiced by those members who wish to practice it. Vedanta, in its purest form, negates all cults, even cults of divine beings.

On the other hand, I personally am a devotee first and a Vedantist second. I flatter myself that I can discriminate —bowing down to the Eternal which is sometimes manifest to me in Swami, yet feeling perfectly at ease with him, most of the time, on an ordinary human basis. My religion is almost entirely what I glimpse of Swami's spiritual experience. I still firmly claim that this isn't a personality cult.

Nevertheless, it is possible that I have encouraged others to practice a cult of Swami. Because, when I talk to people about him, I am nearly always talking about him as the Guru, not as Abanindra Nath Ghosh. Therefore, I am apt to say, for example, that I believe—and I do believe it—that it is a tremendous privilege to set eyes on Swami even once and that a single meeting might have incalculable effects upon an individual throughout the rest of his life . . . I suppose that's certain to be understood as cult talk.

Nineteen

June 1, 1972. Swami told us that people sometimes ask him for a Brahman mantram when they are initiated, but then usually want to exchange it later for a mantram containing the name of some divine personage. The Impersonal God nearly always proves unsatisfactory as a subject for meditation.

July 14. Swami told how Gerald, shortly before his illness, had had a dream in which he was at Belur Math, and Ramakrishna was also there, surrounded by his disciples. As Gerald walked past them, Ramakrishna pointed to him and said, "That one belongs to me." Swami had heard this from Michael Barrie.

July 16. We have been told—as though this were something shocking—that Swami made a scene while he was staying at Trabuco recently: he sent back his piece of chicken to the kitchen, saying that it was undercooked, and that if there was no one who could cook his chicken properly for him he would have to return to Hollywood.

Okay, so the holy man flew into a tantrum. How dreadful! But don't monks (and nuns) need discipline?

July 20. Swami's eyes are getting worse; he strained them by too much reading and writing. His doctor is against letting him have a cataract operation, because of his weak heart.

Swami told us how some young girls who were Krishna devotees once began worshiping Brahmananda as the Baby Krishna. This caused him to go into samadhi. They brought milk and tried to feed it to him as one feeds a baby, but he couldn't swallow it, having lost outer consciousness; it dribbled down his chin . . . Swami hadn't included this story in The Eternal Companion because he felt that Western readers might find it too exotic.

August 3. Supper with Swami at the house in Malibu which a devotee has lent him for his summer holiday.

Once again—nearly thirty years after the event!— Swami referred to Ashokananda's accusation that we had insulted Vivekananda, and to his own reassuring vision of Vivekananda which had followed it. This time, however, he added something to the story which I had never heard before—astonishing us by remarking, almost casually, that, just before he had the vision, he had been considering suicide: "How could I live if I had insulted Swamiji?"

"Surely," I said, "you couldn't have considered killing yourself and leaving your work unfinished? That isn't like you." From my point of view, this had to be either just a bit of Indian hyperbole or a staggering revelation of the depth of his devotion. Well, maybe I don't take his devotion seriously enough, even after knowing him all these years.

Glancing along the bookcase in Swami's bedroom, it

seemed to me at first that his hostess had carefully stocked it with exclusively religious reading matter. But accidents will happen. In between The New Testament in Modern Speech and St. Francis de Sales's Treatise on the Love of God, I came upon Myra Breckenridge.

September 15. When we were alone with him in his room, Swami told us that he can read very little now, because of his cataracts. I asked, "Don't you miss it?" and he answered, with the sweetest significance, "I don't miss anything."

He came into the dining room, to eat supper with the nuns and us. When we'd finished eating, he began to talk about Maharaj and Premananda: "When you were with them, you were in another world." He described how Maharaj would call for his water pipe, take a few puffs, and then become absorbed in meditation—"he'd go away somewhere else." Having remained in this state for a long while, he would "come back" and exclaim with surprise that his pipe had gone out.

The nuns have a microphone fixed in a flower vase on the dining table, so that Swami's words can be un-obtrusively tape-recorded when he is in the mood to talk. Swami was certainly in the mood this evening, but his talk soon left the spiritual heights and became gossip about the progress of the various Vedanta centers in the United States—which swamis had made a success of their work and which had flopped. Swami has followed all this with an interest which would shock some of the more sentimental devotees. I have always realized that he is keenly competitive where the swamis of his own age group are concerned and determined to believe that our Center is the Best in the West. I found him funny and charming in a hard-boiled way, like a veteran actor reminiscing about show biz.

October 4. Swami asked me about my meditation. I said I was finding it helpful to keep reminding myself how near my death may be. Swami then told me that Vivekananda had said: If you are trying to know God, you must imagine that death is already gripping you by the hair. If you are trying to win power and fame, you must imagine that you will live forever.

December 27. Don and I went to the vespers of the Holy Mother puja. Asaktananda was doing the ritual, and he seemed to be behaving with an informality which was surprising and impressive, considering that he has such a serious devotional character. There was a lot of laughter from the monks and nuns inside the shrine room, I don't know what about. When it was my turn to be touched with the relics, Asaktananda said, "Chris, I thought you were still in New York!" and his tone was like that of a host at a party.

February 23, 1973. Swami described a meeting he had had with one of his disciples, whom he hadn't seen for some time. They had had some friction in the past and now the disciple had asked him, "Are you still angry with me?" Swami told me he had answered, "The guru in me was never angry with you—only the man. If the guru had been angry, then nothing in the three worlds could have saved you."

This reply startled and jarred on me; I was shocked by its seeming arrogance. But then Swami explained that "the guru in me" wasn't himself at all; it was the Lord. He added, "I never feel that it is I who am initiating a disciple; it is the Lord."

April 6. I asked Swami, did he fear death. He said no, not at all. But he then repeated a story he has told me before: how, when he was going to have a double-hernia operation and had to fill in a form relieving the surgeon of responsibility in the event of his death, he had felt afraid and had prayed to Maharaj for release from his fear. It had left him immediately.

April 18. Something reminded me that Gerald Heard had once told me, back in 1939, that Swami had talked of arranging for him to take sannyas. I asked Swami if this was so. Swami said that it was, and added: "And you too, Chris—even now—why don't you come back to us?" I said, "I'm not fit to," and he answered, "Only the Lord can judge who is fit." We looked at each other and he giggled.

He giggled again at supper when he told the nuns, "Chris is going to become a monk." I laughed, and the girls laughed, too, watching my face uneasily to see if this really was only a joke. It was very odd and disturbing. Doesn't Swami accept my present way of life, after all? I had begun to believe that he did.

(This was, in fact, the last time that Swami made such a suggestion to me. What had moved him to do it? It was just one of his mysterious impulses.)

At the question period last week he was asked, "Should one regard the guru as being the same as God?"—to which he unhesitatingly answered, "Yes." Then he added: "But I'm not that kind of guru." "What kind of guru are you?" someone asked. Swami answered, "I am the dust of the feet of Maharaj." Then he smiled: "There is some holiness even in the dust."

May 2. When I went to see Swami I got a very powerful vibration from him. It began when I asked him what he does all day, now that he can't read. He said that he feels the Lord's presence. I asked him if he meditates. He said no, not in the daytime. When he meditates, it is either on the Guru in the center of the brain or on the Lord in the center of the heart.

Then he began to recite the formal meditation on the Guru, partly in English and partly in Sanskrit: "He is making with the right hand the sign which dispels fear and with the left hand he is bestowing his blessings on me. He is calm and he is the image of mercy and he is pleased with me . . ."

This recitation was interrupted by the arrival of George, to help Swami get dressed to go to the temple for the class. (This is one of George's prerogatives and I know, without Swami's ever having had to tell me, that I must never help him dress, even if George arrives late.)

Then Swami took my arm for the walk to the temple. (This is my prerogative.) I always try to meditate on the Guru while we're walking, but my vanity at being Swami's attendant and entering the temple with him in front of all those people usually spoils my concentration.

This evening, just as we were about to go into the temple, Swami suddenly continued his recitation with the words, "He is pleased with you, smiling, gracious . . ." I don't know if he said "you" instead of "me" intentionally, but I couldn't help taking it personally and feeling that the Guru was speaking to me through Swami. It was an extraordinary moment.

June 7. Swami told us that he hadn't slept more than two hours the night before. I asked, "So you made japam nearly all night?" And he answered, with a sort of comic ruefulness, "What else should I do?"

June 14. An absurd situation arose when I came into Swami's room. As usual, I prostrated and touched his feet with my forehead. As I started to get up again, I saw his hand extended over me. In my dumb vague way, I thought he was holding out his hand for a handshake, so I tried to take it. Immediately he raised his hand a little, out of my reach. So I reached up for it, rising slightly to do so. He raised it still higher—which was quite awkward for him, since he was still seated in his armchair . . . And then at last I realized—he was blessing me! I was terribly embarrassed, but he didn't laugh.

June 23. Swami's Father's Day lunch. The emergence of Swami from his room, into the garden, was particularly ceremonious this year;, the procession included Pavitrananda from New York, George, Asaktananda, Chetanananda, and me. I had been in Swami's room with the others and tried to slip around and join the crowd. But Asaktananda grabbed my arm and held me firmly. So we took our turn in facing the clicking and flashing cameras of the massed devotees. It was as if we had just gotten married.

At last we were all seated amidst the flowers at the central table, under the colored parachute-silk awnings spanned from the tree limbs—like saints in a farcical heaven. Swami reproved the monks because some of them had started to eat before he did. He was in that kind of a mood. Then came some very tough meat and the usual blush-making songs.

And then Swami spoke. His speech was dismayingly long and rambling—a history of our Vedanta Society, told chiefly in terms of the sums of money donated for various building projects, in Hollywood, Montecito, and Trabuco. Swami also alluded to Heard, Huxley, and me

—saying that, as he put it, "although I am nothing," these famous men had sat on the floor in his presence! There was a vanity in this which Don and I both minded, not because it was vanity but because it seemed so senile. I have never heard Swami talk in this tone before. When it was over, he was obviously exhausted. He went to his room, saying that he wanted to be alone.

October 11. When we went to see Swami yesterday evening, we had already heard rumors of what had happened to him at the Montecito temple, on the 6th. Swami told us the whole story, in his objective way, as though he were describing a sudden attack of appendicitis.

It was during the celebration of the Durga puja. While Swami was offering a flower at the shrine, he was suddenly overwhelmed with emotion, realizing how gracious Mother had been to him. He burst into tears. Chetanananda had to help him out of the shrine room and into the little office room at the back of the building. Chetanananda said to Swami, "This is a sign of the great grace Mother is showing you"—at which Swami began to cry again and couldn't stop for some time. He begged Chetanananda not to mention Mother's name to him again. When he had regained control of himself, he went back into the temple and blessed the congregation, lest they should think he was sick. After this, he became "very jolly." The nuns told him that his face looked changed; it was flushed.

Swami seemed very well when we saw him, though perhaps a bit tired. Now they are getting ready to celebrate the Kali puja here. One of the nuns came in to speak to Swami about the hiring of a boat—to take the worshipers out after the puja is over, so they can drop *the statue of Mother Kali into the sea. Swami immediately got angry: "I don't want to hear about that. It's like arranging the baby's funeral before it is born."*

(After a statue has been worshiped in the shrine room, it must either be disposed of at once or else worshiped daily from that time forward. Perhaps Swami's indignation was due to the intensity of his experience at Montecito, making him more than ever convinced that the Divine Mother actually enters and is present within the material object which represents her.)

December 5. This evening, Swami asked me if I had had any "experiences." That's the word I always use when I ask him the same question. I found myself instantly in a state of strong emotion. I told him that I hadn't had any experiences, but that that didn't matter, because at least I know now that, if I hadn't met him, my life would have been nothing. My voice was shaking and tears ran down my face. Swami didn't say anything but his face became aloof in that way it does when he is in a spiritual mood—"deserted," one might call it, because one feels that he is "out of himself." We were silent for a long time.

December 27. Yesterday was Swami's eightieth birthday. Before lunch, talking to the monks from Trabuco, he really gave forth power. He retold the "lovest thou me?" story about Brahmananda, and then added: "And I didn't love him."

Despite all my years of indoctrination, my reactions are so conventional that I was puzzled and shocked, and I asked him almost indignantly, "What do you mean?"

And Swami answered, in that matter-of-fact tone in which he sometimes talks about the deepest mysteries:

"How many of us can love God? How many of us can return that love? It's too big for us. We can't understand it. He loves all of us, everybody, without any motive. How can we understand that?"

After lunch in the dining room, he signed to me to take his arm to help him walk back to his room. However, on the way there, he had to stop and receive the pranams of every single monastic member who was visiting the Center that day. My first instinct was to withdraw my hand, but he held it firmly under his left arm. So there I stood, like an inferior Siamese twin, attached to this being, through whose right hand Brahmananda's blessing was conferred, again and again, on these bowed heads! All I could do was to keep my eyes lowered and try not to seem to participate outwardly in the giving of the benediction. It was an absurd and embarrassing and beautiful situation to be in.

January 14, 1974. I read the Katha Upanishad at Swamiji's breakfast puja. Asaktananda did the worship but Swami felt well enough to come into the shrine room and sit on a chair.

When the breakfast tray was brought in, Asaktananda made mudras in formal style over the food, before pouring the coffee and lighting the cigarette. Swami objected to this strongly. He was so concerned that he got out of his chair and down on his knees behind Asaktananda and reproved him, telling him that this isn't a ritual offering like others and that one shouldn't make mudras—"because Swamiji is alive."

I felt that Swami shouldn't have corrected Asaktananda like that. It embarrassed him in front of all of us. I saw that Asaktananda was deeply hurt. He showed this at breakfast by becoming silent and very Asian. He wore his scarf over his head with his cap on top of it, which reminded both Don and me of women wearing snoods under their hats, during the forties. This, too, seemed somehow a kind of protest.

Perhaps Swami himself felt that he had been unkind. When we saw him later, he indirectly defended his behavior by saying that Sister never used to make mudras at this puja. She simply served the breakfast, as she had served it to Swamiji when he was physically present.

February 11. Yesterday I saw Swami, who is leaving with George and Len to stay at a house near the Montecito convent. Len describes Swami as being "testy." To me he seemed only rather remote. He made me think of an animal which waits passively—until it either feels better or stops living.

Then, with sudden nervous energy, he began instructing a somewhat intimidated junior nun how to pack his bag. She was told to put in his winter socks and his black-and-white scarf. (It is black and gold, but she didn't dare to point this out to him.)

George was there, too, unflappable, getting scolded and taking it as a grace. Why should he ever worry about anything, any more? He has it made.

Swami asked me, when I go to New York, to visit the swami who is now running Nikhilananda's former center. I remarked that I have never yet seen the inside of that building—I never once visited Nikhilananda there. Swami seemed pleased, although I certainly hadn't meant it as a declaration of my loyalty to him. He smiled and said, "Nikhilananda was always jealous of me, because of my disciples." This touched me because the memory seemed to come from such a long way back—it was like an old woman remembering the suitors of her girlhood.

February 24. To the vespers of the Ramakrishna puja. Swami came into the shrine room to have the relics touched to his forehead before it began. He is very frail. Seeing him shuffle back to his room and totter up the steps, I thought to myself: There goes all that's left of the boy who met Brahmananda on the balcony at the Belur Math.

March 14. Last night, we saw Swami briefly. He complained that his pulse was too rapid but admitted that the doctor hadn't been able to find anything particularly wrong with him. I could see that it was a strain on him, just trying to attend to what we said. When Don said something and then I said something, his head jerked back and forth painfully; he was like an old animal being teased by two people competing for its attention.

Most of the nuns and monks who are looking after Swami agree that this is the beginning of the end. "Swami isn't gaining any ground," they say. "He is failing." This must be true, but I much prefer the attitude of Chetanananda, who says, "Swami is becoming more and more indrawn." Chetanananda sees Swami as deliberately preparing himself for his departure, not just passively "failing" physically.

April 10. After describing the new diet the doctor has given him, in the most minute detail, Swami suddenly began to speak ecstatically about Rama. The room was filled with his joy. I forget everything he said—the words didn't matter. I went into the kitchen afterwards, and George was there. I loved him because I knew he would have felt what I had been feeling. I might have talked about it, but other people were present. All I could find to say to him was, "Oh, I'm so glad to see you!" George seemed to understand immediately; he must somehow have guessed what had been happening to me. We beamed at each other in delight.

May 8. I asked Swami if he had had any experiences and he answered no. "If I have another one, it will be the end of me." He said this quite casually, with a certain amusement. "I couldn't stand it," he added.

May 22. Swami talked about Ramakrishna and Girish Ghosh. They once had a competition to find out which of them knew the bigger number of risqué words. (It was amusing to hear this corny French adjective pop up out of Swami's vocabulary.) After they had both said all the risqué words they knew, Girish bowed down and told Ramakrishna, "You are my guru in this also."

June 16. Yesterday, we went up to the Center for the Father's Day celebration. This year, there was no lunch, lest it should be too tiring for Swami. Only a kind of darshan, with fruit punch and cookies, in the puja hall. Swami told several stories about Maharaj.

This morning, Swami phoned me and came nearer than he has ever come to giving me a bawling out. He said he had been "shocked" by two questions I had asked him while he was speaking yesterday. "You were not yourself," he said—as if he were accusing me of having been drunk.

The worse of my two offenses was as follows: when Swami told how Maharaj had jokingly asked someone, in the presence of a number of young women, "Which one do you like best?" I had asked Swami, "Did Maharaj say that to you?"

My question had shocked Swami because it suggested that Maharaj could conceivably say such a thing, even in joke, to a boy who was then already a monk. Actually, he was speaking to Ramlal Dada, Ramakrishna's nephew, who was a married man. Swami said that he had made this point absolutely clear, and I have no doubt that he did. The heat was stupefying inside the puja hall and I wasn't attending properly and indeed only asking these questions to encourage Swami to continue telling stories. Prompting Swami on such occasions is one of my functions, because the majority of people are unwilling to ask him anything in public. Anyhow, I can't see anything shocking in the idea that Maharaj should make a joke of this kind, even to a young monk. Surely, purity such as his gives one a great deal of license?

My other offense: when Swami told us that Maharaj was able to inhibit his sense of smell completely, I asked, "Do you mean he did that permanently?" Admittedly, this was sheer idiocy on my part—also due to the heat. I asked him to forgive me, and he laughed and said, "How should I not forgive you? You are my disciple and my child." "A very silly child," I said. "Oh no, Chris, you are the most intelligent of all my children."

Right after our conversation was over, I felt that his scolding had truly been a blessing. But already, such is egotism, I am beginning to indulge in resentment, because I am certain that someone at the Center must have commented on my mistakes to Swami and thus put the idea of scolding me into his head. He has become much more suggestible lately, I suspect.

June 23. This morning, I drove up to Montecito. I saw Swami briefly in his room, constipated and uneasy. He now dislikes spending a night anywhere except in his room at the Hollywood Center.

He gave his lecture seated and wearing Western clothes. He says he is apt to trip over his gerua robe while walking from the car into the temple. At the end, he blessed us all. Then he made a gesture toward the shrine—as if of acknowledgment—and said, "Who spoke through me." It seemed perfectly obvious that he meant, "It was He who spoke through me." But several people who talked to me later were puzzled. They had taken Swami's statement as a question, "Who spoke through me?" Meaning, I suppose, that Swami was uncertain whether he had been inspired by God or the Devil! Maybe such apparent stupidity isn't stupidity at all, but an obstinate desire for mystification. How they love to be puzzled!

August 21. When I went up to the Center, Swami didn't feel like seeing me; he felt too weak, he told them to tell me. This may also have been because he didn't want me to ask him any questions about spiritual matters— he had told the girls that he mustn't talk about such things, and had turned on the radio and started listening to the news. He has been very cantankerous about his food lately, complaining that it isn't cooked just right. And then he says, "I don't scold you for now but for after I'm gone."

A., in her dry, matter-of-fact, hospital nurse's tone, told me: "Yesterday morning, he said something that didn't sound so good. He said, 'I've been dancing with Maharaj.' "

Although I realized how she meant "didn't sound so good," and how serious its significance might be, I very nearly burst out laughing—because it reminded me of Mistress Quickly describing Falstaff's death in Henry V: "I bid him a' should not think of God, I hoped there was no need to trouble himself with any such thoughts yet."

(Incidentally, this was one of Aldous Huxley's favorite Shakespeare quotations.)

November 13. This afternoon, when they were getting the shrine room ready for the Kali puja tonight, Swami came in to look at the image and said, "My hair is standing on end." Then he prostrated in front of the image, lying down full length on the floor. Then, coming out of the temple, he said to some people who were in the garden, "You are all Shiva."

"But," said A., after telling us this when we arrived to see Swami, an hour later, "he's quite all right now."

December 11. In three days, we leave for New York. Today we went to say goodbye to Swami. He was in good spirits. He talked with scorn about some new regulations concerning the giving of brahmacharya. They have been proposed by someone at the Belur Math. One of them was that every candidate for brahmacharya must have a recommendation from his guru, stating that the candidate is devoted to God.

"What nonsense!" Swami exclaimed. "As if one can say that anyone is devoted to God! It is only when you feel that you are not devoted that you are devoted!"

However illogical and inconsistent this remark might seem to an outsider, Swami's indignation made it beautiful.

January 29, 1975. Swami told how, long ago, two of the male devotees played a joke on him—sending him a fake letter from a girl which said that she was in love with him and wanted him to call her at a certain number. Swami said that he recognized this number as belonging to one of these devotees, so he wasn't fooled.

I said, "I suppose you must have had a lot of trouble with women, while you've been in Hollywood?"

"Oh yes," he answered, frowning and shaking his head comically, "terrible—you have no idea." Then he added, with truly sweet simplicity: "You see, Chris, I used to be very handsome."

February 26. Before I saw Swami this evening, they told me that he had had another spiritual experience while he was at Montecito the other day. He was quite ready to speak about it himself. It was a vision while he was sleeping. He was feeding Holy Mother and he began to weep.

"I could have wept myself to death," Swami told me. "When the doctor examined me, he said, 'You have had a shock.' It was like a heart attack . . . When I wish to die, I can die. Whenever I wish. But I don't want to die yet—not until this place is saved." (Meaning, not until a senior swami is sent by Belur Math to succeed him.)

Then he talked about the lower samadhi—how doubts still remain, even after you have experienced it. "Do you still have doubts, Swami?" I asked. "Oh yes—well, not doubts, exactly. It's what you call 'divine discontent.' You know, Maharaj used to tell me, 'What's wrong with you is, you're too contented here. You shouldn't be contented in spiritual life. You should always want more.' Well, now I always want more—<u>more!</u>"

June 5. When I saw Swami yesterday, he told me that he had refused the application of a lesbian who wanted to be a nun. Put like that, the statement sounded bluntly sexist, and I suppose my face showed my disapproval. Today he phoned to assure me that he hadn't refused to take the girl because she was a lesbian but because she had got into a fight with one of the nuns and was, anyway, over the prescribed age limit for joining the convent.

Then why did Swami even mention that she was a lesbian, in the first place? Probably because that made her my fellow tribesperson. For a long time now, he has been treating me as a sort of official representative of all the homosexuals he comes in contact with; my opinion on tribal matters has to be consulted, even if it is overruled!

August 21. George has been suddenly subjected to a stoppage of the bladder. I visited him in hospital today. He was lying doubled up, in great pain. Being with him was marvelous, not because he was suffering nobly and patiently—he was grunting and muttering to himself like any normal impatient patient—but because of the atmosphere he had created around him in the room. After staying there about ten minutes, during which we hardly spoke, I felt so uplifted that I went into the hospital chapel and knelt for a while before its hideous arty modernistic altar.

August 22. Talked to Swami today about the ultimatum from Belur Math; they won't send another swami until Swami agrees to separate the monks and nuns more completely.

Swami seems to have accepted this fairly calmly. However, he remarked that it was such a pity I wasn't a swami, because then I would have been able to help a lot during this interim period. So I said, smiling, "Perhaps in my next lifetime—"

"What do you mean—next lifetime?" he exclaimed indignantly. "You will not be reborn! You will go straight to the Ramakrishna loka!"

"Well, Swami, if I do, I'll be sitting right at the back."

August 28. I had almost forgotten this when, yesterday, Swami phoned and said—picking up our previous conversation, as he so often does—"In God's eye, it is all the same." He then went on to assure me that, in God's eye, there is absolutely no difference between me and George and himself.

It's easy to accept this theoretically, but, as far as I'm concerned, it's only theoretically convincing. I can grasp the idea that the Eternal sees nothing but the Eternal in everyone and everything. To Swami, this is a fact, because Brahmananda told him that he sometimes saw everybody as God, playing in various forms.

I think, however, that Swami was perhaps saying this to me as a gentle rebuke to my overindulgence in humility, in my relationship with him. He is fond of telling other people how humble I am about my literary reputation. But he must know perfectly well what my humility really is—the other half of my vanity. It is so cozy and relaxing to play at being the lowest of the low, within his circle—which only tends to make me feel all the more sophisticated and superior in my attitude toward uninitiated outsiders, especially when they are literary intellectuals.

December 31. When we went to see Swami on the 26th, to bring him a crystal drinking glass for his birthday, he amazed us by at once peering at Don—his sight is now very poor—and saying, "There's something different." He had noticed what nearly everybody, including Don's parents, has failed to notice—that Don has cut his mustache off.

Twenty

During the first months of 1976, I was working under pressure to finish *Christopher and His Kind*. This made me give up my diary keeping, and thus there is no record of our last visits to Swami. We saw him at least fifteen times before we left for New York and England, on May 21.

On May 29, while staying at the Montecito convent, Swami had a slight stroke and a fall. He was brought back at once to the Cedars-Sinai Hospital in Los Angeles, where he was put into intensive care.

On May 31, Chris Wood died. When we had seen him, just before leaving Los Angeles, we had wondered if this might not be for the last time. Chris had already had several strokes and had turned into a skinny little bent-up man. But he hadn't lost his dry-toned, slightly amused self-possession. "I'm perfectly happy at present," he had told us. "When I stop being, I shall be quite ready to go."

On June 1, Swami was taken out of intensive care but

remained under cardiac observation. A few nuns from the Center were with him throughout much of the day. He remarked, "Tomorrow I'll be normal."

Nevertheless, this day was like a rehearsal of dying. Sometimes, Swami's expression was indrawn, or he gazed into space with a fixity which seemed visionary. Sometimes, his face had a wondering, blissful smile on it and his hand was slightly raised in a gesture of blessing. This is preserved in a photograph which George took.

But, most of the time, he was in a state of normal consciousness. When they tried to make him more comfortable by screwing his adjustable bed up and down, he declared every position to be the wrong one. A nurse turned his bed toward the window, so that he should have a view of the Hollywood hills. He grumbled, "I've seen the Himalayas, I've seen the Alps—so what do I need this view for?"

Another nurse came to check the instrument which monitored Swami's heartbeats. "Hi," she greeted him. "Hi, honey," he replied. When she told him, "Goodbye," his answer was "Okay." After she had left the room, he said, "Okay's the only word they know here."

He also spoke in Sanskrit or Bengali, which some of the nuns understood. He said, "*Ananda mrtu*," meaning "blissful death." Also, something about a chariot—how it comes to take away the departing soul. Then, in English, "You remember, 'Swing low, sweet chariot'?"

He began to chant his mantram, which, of course, they had never heard before. He told them, "I'm saying the mantram out loud—this is a sign of death." He made them all chant with him, as loud as they could, and he waved his arms vigorously like a conductor, although they urged him not to exert himself.

A disciple who had just come into the room exclaimed:

"How beautiful you look!" And Swami, as if standing aside and regarding himself, said, "I look beautiful in my death."

Then he said, "Tell my children to come." So the nuns phoned the rest of the monastics, who were already waiting near their telephones for news, to come to the hospital. About thirty-eight of them came. The nurse who had given permission for Swami to be visited was horrified when she realized, too late, how many had been admitted. But Swami's manner, at that time, had such authority that nobody could refuse him. He spoke to each monastic privately, giving him or her a few words of instruction for the future.

On June 2, just as he had predicted, he was much better.

On June 3, Don and I, in London, got a belated cable which had been sent on June 1 to warn us that Swami was gravely ill. We immediately phoned Los Angeles and were told that he was out of danger. So this seemed to me to be yet another of Swami's dramatic crises and recoveries. I was no longer seriously worried, and we decided not to return home earlier than we had planned, unless we got another warning. We never did.

On June 18, Swami was well enough to be brought back to the Center, where he would have trained nurses in attendance.

On June 21, he asked, "Is it July the first?" as if in expectation of some event.

On June 29, he began taking daily walks, supported by a nurse.

On July 3, he was weaker but could nevertheless be helped to walk around the temple. This was shortly after seven in the morning, because the garden was deserted at that time and there was no danger that he would be accosted by well-wishers.

That afternoon, he had a heart attack. He said firmly, "I don't want to go to the hospital." Later he said, "I am dying." One of the nuns began to chant softly, "Hari Om, Ramakrishna," but Swami stopped her, saying, "Don't remind me now."

That evening, he said, "Maharaj, why do you let me suffer?" Also, "Maharaj, I will come" or "Maharaj will come"—they couldn't be sure which.

About an hour after this, he asked, "What time?" and was told eleven-fifteen. He said, "No, too soon—it must be midnight." (It is generally agreed that Swami wished to wait until July 4, because that is the day on which Vivekananda left his body, in 1902.)

Just before midnight, Chetanananda was called. Swami's lips were moving and his eyes were turned upward. Those who were in the room stood well back from the bed, for Swami's breathing had become labored and they wanted to let him have as much air as possible. The window shades had been opened so that those who were gathered outside in the garden could see in.

Just after midnight, Chetanananda touched Swami's head and began chanting, "Om, Hari Om, Ramakrishna." With the first "Hari Om," Swami gently exhaled and died.

A disciple who was a doctor had been called, but the message reached him too late. When he finally arrived, he said he was glad of this because, if he had come earlier, he would have felt obliged, as a medical man, to try mouth-to-mouth resuscitation, although, as a disciple, he would have realized it was presumptuous to do so, since Swami had obviously wished to die exactly when he did.

After the prescribed interval of two hours, Swami's body was dressed in monastic robes. And now the disciples began to keep a vigil in his room, which continued on into the morning. (After Don and I had got back to Los Angeles, some of them described to us what they had experienced: "We none of us wanted to leave. Swami was such a presence there. You felt such power, such awe. One of the nurses said, 'I've seen so many people die, but with him it was different. I couldn't feel he was dead.' ")

In the afternoon, when the morticians had come, Swami's body was carried three times around the temple and then placed outside its open doors, with the head pointing toward the shrine, before being taken away to be cremated.

In October of that year, George flew to India with Swami's ashes. Some of them were put into the Ganges opposite the Belur Math. Then George went up to Hardwar, to which Abanindra had run away from college to be with Maharaj, sixty-five years earlier. There George left the rest of the ashes, in waters which are held to be especially sacred, where the river comes down out of the great mountains.

Three Years Later

The reader may ask: Now that your Swami is dead, what are you left with?

I am left with Swami. His physical absence doesn't make nearly as much difference to me as I had expected it would. I think about him as constantly as I ever did. What I do seem to be losing touch with is Swami's Hindu pantheon of gods, goddesses, and divine incarnations. My Occidental consciousness is in the process of rejecting them, it seems, as imperfectly transplanted, culturally foreign bodies. Meanwhile, Ramakrishna, Brahmananda, Vivekananda, and Holy Mother remain to inspire me as powerfully individual figures—though Swami used to tell us that they are "all the same."

Toward the end of his life, Swami seemed to identify the Divine Mother, God's female aspect, almost completely with Holy Mother. He had one of the photographs of her enlarged and hung in his room. I meditate before a print of that same photograph—partly because I associate it particularly with Swami; partly because I need a mother figure through whom I can feel a more loving acceptance of my own mother, now that she is dead and my hostility toward her has left me.

I have had no visions of Swami since his death; no dreams of him, even, which were memorable. I have found myself saying to myself, "He knows everything about me, now"—which merely means that I no longer feel guilty when I do something that I wouldn't have wanted him to know about during his lifetime. But this is child's talk. I am only referring to Abanindra Nath Ghosh. The contact I sometimes think I feel isn't with him but with what I believe he has now become, the Guru, a being who exists only to help his disciples. While the Guru was still within the body we called Prabhavananda, he gave us our mantrams. It is when I am saying my mantram that I very occasionally feel I am in communication with him. The mantram was a gift of his love, and love is communication. The mantram is all I have of him and all I need.

Such moments reassure me that "the real situation" does indeed exist and that an acceptance of it is my only safety. I recognize this in a flash of sanity from time to time. Then I lose it again.

Now that I am nearly seventy-five, I am mindful that death is near. I no longer avoid the thought of it; indeed, I dwell on the thought, as Vivekananda advises. My fear, insofar as I feel any, is of the manner in which death may come—or, worse still, of the manner in which it may be painfully, tediously delayed.

In the old days, I often said to myself that I should feel no fear if I could actually die in Swami's presence. Suppose that I can somehow feel his presence right at the moment of death, and so die fearless—only to find that death is total extinction? Well, I see nothing terrible in that possibility.

There is a second possibility—that there is life after death, but not the kind of life Swami promised us. Eternal hell, for instance, with torments. Or an endless limbo of boredom, loneliness, regrets.

But here I suddenly feel on firm ground. Quite irrationally, I find I have faith in Swami's faith, to this extent: if death isn't the end, then I believe that the life to come will be more or less what he led us to expect. There will be "the real situation" and there will be the many who are still unable or unwilling to accept it. There will be a continuity of individual problems which remain to be worked out.

My own problem will be, presumably, that I find myself in the Ramakrishna loka—and how my individualistic ego shrinks from *that* prospect! I remember how often, despite my love for Swami, I used to draw a breath of relief when I left his room. I was like a child escaping from the presence of an elder, simply because he needs to breathe a less rarefied atmosphere, to feel himself free to chatter and be silly. How could I endure the combined presence of Ramakrishna, Holy Mother, Maharaj, and Swamiji? Well, I suppose that is what the concept of purgatory is all about. You hate it until you slowly and painfully learn to love it, and when you do, it automatically becomes paradise. Don, of course, would be arriving there too, before very long. And that would help me enormously.

Meanwhile, my life is still beautiful to me—beautiful because of Don, because of the enduring fascination of my efforts to describe my life experience in my writing, because of my interest in the various predicaments of my fellow travelers on this journey. How I wish I were able to reassure them that all is ultimately well—particularly those who are quite certain that it isn't; that life is meaningless and unjust! I can't reassure them, because I can't speak with the absolute authority of a knower.

All I can offer them is this book, which I have written about matters I only partially understand, in the hope that it may somehow, to some readers, reveal glimpses of inner truth which remain hidden from its author.